THE
HARMLESS
PEOPLE

THE
HARMLESS
PEOPLE

REVISED EDITION

by
Elizabeth Marshall Thomas

VINTAGE BOOKS

A DIVISION OF RANDOM HOUSE, INC.

NEW YORK

Second Vintage Books Edition, September 1989

Copyright © 1958, 1959, 1989 by Elizabeth Marshall Thomas

Copyright renewed 1986 by Elizabeth Marshall Thomas

Library of Congress Cataloging-in-Publication Data
Thomas, Elizabeth Marshall, 1931–
The harmless people / by Elizabeth Marshall
Thomas.—Rev., with
a new epilogue, 2nd Vintage Books ed.
p. cm.
ISBN 0-679-72446-X : $8.95
1. San (African people) I. Title.
DT764.B8T4   1989
968.83′004961—dc20   89-40157
                                            CIP

Manufactured in the United States of America
579B864

To Stephen

CONTENTS

GIKWE

CHART OF UKWANE'S FAMILY

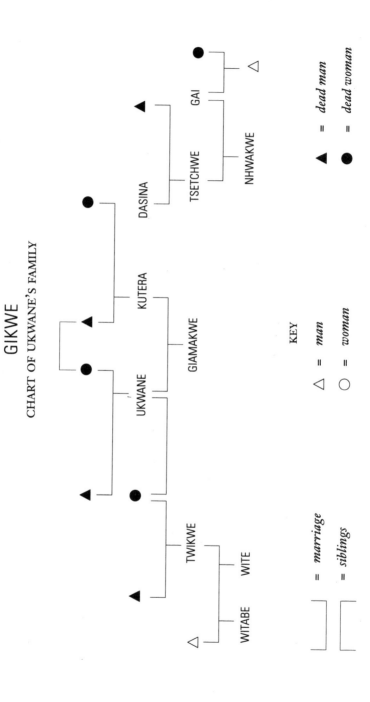

KEY

△ = man

○ = woman

▲ = dead man

● = dead woman

⊔ = marriage

⨆ = siblings

KUNG
CHART OF TOMA'S FAMILY

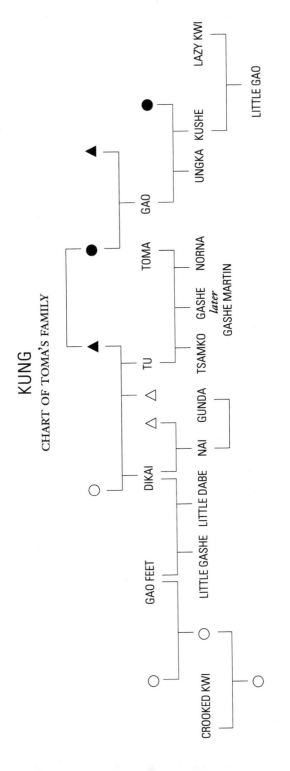

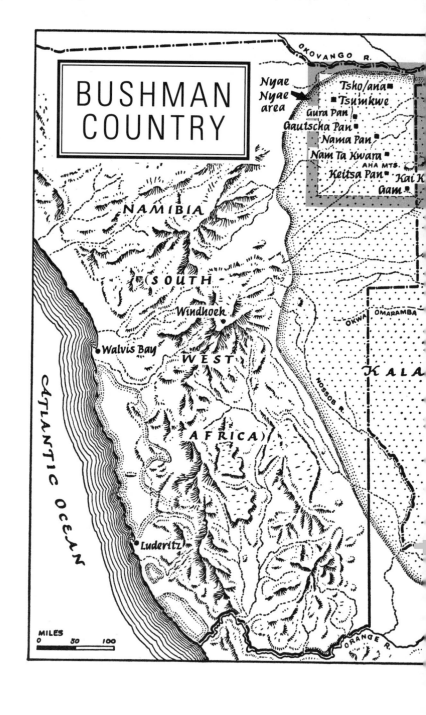

BUSHMAN COUNTRY

OKOVANGO R.

Nyae Nyae area

Tsho/ana
Tsumkwe
Gura Pan
Gautscha Pan
Nama Pan
Nam Ta Kwara
AHA MTS.
Keitsa Pan
Kai K
Gam

NAMIBIA

SOUTH

Windhoek

Walvis Bay

WEST

AFRICA

OKWA
OMARAMBA

KALA

NOSSOB R.

ATLANTIC OCEAN

Luderitz

ORANGE R.

MILES
0   50   100

ZAMBEZI R.

Livingstone

RHODESIA

Bulawayo

Tsau

L. NGAMI

hanzi   BOTSWANA

Okwa   Chukudu

(Formerly BECHUANALAND)

Ai a ha'b

HARI

LIMPOPO R.

DESERT

Molepolole   Mochudi

Gaberones

TRANSVAAL

Pretoria

Johannesburg

MOLOPO R.

Kuruman

VAAL R.

palacios

THE
HARMLESS
PEOPLE

N O T E

- - - - - - -

The spelling of Bushman words and names is at best a rough approximation. Most Bushman words and names have clicks in them, usually clicks acting as consonant sounds. For the purpose of simplicity, the clicks have been omitted.

CHAPTER ONE

- -

The Desert

THERE IS A vast sweep of dry bush desert lying in South-West Africa and western Bechuanaland, bordered in the north by Lake Ngami and the Okovango River, in the south by the Orange River, and in the west by the Damera Hills. It is the Kalahari Desert, part of a great inland table of southern Africa that slopes west toward the sea, all low sand dunes and great plains, flat, dry, and rolling one upon the other for thousands of miles, a hostile country of thirst and heat and thorns where the grass is harsh and often barbed and the stones hide scorpions.

From March to December, in the long drought of the year, the sun bakes the desert to powdery dry leaves and dust. There are no surface waters at all, no clouds for coolness, no tall trees for shade, but only low bushes and grass tufts; and among the grass tufts grow brown thistles, briers, the dry stalks of spiny weeds, all tangled into knots during the rains, now dry, tumbled, and dead.

The Kalahari would be very barren, very devoid of landmarks, if it were not for the baobab trees, and even these grow far from each other, some areas having none. But where there is one, it is the biggest thing in all the landscape, dominating all the veld, more impressive than any mountain. It can be as much as two hundred feet high and thirty feet in diameter. It has great, thick branches that sprout haphazardly from the sides of the trunk and reach like stretching arms into the sky. The bark is thin and smooth and rather pink, and sags in folds toward the base of the tree like the skin on an elephant's leg, which is why a baobab is sometimes called an elephant tree. Its trunk is soft and pulpy, like a carrot instead of wood, and if you lean against it you find that it is warm from the sun and you expect to hear a great heart beating inside. In the spring, encouraged by moisture, these giants put out huge white flowers resembling gardenias, white as moons and fragrant, that face down toward the earth; during the summer they bear alumlike dry fruits, shaped like pears, which can be eaten. In the Kalahari there is no need of hills. The great baobabs standing in the plains, the wind, and the seasons are enough.

Usually in the hot months only small winds blow, leaving a whisper of dry leaves and a ripple of grass as though a snake has gone by, but occasionally there is a windy day when all the low trees of the veld are in motion, swinging and dipping, and the grass blows forward and back. When there is no wind, heat accumulates in the air and rises in thick, shuddering waves that distort everything you see, the temperature rises to 120° Fahrenheit and more, and the air feels heavy, pressing against you, hard to breathe.

June and July are the months of winter. Then water left standing freezes at night, and with the first light of morning all the trees and grass leaves are brittle with frost. The days warm slowly to perhaps 80° at noon, but by night when the sun sets yellow and far, far away over the flat veld the cold creeps back, freezing the moisture from the dark air so that the black sky blazes with stars. In winter the icy wind, pouring steadily across the continent from the Antarctic, blows all night long.

There are only three months of rain in the whole year, and these begin in December, ending the hottest season when the air is as tight and dry as a drum skin. Under the rain—which is sometimes torrential, drenching the earth, making rivers down the sides of trees, sometimes an easy land rain that blows into the long grass like a mist—the heat and drought melt away and the grass turns green at the roots. Soon the trees flower, and in the low places the dry dust becomes sucking mud. Towering clouds, miles away, widen the horizon, and all the bushes which stretch in an unchanging expanse over dune after dune now blossom and bear white or red or violet flowers. But the season is short, and the plants bud, flower, and fruit very quickly; in March the drought creeps in, just as the veld fruits ripen and scatter their seeds.

When the rains stop, the open water is the first to dry, making slippery mud and then caked white earth. By June only little soaks of waterholes remain, hidden deep in the earth, covered with long grass. These, which are miles apart, dry up by August, and then travel in the veld is nearly impossible. Because of this, large areas of the Kalahari remain unexplored.

We have crossed this desert three times, my family and

I, on three expeditions, which usually numbered between ten and fourteen people and included my father, my mother, my brother, and myself, as well as other Europeans who were linguists, zoologists, botanists, or archaeologists, sent by universities of the Union of South Africa, England, or the United States, as well as four or five Bantu men—several interpreters, a cook, and a mechanic—who were the staff. We usually traveled in four big trucks and a jeep, and had to carry all our food and water, gasoline, and equipment in supplies to last us for several months. We crossed great drought areas, once crossing four hundred miles of the central desert of Bechuanaland where there was no water at all, and once traveling every day for two weeks into an unmapped part of the desert of South-West Africa, close to the Bechuanaland border, where we found a waterhole and refilled our empty drums. All this was for the purpose of filming and studying the life and customs of the people of the Kalahari, who are called the Bushmen.

- - -

Bushmen are a naked, hungry people, slight of build and yellow-skinned; the only feature they have in common with their large-boned, darker-skinned neighbors, the Negro or Bantu tribes living at the edges of the Bushmen's territory, is their peppercorn curly hair. Otherwise, Bushmen are very like the Asian peoples, often having Mongolian eyefolds and rather broad, flat faces with almost no noses at all. Because of the dust, perspiration, and the blazing sun, their skins darken to a copper brown, but under their arms where sweat has washed the dust away the yellow skin shows. Bushman babies, in fact, are born pale pink, often with a dark, pigmented area at the base of their spines which Kung Bushmen call "the jar"—because, they say, the mother carries her baby and her water jar together in the pouch of her garment—but which we know as the Mongolian Spot.

Physically, the Bushmen are a handsome people, though short of stature—a man being a few inches over and a woman a few inches under five feet—and a little sway-backed of carriage, which makes their bellies stick out. They are handsome because of the extreme grace in their way of moving, which is strong and deft and lithe; to watch a Bushman walking or simply picking up something from the ground is like watching part of a dance. This is not a beauty of the flesh, and therefore exists in everyone who is not an infant or stiff with age. Bushmen have long, slender arms and legs, and the men are built for running, all lean muscle and fine bone, and consequently they often seem younger than they are. They are delicate of proportion, too, and they speak very softly.

Bushmen dress themselves in the skins of animals, a man wearing only a leather loincloth and a woman a small leather apron and a big kaross, a leather cape made from a whole animal hide, belted at the waist with a sinew cord, knotted at the shoulder, forming a pouch in back where a baby can ride, and where the woman carries her blown ostrich eggs, which are used as water containers. Bushmen are a very neat people; they keep their clothes tidily about themselves, and though they do not really need haircuts because their curly hair breaks off by itself, they prefer to keep their hair cropped close to their heads. White orna-ments of ostrich-eggshell beads dangle from tufts of their hair and are strung in tiny bands around their arms and knees. Sometimes they wear leather sandals, but mostly their hard brown feet are bare.

- - -

The first time we came to the Kalahari, we spent several months looking for Bushmen. It was very hard for us to find them because they are shy of any stranger. If they believe that you are coming, they run away like foxes to hide in the grass until you have gone. Their tiny huts, dome-shaped and made of grass, are also inconspicuous. I once walked right into an empty werf, as their tiny villages are called, and didn't see the little scherms, or huts, hidden in the grass until I noticed a small skin bag dangling in a shadow, which was a doorway. Then I saw the frame of the scherm around it, then the other scherms as well. The werf was abandoned, all the people had slipped away, but I heard two voices whispering in the grass nearby. You can tell by these werfs that there are Bushmen in an area, and also by their footprints on narrow trails which they share with the game and which run all through the desert. You may find footprints or you may see a little pile of white ash, the fire that a Bushman kindled where he spent the night. Otherwise, to find them you must depend on luck or on the fact that the Bushmen of an area may have heard something good about you and will not be too afraid.

Culturally and historically, the Bushmen are an interesting people, for they and the Hottentots, who belong to the same racial and language groups, are the earliest human inhabitants still living in southern Africa. There are now from thirty to fifty thousand Bushmen, who are divided into several language groups. Their languages are related to each other and to the Hottentot language, and are in what is known as the Khoisan language group, made up of most of the click languages spoken in South Africa. A click language has sharp pops and clicks made with the tongue in various parts of the mouth, combined with an implosion of the breath, very difficult to understand, harder still to pronounce, as the slightest mistake may change the meaning of a word entirely. For example, the word //kx'a, which in one of the Bushman languages means *mangetti*, a certain kind of nut-bearing tree, is pronounced by making a lateral click for which the tongue is pulled sharply away from the sides of the mouth, producing the click one makes when calling a horse, followed by a scraped *k* turning to a *g*, followed by a glottal stop—a slight pause or tiny choking sound made as the back of the tongue stops the breath—which is followed at last by the vowel. To make a mistake is easy, and that is why non-Bushmen have a hard time learning the language, and why, when they do learn, they are often misunderstood.

The Bushmen are one of the most primitive peoples living on earth. Although most of their groups own some metal objects, Bushmen do not smelt or forge metal but get it in trade from their Bantu neighbors. They use soft metal in the making of a few tools such as knives, arrowheads, and little axes, cold-hammering the metal into shape themselves. Bushmen make the other tools they use from wood and bone, grass and fiber, the things of the veld. They dig roots and pick berries to eat because they have no crops. The desert is too dry for anything but desert plants to grow naturally, and Bushmen, who quickly consume all the wild food available in one place, cannot stay anywhere long enough to tend crops or wait for them to grow.

There is not enough water to water livestock, and for this reason Bushmen have no domestic animals. Most of their groups do not even have dogs. Instead of herding, Bushmen hunt wild antelope with tiny arrows, sometimes made of soft, traded metal, sometimes made of bone, and poisoned with a terrible poison extracted from a certain grub, a poison which affects the nervous system of a creature and which is so deadly that an antelope shot early in the morning with a single arrow well placed in the body dies within the day. Hunting is very difficult, for travel in the veld is thirsty and rigorous and the antelope are clever, but as often as not the Bushmen hunters shoot one and then they use it all. Most of the meat is dried to preserve it, causing it to last at least a few weeks, but sooner or later every last bite of it is eaten, even the mucous lining of the nostrils and the gristle inside the ears. They sometimes eat the hide, sometimes work it into leather to use for clothing, and if the antelope bones are not all cracked for the marrow, pieces are worked into arrow points to shoot another antelope.

In order to live as they do, Bushmen must travel through the veld, changing their abode every few days in search of food. Because of their way of life, they do not need villages to live in, so they rarely bother to build strong scherms, making small domes of grass for themselves instead, just a little shade for their heads, grass which the wind soon blows away. Sometimes they do not even bother with this, but push little sticks into the ground to mark their places. They sleep beside the sticks and arrange their few possessions around them, symbols of their homes.

Although Bushmen are a roaming people and therefore seem to be homeless and vague about their country, each group of them has a very specific territory which that group alone may use, and they respect their boundaries rigidly. Each group also knows its own territory very well; although it may be several hundred square miles in area, the people who live there know every bush and stone, every convolution of the ground, and have usually named every place in it where a certain kind of veld food may grow, even if that place is only a few yards in diameter, or where there is only a patch of tall arrow grass or a bee tree, and in this way each group of people knows many hundred places by name. Even if you are traveling randomly with Bushmen and ask at any time on the journey for the name of the place where you happen to be standing, they will probably be able to tell you.

The social structure of Bushmen is not complicated. They have no chiefs or kings, only headmen who in function are virtually indistinguishable from the people they lead, and sometimes a band will not even have a headman. A leader is not really necessary, however, because the Bushmen roam about together in small family bands rarely numbering more than twenty people. A band may consist of an old man and his wife, their daughters, the daughters' husbands, perhaps an unmarried son or two, and their daughters' children. Bushmen are polygynous, and a man is allowed by custom to have as many wives as he can afford, depending on how well he hunts—usually a man can afford only one wife, sometimes two (often sisters), and once we heard of a man with four wives. For this reason there are often more women than men in a band.

The immediate family, a man, his wife, or wives, and children, is the only solid social unit; otherwise the small bands are always breaking up and recombining with other small bands as the structures of single families change, through marriages, divorces, deaths, or as the family decides to pay a prolonged visit to a different group of relatives.

Any Bushman will either be related by blood or marriage or will be acquainted with all the other Bushmen in his area but this is as far as Bushmen go in their affinities. They do not recognize as their own people strange Bushmen who speak the same language; in fact, they suspect and fear them as they do any stranger.

We have visited four of the Bushman language groups, two of which we stayed with for long periods of time. In 1951, after a survey expedition to learn where Bushmen could be found, we went into the Nyae Nyae area of South-West Africa, close to the border of Bechuanaland, to look for Kung Bushmen. We found a band living near a waterhole, as it was June, the drought of the year, and we stayed with them for four months. At first only a few Bushmen were there, but as the news spread that we were friendly, more and more people came to visit us and receive presents of tobacco and salt, for Bushmen love to smoke but rarely have tobacco, which they get in trade. Also, most of the

Bushmen had never seen a European before, none had ever seen a European woman, and they came by dozens to sit together in a cluster at a distance to observe my mother and me. By the end of our stay we had become friendly with them, and in 1952 we visited them again. We found them waiting confidently for us, living beside the track our trucks had made, as we had told them that we would come back if we were able, and this time we stayed with them for a year. In August 1955 we returned to them again, but before we did so we spent four months in Bechuanaland. We lived one month with a group of Naron and Kõ Bushmen at a place called Okwa (the two groups were mixed together because their territories happen to meet at that place), and almost two months with Gikwe Bushmen in the four-hundred-mile stretch of empty desert between Ghanzi, near the border of South-West Africa, and Molepolole, near the border of the Transvaal. Ghanzi is a small town with a post office and a store, the center of a group of rather extensive European farms. Molepolole is a great Bantu village of the Bakwena (Crocodile) Bechuana people, where a Chuana chieftain lives. The other month we spent traveling to the Gikwe, because they are very remote.

- - -

Nobody knows where the Bushmen originated, from what racial stocks they came, or when they came to Africa. But here and there throughout southern Africa, in mountain caves and on sheltered rocks, paintings and engravings are found which are known to have been made centuries ago, and are believed to have been made by Bushmen. It is hard to say for certain that Bushmen made the paintings because, to my knowledge, Bushmen do not paint on rocks or in caves now. However, Kung Bushmen do scratch designs on the bark of trees and on their ostrich eggshells. During each expedition I asked Bushmen to paint for me with paints and paper which I provided. Though none of the Bushmen we met had ever seen paintings, photographs, or drawings of any kind, the paintings they made for me could be said to resemble the paintings and engravings on the rocks.

If there is a resemblance, it is not surprising. The Bushmen, together with the Hottentot peoples, are known to have lived in South Africa long before the Bantus came. At one time it all was theirs to roam in, all the riverbanks and all the grasslands, all the hills and valleys where cedar trees grow, from the Cape to Rhodesia, from Angola to Mozambique. But during the waves of the early Bantu migrations, when the taller, energetic Bantu people with their chiefs and kings, witch doctors and armies of soldiers, their metal spears and axes, shields and maces, came walking down from central Africa driving their great herds of cattle before them, the Bushmen yielded their land to the stronger newcomers, after a few struggles, surely, and most of them were killed, enslaved, or driven farther and farther back into the most remote parts of the country, where the Bantu people and their livestock could not live. But the Bushmen are very tough and hardy, all sinew and wire, with not an extra ounce of flesh to carry, and possess great endurance of hunger and thirst, endurance to search through the grass roots all day looking for a vegetable to eat, or endurance to chase the antelope they shoot, which may take as many as four days to die and may walk as far as a hundred miles if the arrow was not particularly well placed. Bushmen are extremely observant, too, and can follow the spoor of their wounded antelope over the hardest ground or recognize it among the spoor of a herd of other antelope of its kind, and if they miss the spoor and find it again, they know from individual characteristics of the footprint that it is their antelope and no other. Even a Bushman child walking along in the veld can tell his mother's footprints, can see at once the tiniest dry stalk among the grass that marks an edible root, or see a scorpion hidden in the dust and jump over it. So Bushmen survive in the most rigorous places; they survive in the dense, mosquito-ridden papyrus swamps of the Okovango River, steaming like a jungle and dangerous with snakes and fever, where the River Bushmen live, the only Bushmen with plenty of water; they also survive on the vast, rolling steppes of central Bechuanaland, the territory of the Gikwe Bushmen, who for the nine dry months of the year have no water at all and do without it.

Besides the fact that Bushmen alone can live in the land they occupy, there is another reason for their remoteness and shyness. They are in many instances exploited by the Bantu farmers, and by a few of the European farmers, usually those who need free or almost free labor. Many Bantu farms and households have Bushman servants, or serfs, rather, as they usually come from the land on or near the farm, and when working they are paid nothing but are given food, tobacco, and sometimes cast-off clothing as wages. Some European farms in Bechuanaland and some in South-West Africa have Bushman laborers too, though most European farmers do not depend on Bushman labor. Those European farmers who do employ Bushmen usually pay wages, about ten shillings a month, plus a ration of food to each Bushman who is working, though not necessarily to his family, consisting of about a pound of cornmeal and a quart of milk a day, meat occasionally, and weekly a ration of tobacco. Perhaps the employer will add a set of clothing—that is, a pair of cast-off pants and a shirt—and perhaps a blanket every year, but occasionally they pay their labor in cast-off clothing and omit the ten shillings altogether.

European clothing is esteemed among Bushmen, for it is symbolic to them of a people mightier than themselves, and also because, made of cloth instead of leather, it is more clinging, therefore warmer and more comfortable, and dries faster when wet. It is sought after and desired, it is got through employment; yet, even so, Bushmen hesitate to seek employment because they believe that they will be badly treated (as they sometimes are) and they often find the customary wage and food ration to be inadequate for anyone who must support a family. Supposedly, the wives of Bushmen laborers are free to look on the farmer's land for roots and berries, as they would if they were living in the veld; but, as it happens, after a few years the supply of wild food around a farm becomes exhausted.

The Bantu farmers, being as a rule much poorer than the European farmers, are less generous to their Bushman serfs. They also give a food ration of cornmeal and milk but almost never meat, for any meat that may come into the Bantu kraal is eaten by the Bantus unless it is the carcass of a hyena or a leopard which the Bantu masters have killed for the pelt. The Bantus say: "Our Bushman servants are like our children; they herd our cattle for us and we feed them. A child does not ask for wages when he helps with the family work."

Besides this, the Bantus badly cheat the Bushmen who come in from the veld to trade cured antelope hides for metal and tobacco, sometimes asking several hides, worth several pounds apiece, for enough tobacco to fill the palm of the Bushman's hand, or for a piece of wire long enough to make an arrowhead. All in all, it does not benefit the Bushmen to live anywhere near Bantu or European settlements, and that is why the Bushmen of the veld run and hide when they see Europeans coming, believing that they may be taken by force (as they sometimes are), and why they avoid going to a Bantu settlement except to trade for tobacco when they feel they must smoke, or when they are dying of thirst and must come in to beg for water.

- - -

Once I talked with a young Bushman who had visited one of our camps in Bechuanaland many times, who spoke

Afrikaans, and whom I shall call Tami. I could speak a little Afrikaans, so he and I could talk together. He was in his early thirties and had been working for some time for European farmers. When I met him he was married, and as his wife had just had a baby, he felt that his ten-shilling-a-month wage was inadequate and he planned to move to another part of the country where he hoped to be paid more. As it is rather unusual for a Bushman to uproot himself from his own country, no matter how long he has been on a farm and away from his own people, I asked him where he had come from and how he had learned Afrikaans.

"Oh," he said, "I learned Afrikaans in the places I have been. I have worked for white men since I was a young boy and I have always been fast to learn their languages. In the same way I have learned the languages of the black people."

"Where did you live before you worked for white people?" I asked.

"We lived not far from Nurigaas, at the edge of the police zone. I am a young person still, but I remember that Nurigaas was all wild then. We always lived there."

"With your parents?"

"Yes, until the police boys took the old man my father."

I asked him what had happened, and he said: "We lived at the edge of the police zone, you know. We lived with other Bushmen there, and my sister, she was there. My mother's father was still alive then, but he was too old, he couldn't even carry water, and my mother had to do everything for him. She was his daughter, so she was glad to do it, but my sister and I thought he was just an old man who sat and coughed and spit. He didn't like the Europeans or the black people either, and my father didn't either, and that is why we lived on the other side of the police zone. On one side were the police boys with camels—

that was in the old days with the camel patrol*—and on the other side the lions and the Bushmen asked for your pass.

"One day my father went hunting and he was gone two days. Then my sister said: 'He must have shot a giraffe.' A giraffe is royal game, you know, and you can go to jail if you kill one, only my father didn't know it then.

"Yes, and that day two police boys came on camels and a white man on a camel. The police boys had a rifle and the white policeman had a rifle and a little gun in his hand. They had a Nurigaas Bushman walking with them, but he didn't come near us because he was ashamed. One police boy spoke the language of the Bushmen, and he said: 'Where is the old man who lives here?' and my mother pointed to my grandfather and she said: 'This is the one,' but the police boy said: 'Not that one, I want your husband. Where is he?' 'I don't know,' said my mother, but the police boy said: 'How can an old woman like you lie to me?' and my mother just covered up her face and said nothing. Then the police boy and the Nurigaas Bushman found my father's spoor off in the veld, and they all followed him, with the police boy and the Nurigaas Bushman walking and the white man and the other police boy on the camels. Next morning they came back with my father, they had his hands tied behind and a rope around his neck and he was running behind the camel. His face was all thick, you know, and he had to hold his head back because the rope was choking. My mother, she ran after the police boys and called them to stop. She said: 'I will speak with the old man before he dies.' But the police boys had no time and they went off

*Until quite recently, the police who had occasion to go into the desert rode on camels because camels could endure desert conditions far better than horses, and could go through soft sand where trucks could not.

with the camels' heads going up and down and the old man running, running, running, behind.

"And my mother fell down in the dust and cried, and my sister did too, but I didn't, I watched my father instead because I didn't know when I would ever see him again. I told them so and I was right, because later a Bushman who came up from the south told us that they rode the camels through a river and my father was drowned. It was the rope around his neck that choked him, though. That is what happened, and I remember it all, but it happened a long time ago.

"After that, my mother wouldn't stay in the veld without a man and she took us near the waterhole of Nurigaas because the veld was no place for us when my father was dead. But I would like to find that Nurigaas Bushman who followed my father's tracks.

"Then one day a European farmer came in his ox wagon and he said to my mother: 'Who will give me a boy for this pound of tobacco?' And my mother was afraid, so she took the tobacco and said to me: 'He wants you to go with him.' I cried, but the white man took me and put me in his ox wagon and gave my mother another cup of tobacco, but she told him she didn't want it and wanted me to come back. But the white man drove away and my mother ran along beside, crying. She said: 'Wait! Where will I get another boy when he is killed like my husband?' But the farmer didn't hear her. I got sick riding in the wagon and my bowels opened and I was ashamed because the farmer's Bushmen were riding in the wagon too, and they said: 'Why are you crying? Don't be afraid.' But I was afraid because my grandfather told me that white people used to hunt Bushmen and wanted to kill us for our land. The farmer took me to his farm and I pulled weeds and watched his cattle. He gave me milk and cornmeal, but I didn't like it.

I told him milk was for babies and I wanted him to take me back to my country, but he laughed at me.

"He called me Goliath because I was so small. Goliath, come here. Goliath, watch my calves. And later he gave me a shirt to cover my body and then I went to work for another master, who gave me a goat, and then I worked for my last master, who paid me shillings. But I am leaving here too because in South-West Africa they pay better. I am a father now, you know."

The day Tami left, I walked over the veld toward a road to say good-bye to him, and when I got halfway there I found that he had come halfway to say good-bye to me. He was holding his goat by the horns, and behind him his wife, wearing a horrid rag of a European dress, was standing with the baby inside the front of the dress. I gave Tami a knife and his wife a scarf of mine, although I had nothing to give to the baby, and they said good-bye to me and turned, Tami dragging the goat around, pretending to be very jaunty, and they set out walking toward the road that leads to South-West Africa.

Times have changed since Tami's father died. In those days, to be sure, there was a great deal more friction between Bushmen and non-Bushmen than there is now because the Bushmen who lived near the farms of European or Bantu farmers quite often killed cattle. It is sometimes said that they did so because they were unable to distinguish between cattle and wild game, or that the cattle drove away the wild game so that the Bushmen would have had no meat if they had not killed the cattle, but I very much doubt that either of these things was true. Most probably, the Bushmen found that hunting cattle was extremely easy, and also, very probably, they wanted to revenge themselves upon the owners of the cattle, whom they believed to be encroaching upon the land they considered their own. Today, largely because the ownership of the land has been determined, many fewer cattle are killed by Bushmen.

Of course, it is quite against the law for any farmer to keep Bushmen against their will and without recompense, but in the most remote outposts, on many farms, the laws cannot always be enforced. In the Bechuanaland Protectorate today, and also, I believe, in South-West Africa, the governments are trying to set wage scales and provide education for Bushmen, something very difficult for these governments to do as the Bushmen represent only a small fragment of the population, pay no taxes whatever, of course, and are in great demand as laborers; but the only Bushmen who so far can benefit from this are those who already live on the more central farms. Most Bushmen live in the veld, many in almost unreachable parts of the desert, and these people are still being taken by farmers and made to work almost as slaves.

Usually Bushmen do not run away from their masters unless a very good chance presents itself, such as the master's departure for a time, in which case he may return to find that all his Bushmen have run. But to escape is not always easy; the Bantus usually ride after the escaping Bushmen and drag them back, sometimes beating them severely as well. We once learned of a Bushman who, trying to escape, was captured by his Bantu master and beaten to death, his potential labor being sacrificed to set an example for others.

A European farmer can sometimes get police help in recapturing his escaped Bushmen if the farmer has paid the Bushmen some wages in advance and is owed the Bushmen's labor. European farmers are also not always lenient with Bushmen who try to escape. But to escape from any master is by no means impossible; Bushmen are not locked up at night or guarded during the day. Even the chain gangs of Bushmen that you may see in European settlements (Bushmen living near the farms are put in jail occasionally for killing giraffes or stealing cattle) are always straggling down a road with a defenseless guard trailing far behind, and we often wondered why Bushmen were so docile, so easy to exploit, allowing themselves to be badly treated and taken away from their homes. Some people, like Tami, have no choice because they have forgotten the fine skills required to live in the veld and would die there. Some young Bushmen find the promise of European clothing and customs too alluring to resist and are willing to give up their own ways and customs for a shirt or a ragged dress. Perhaps others welcome the promise of food every day, even though they find that on the farms they are poorer than ever, having little enough food, and when their leather clothes fall into rags they cannot hunt to get new ones. Perhaps, too, they are surprised to find their Bantu or European masters not always as dangerous as they feared.

But these things are not true of everyone. Many servants long for their homes; many veld Bushmen hide from Europeans for fear they will be taken away, for they know that a European does not have to force them to come with him, only to persuade them, and since they are afraid of him they hear themselves agreeing to go, and, shortly after, find themselves working on his farm, angry with themselves and filled with remorse.

We learned two reasons for the submissiveness of Bushmen. One reason is that it is not in their nature to fight, not in their experience to deal with people other than themselves. They would much rather run, hide, and wait until a menace has passed than defend themselves forcefully, quite unlike the Bantus, who in the past have waged great wars. But Bushmen misunderstand confrontational bravery. The heroes of their legends are little jackals who trick, lie, and narrowly escape, rather than larger, bolder animals such as lions (who in the Kalahari are something of a master race). In the Bushmen's stories, lions are always being scalded, singed, duped, cuckolded, or killed.

Bushmen cannot afford to fight with each other and almost never do because their only real weapon is their arrow poison, for which there is no antidote. But even were they to disregard this danger, Bushmen would try not to fight because they have no mechanism in their culture for dealing with disagreements other than to remove the causes of the disagreements. Their hold on life is too tenuous to permit quarreling among themselves. A Bushman will go to any lengths to avoid making other Bushmen jealous of him, and for this reason the few possessions that Bushmen have are constantly circling among the members of their groups. No one cares to keep a particularly good knife too long, even though he may want it desperately, because he will become the object of envy; as he sits by himself polishing a fine edge on the blade he will hear the soft voices of the other men in his band saying: "Look at him there, admiring his knife while we have nothing." Soon somebody will ask him for his knife, for everybody would like to have it, and he will give it away. Their culture insists that they share with each other, and it has never happened that a Bushman failed to share objects, food, or water with the other members of his band, for without very rigid co-operation Bushmen could not survive the famines and droughts that the Kalahari offers them.

The other reason for their submissiveness is that Bushmen, whose possessions are only sticks and bones, beads made of eggshell and fragments of leather, are overwhelmed by the possessions of Bantus and Europeans—horses and cattle, dogs, melon lands, medicines, rifles, boots, and trucks— as well as their enormous size, heavy necks and arms, great beards, and roaring voices. Europeans are beyond the powers of Bushmen's imagination, more awesome in stature, in possessions, in might, than even the Bushmen's god, who can be cajoled, who hunts with a bow and arrow. Bushmen consider the Europeans and the Bantus to be superior beings. Bantus and Europeans consider the Bushmen to be inferior beings, and, without resisting, a Bushman always bows to a European or a Bantu person's will.

Once an old man, a veld Bushman, told us the story of the reim and the grass fiber. A reim is a leather rope which the Bantus make by skinning a cow with a long, spiraling cut that goes around and around the body so that the hide comes off all in one piece a few inches wide and many yards long, which is then stretched and cured, making a piece of leather useful for harnessing oxen or building a hut.

"In the earliest days," the old man said, "the Bushmen and the non-Bushmen were all one nation, and the great god came to earth and gave them a rope. Half the rope was made of reim and half was made of grass fiber. The great god told all the people to pull on the rope, and the non-Bushmen came away with the reim, but the Bushmen got only the grass fiber. After that, the non-Bushmen had cattle and reims and all those things, but the Bushmen had only the things that are in the veld. If this ever happened again," the old man said, "I would tell the Bushmen to make sure they got the reim half."

So the distinction between people was caused by the great god, and the Bushmen, who want only to be left in peace, do not compete in issues which they cannot win. They are only frightened by other peoples and hope to be spared their attention. Kung Bushmen call all strangers *zhu dole*, which means "stranger" but, literally, "dangerous person"; they call all non-Bushmen *zo si*, which means "animals without hooves," because, they say, non-Bushmen are angry and dangerous like lions and hyenas. But Kung Bushmen call themselves *zhu twa si*, the harmless people. *Twa* means "just" or "only," in the sense that you say: "It was just the wind" or "It is only me."

- -

CHAPTER TWO

The Road

AFTER WE LEFT Chukudu, a tiny village of Bantu people, the last marked place on the map of Bechuanaland between Molepolole in the east and Ghanzi far in the west, we had no path to follow. We took a course out over the veld set by a Bushman, Gishe, who rode in the jeep at the head of our convoy of four trucks and, remembering the land from his childhood—for he was a Gikwe Bushman—pointed the way.

That was in winter, the last of June 1955, and there were fifteen of us on the expedition, a larger group than we had traveled with before. Besides my father, my mother, my brother John, and myself, there were three South Africans with us, who were Dr. Robert Story, of the Division of Botany in the Department of Agriculture at Pretoria; Theunis Berger, once a health officer of the government of the Bechuanaland Protectorate; and Cass Kruger, a mechanic. There were two other Americans—Daniel Blitz, an expert in sound-recording and photography, and William Donnellan, a doctor. There was also a staff of six African and colored men, who were Philip Hameva, the cook; Ledimo, an interpreter who spoke English, Afrikaans, Herero, Sechuana (his native language), and Kung; Simon, a mechanic's helper; William Camm, also an interpreter who spoke Afrikaans, some English, and Gikwe; and Gishe and Dabe, two Gikwe Bushmen who lived on Theunis's farm.

We were looking for Gikwe Bushmen, as we had heard that there were some who lived in the area. We hoped that if we found some, Gishe or Dabe might discover a relative and enable us to make friends.

- - -

We traveled for many days, all day long, for, not knowing where the Bushmen were, we hoped to come across some of them somewhere, or find a trace or track that might show us in what direction they had gone. We did not find anyone, though, and we saw nothing but the series of long, broad plains that dipped and tilted ever so little; we would find ourselves down in a wide, shallow bowl of grass, then at the rim of the bowl, where we would see the next plain rolling for miles away. Occasionally we came to an acacia forest, but mostly the country was open grassland with tiny thorn bushes down in the grass to catch us. Because it was June, the beginning of the dry season, there were many veld fires, and although we never came upon any, every day we saw their smoke, gray and misty on the horizon, all around us in a ring.

Sometimes we saw a small herd of game running far away from us, raising a little cloud of dust. We saw gemsbok, handsome, large, beige antelope, striped black on their sides, white-bellied, with long, straight horns. We saw gray, tousled wildebeest with curved horns like the horns of cattle. Once we surprised a herd of three eland, a bull and his two wives, which had been eating behind a clump of bushes. They threw up their heads when they saw us, eyes catching the sun and shining pale green like fires. They wheeled, hoofs scraping, and ran, their red bodies swaying, their heads held high with their straight horns down on their backs; they neither leaped nor galloped, but paced majestically away, the great folds of flesh from their chins to their chests swinging. The bull left a string of saliva hanging, shining in the air.

Once we even saw a giraffe, but miles, miles away from us, alone under the clear sky among the thorn trees on the horizon, and we could see its silhouetted head and long neck turned to watch us; it seemed very lonely, very small, and very far away on the yellow flats; when the noise of our trucks reached it, it was frightened and began to run, heaving itself up and down. It ran away from us for a long time and got even smaller but never out of sight. At last it reached the horizon.

Later we came to some soft sand in a little forest of low trees where we found the footprints of a family of lions. Beside the great, splayed pads of the lion, bigger than the span of my hand, went the smaller, neater pads of the lioness with little ridges of dust between the toes, followed by the tiny prints of two almost newborn cubs with feet no bigger than the print of my thumb. The marks had been made less than an hour ago, so John, Theunis, Gishe, and I, who had been in the jeep and were a good distance ahead of the heavier, slower trucks, decided to follow a little way after the family to see what they had been doing. It was during the day and warm, and the lions had been doing nothing except resting in the shade. We found the furry prints of the chests of the adults, made in the shade of a bush, and the prints of two more tiny cubs which the parents must have been carrying. We believed that they were near us because we heard some creature breathing in a tangle of bushes not far away, and we decided not to follow them because the lioness might become anxious and charge. We had only wanted to see them and perhaps photograph them, but we had no rifle and decided it was too dangerous for us there, so we withdrew. We should have loved to see them, and we were sorry to leave their patch of bush.

We looked in the open ground near the lions' thicket for signs of Bushmen, but we found none, so we went on over the flat plains and the next day we came to a long dip in the country, forested with small trees, the last place, said Theunis, where anyone except Bushmen lived. It was the rainy-season village of a few Bakalaharis, a Bantu people who years ago lost all their cattle and went into the desert, where they live a life very much like the life of Bushmen except that they raise goats. During the rains they graze their goats at little posts of theirs, far away in the veld. We set off toward the village, planning to ask the people there if they knew of Bushmen farther on, but as we went over the ridge and down into the valley we came upon all the villagers walking toward us, driving donkeys and herds of goats, a surprising sight in that lonely country. There were about sixty people in all, tall, dark-skinned Bakalahari men carrying bows and arrows, followed by their women, who carried heavy bundles on their backs, supported by tump-lines around their foreheads, which made their eyes bulge and their lower jaws stick out. Among them walked their Bushmen servants, old wrinkled men and women, young girls with their babies, lithe young hunters, small, light-skinned, all carrying great loads of household goods belonging to the Bakalaharis, with the youngest Bushman children riding on top of the loads. Some of the Bushman

boys were driving herds of goats, some of the older Bushman women drove herds of scrubby gray donkeys which
were also heavily loaded with bundles of hides, sticks used
to build houses, bags of belongings, and baby goats too
young to walk.

We were surprised to see them and we stopped. Some
of them stopped when they saw us, halting the donkeys;
the rest, hot and feeling the weight of their bundles, walked
by us in a long procession on either side, glancing at us but
not stopping, anxious to get to their camping place as soon
as possible although it was only morning and they still had
a long way to go. Their company did not follow a path,
but spread out all through the bush in a dusty crowd, the
adults walking silently, saving their energy. The children
shouted, the goats bleated, and the skinny dogs whined and
barked.

A Bushman woman driving a herd of goats almost
walked over us, and a donkey driven by a child crowded
against us, loaded with clusters of pottery jars that were
strung together like melons on a vine, each of which con-
tained a chicken, thrust in with its head down and its feet
protruding from the mouth of the jar, the theory being that
the chicken, finding itself upside down and so confined,
gets confused and does not try to escape. Muffled squawks
echoed from the chickens, an eerie sound.

One old man, a Bakalahari, came up to talk with us.
He was very poorly dressed, in ragged shorts, and was very
suspicious, perhaps assuming from our questions about
Bushmen that we wanted his servants for laborers, and he
stood apart from us and called out his answers to us, glancing out of the corners of his eyes at the people pouring by
him, worrying perhaps that they would leave him behind.
I was sitting on the ground listening to the conversation
when I heard someone come up behind me, and I looked
around to see a pair of long, dark legs almost standing on

me, then up into the shadow of a wide-brimmed hat which almost covered a young man's face. He had a beautiful body, clad in a pair of shorts, but of his face under the hat brim, only the eyes, dull white, showed clearly. The rest of his face had been eaten away by yaws into a mass of holes and pits, some large, some small, some around his nose showing black caves, the insides of his nasal passages, some, around his mouth, showing a tooth or two. The wide strap of his hat was arranged over his face to cover the hole where his nose had been. He spoke, a belch, for the insides of his mouth and throat were gone, and his voice was deep and echoing, like a voice in a cavern. It did not sound like the voice of a human being.

He stepped over me as if I weren't there and, shouldering the old man aside, told us that he was the headman of the village. The old man hurried on, and we asked the headman where all the villagers were going. He told us that they were moving back to Chukudu, their winter quarters, for the veld was particularly dry that year and they could no longer live there. We asked him if he knew of any Bushmen farther on in the desert, but he said that none were left. Lions, he told us, had eaten them all. This was impossible, of course, although it meant that he suspected us and did not wish to talk. The condition of his face made him self-conscious, for he kept arranging the strap of his hat over the holes, and didn't talk with us long, but lifted his hand in a salute and turned away, following his people up the path that they were leaving behind them, for the sharp feet of the donkeys and goats trampled a swathe through the grass.

We watched them go, and soon they were out of sight among the bushes. Only their heads showed, bobbing above the tops of the bushes; we saw the headman's hat—he had hurried and caught up. In a moment the procession had reached the rise of ground and there a group of young

Bushman women, who were the last of the procession and were scattered all over the hillside waist-deep in the yellow grass, turned their heads to look back at us; like vixens they watched us over their slender shoulders, neither smiling nor speaking, just watching with blank faces and great eyes.

- - -

We went on, and traveled for many days, breaking camp before dawn, stopping only for a minute for a bite at noon, not stopping again until it was almost dark. We saw no people, no animals, but only the miles and miles of yellow-silver grass and black bushes, and the wind that blew across the country twisting the grass from silver to gold, gold to silver. It may have blown for thousands of miles before it touched us, perhaps blown over a Bushman werf tucked away somewhere, one point in the enormous, vast veld that ran all the way to Molepolole and all the way to Ghanzi, hundreds of miles to the south and north to the great river; the veld was just grass, occasionally marked by a little nameless pan, a little salt flat, or a few bushes or thorn trees; it was inhabited only by lonely birds, a few antelope in small herds, a few families of lions, a few Bushmen, as far apart from each other as the stars. The only sound there was made by the wind in the grass or the voices of a few birds singing, the only movement the slow turning of the sun, the moon, and the cold stars, very far away.

Every morning the sun rose straight up from the flat horizon, salmon red and in a haze of yellow, distorted by the haze into an oblong, and always gigantic, like a monster looming above the poor, dry, stumpy bushes of the veld.

- - -

As we went farther and farther into the desert we saw less and less game. The great herds that had once been there were gone, perhaps because it was too dry, although the game antelope do not need to drink water, for they get enough moisture from the grass and roots they eat; perhaps because the great veld fires had burned away the dry grass farther in the north, causing new green grass to spring up, luring the antelope to come there. We saw fires very near us and we wondered if the Bushmen had followed the game to the north.

One day we came to a tiny, low forest where we decided to camp for the night. As we searched among the little trees for firewood, we came upon three scherms, three little huts, built by Bushmen and abandoned very recently. The ashes of the fires were still warm. The people who lived there had surely heard us and had run away, leaving many of their possessions behind. We found a pot, burned black from use, a few white beads, a quiver with arrows, and a digging-stick, which is a branch a few feet long with the bark peeled off and the twigs trimmed away, sharpened at one end and used by Bushmen as a spade to break the hard ground when they dig roots. We then found footprints made by the people when they had rushed off in all directions; and later, as we followed the tracks, we even found the prints of hands and knees where someone had crawled hastily across an open place.

The discovery of these huts made us very hopeful, as we had traveled much farther than we had expected. We felt confident that Gishe, who had been born near our very campsite, would be able to track the people and find them, or that they would be plagued by curiosity and finally visit us. They did not, however; nor did they come back for their possessions, nor was Gishe able to find them. He had been living on a farm for many years and was no longer an expert tracker; and after the night dew had fallen during the evening that we found the werf, the tracks were old.

Of course, it was useless for us to wander around the veld hoping to stumble upon fresh tracks, although we tried the following day without success. We also sent Gishe to look for the people, but all he did was set the veld on fire;

he had been careless when lighting his pipe. He had asked to have matches to start a fire in case a lion saw him, so that when we saw smoke rising from the direction he had taken, we ran to the spot, then had to run back again to save our trucks when the wind turned the fire toward our camp. After that, we were about to give up and move farther into the veld, thinking that the Bushmen had perhaps gone far away. We had only the water that we carried and we were wasting it by waiting; but in the evening, in the quiet, cold air, when some of us happened to be standing at the edge of camp, we heard an ax ringing as somebody chopped wood far away, the sound carried to us on the wind. It was surely the people; there is no other sound in the world exactly like an ax ringing, and we decided to wait a few more days.

We set up a permanent camp. We arranged our trucks, pitched our tents, and waited. The third night that we waited there, all scattered in our blankets over the ground, three lions walked among us as we slept, sniffed us, and watched us with their yellow eyes, although we didn't know until morning when we found their tracks.

The fourth night a veld fire passed us. We were awake then; we saw the bright flames leaping at the trees, smelled the smoke, and heard the fire roaring as the wind pushed it forward into the grass.

CHAPTER THREE

- -

The Bushmen

ON THE MORNING of the fifth day, when we felt that we could wait no longer, Gishe guessed that we might find Bushmen farther ahead, and we decided to try. Breaking a track is such a slow and tedious process that my brother John, Theunis, Gishe, and I loaded one truck and set off in it, leaving the other people to load the other trucks and follow later, traveling faster in our tracks.

We rode west all morning, and at noon we came to an open pan where fine, soft grass as fine as hair was blowing, and we saw a lion there, a big male with a black, tangled mane growing all the way down his neck and ending between his shoulders. He had the muscled neck and shoulders and the wide, swelling jaw of male creatures, and when he raised his head to look at us we saw that he was old. His face was wrinkled and massive, and he looked straight at us with a direct, indifferent look, the blind gaze of cats. His paws were enormous, his fur was the color of gold. He seemed so huge and bright in the sunlight, his eyes so cold and pale, that he fascinated us the way a cat fascinates birds. At that moment he could have walked up to us and carried one of us away.

Bushmen believe that certain famous sorcerers, once medicine men who chose to be poisoners and magicians instead of healers, have taken the form of certain lions, which can always be distinguished from ordinary lions by their great size and their ability to float in the air. Also, Bushmen say, the eclipses of the moon are caused by lions, as on very bright nights a lion may cover the moon's face with a great paw, giving himself darkness for better hunting.

Usually, when a lion sees you, he skulks away or bounds off in great, ungainly leaps, in clumsy dodges, making a fool of himself because he is frightened; but when one raises his head and looks right at you, then turns as this one did, and walks off without even looking back, you understand at once why Bushmen believe the things they do.

As the lion walked away into a thicket of acacia trees we climbed off the truck and followed him. It was rash of us, but we were not afraid of him. We wanted a photograph. However, he had disappeared, and as we were looking cautiously around among the trunks of little trees we heard a motor roaring, gears grinding; and finally, as we watched, the jeep arrived with Cass and Bob (Dr. Story), who told us to go back to camp as fast as we could. Two Bushmen had arrived.

We started back at once and got there late in the afternoon, and there we found them, two small men, one old, one young, in silhouette as they squatted by the fire, turning as we came to look at us, very nervous and very ill at ease. They had been given food and tobacco—a blue cloud hung above their heads—and a bucket of water, but during the course of the afternoon they had drunk the bucket dry. As Theunis and Gishe, the only people who could have spoken to both them and us, had been away, the rest of the expedition had had to wait anxiously for our return, unable to communicate a single word.

Both men were thin, brown-skinned, and wore nothing but loincloths, and they looked very out of place next to us, among our big trucks and boxes of equipment, squatting naked like two frogs against the long grass and reddening sky of their country. We sat by the fire to talk with them, and it was the old man who answered our questions. His name was Ukwane, and he seemed very old, for he spoke with a hesitant, cracked voice that faded into a whisper at the end of every phrase, and whenever some of us would leave or join the group at the fire he would stare intently at us, frowning, leaning forward a little because he could barely see us, his eyes being filmed with cataracts, hazy blue.

Ukwane had great wrinkles lengthwise down his belly. His hands were knobbed and his shoulders stiff, yet his legs were as supple as a baby's, for he sat crouched with his knees in the air and his heels tucked up tight against his buttocks. His skin looked old, too, like old leather, hardened and black like a glove that has been left in the rain, and his curly hair was disheveled, uncut, untidy with pieces of straw.

Our questions frightened Ukwane, and often he was at a loss for something to reply. He thought we were policemen coming to look for some lost horses, for somehow a rumor had reached into the farthest corners of the veld that a European farmer had lost seven horses and all the people in the veld were afraid for their lives. The first thing he said was that he hadn't seen any horses and certainly hadn't taken them himself. He was too old, he said. We told him that we were not policemen and besides, had never heard of the horses, but he was not reassured. He coughed and turned to the young man, who looked at us with nothing to say.

The young man was also very shy, but had a greater dignity than Ukwane because of his cool, proud bearing. He said very little, and when he did speak it was in a voice so soft that it was almost inaudible. Also, he held his hand in front of his mouth with a finger against his lips, which muffled his words so that only Ukwane could understand them. This was what the young man intended; he meant for the old man to speak for them both and only wanted to help him through tight spots in the conversation.

The young man told us his name, though, which was Gai. Gai sat crouching too, like Ukwane, and kept self-consciously shifting his position, pretending to be unconcerned. He glanced at us out of the corners of his eyes and smiled skeptically from time to time, for although he did not know us and, as we learned later, had not seen Europeans before, therefore had no way of judging our remarks and our expressions, he was younger than Ukwane, and prouder, and was afraid of showing his naïveté, afraid of seeming to believe a lie or disbelieving something that everyone should know was true.

Gai was extremely handsome. In fact, he was one of the most beautiful human beings I have ever seen, tall for a Bushman, his head shaved, showing a strong, domed skull. His face was strong, too, a little heavy of bone, with a big jaw which he carried thrust forward and up so that he looked at you from the bottom of his eyes, a reserved gaze. His body was smooth and brown, built compactly, the body itself long in proportion to the arms and legs. Like all Bushmen, he was narrow of shoulder and hip, with a deep chest and a large belly, and when seen from the side as his belly relaxed he seemed wider from front to back than he was from side to side, very like a hunting animal whose chest is deep but narrow. Gai was also well dressed, not with a strip of leather like Ukwane, but with a beautifully designed, worked, and fringed loincloth with two wide tabs at the back which he could spread to sit on. He wore a band around his hips, too, as a belt for the loincloth, with a fringe of leather strips so long that when he sat down the fringe lay on the ground.

We asked them where they lived, and Ukwane, who was afraid to answer, said he was old and did not remember. Gai said they lived many days' journey to the east. We asked if the huts beside our camp belonged to them, and they said no, they had never seen them before, neither did they have the slightest idea how they came to be there.

We gave them some more tobacco as a gesture of our good faith and we told them that we had come from America, hundreds of days' travel and across a great body of water, but of course they had never heard of America or the ocean and thought we meant the Okovango River, and at that they didn't really believe us, although they were too polite to tell us so. "Merica," they said softly, with a beautiful, curled *r*, almost a *d* or an *l*. We said that we had come to visit them and to give them presents. We said that we were the friends of many Bushmen in the west where we had lived for a year, and had been given Bushman names, so we weren't entirely strangers. We told them the names, which made them smile, because of course they weren't Gikwe names, but Gai and Ukwane softened a little with this and admitted that, after all, the huts were theirs.

Finally they told us that a few nights ago they had been sitting at their fires, the two men, their wives and children, and one other family, when they had heard the sound of our trucks, which had frightened them so that they had run off into the veld in all directions, taking nothing with them except the few possessions that had come first to hand. Ukwane, warming a little, said that he had been so terrified that he had crawled away on his hands and knees, afraid to show his head above the tops of the bushes.

Presently they had found each other again and had settled into a new place, although now they had no scherms. For the next days they had waited and listened, and when they had heard our truck leave they had assumed that we were gone, and had returned to get the rest of their things. Then they had noticed our trucks, and believing that they were surrounded and had fallen into our trap, they had come to surrender. Ukwane felt more relaxed and laughed at this, a warm, wheezy chuckle, showing a few teeth, slapping his chest and coughing from the smoke which he had been inhaling deeply. Seeing Ukwane, the rest of us laughed, too, but Gai only stiffened and smiled an icy smile. Behind his head the sun was setting, small and red, away over the edge of the flat plain, making all the little, distant trees against it look black and very lonely; and the new moon followed after into the salmon light, a heavy crescent flat on its back and bow-shaped, yellow and malevolent like the smile.

Before they went to sleep that night, the two men accepted a second bucketful of water as a present. The bucket they would return, but the water was for them alone, an enormous present in the desert, for which they were very grateful. They began to drink from it, scooping the water up with their hands and, later, lifting the bucket to drink from its rim. After that they lay down, naked as they were on the bare ground, close to the fire, with their knees bent, letting as much skin as possible be exposed to the heat. The warm smoke and ashes blew over them and they went to sleep on their sides as Bushmen always must, with one ear on the ground but with the other up and listening, to hear what comes along. Because it was cold they woke up often, and every time they woke they drank, so in the morning only the bottom of the pail had water in it, frozen into a circle of ice.

The next day the two men agreed to take some of us to their werf, and we drove off with Ukwane in the jeep and Gai on the hood to point the way. From his higher position he noticed the long horns of a gemsbok in the grass and he signaled for the jeep to stop. Then he, John, and Theunis, taking a rifle, slipped out of the jeep and ran off after it, bent over and crouched so low that only their backs showed, as the backs of animals would, gliding above the grass. The gemsbok saw them and ran away toward a patch of heavy bush in the plain, the great V of horns a crown over its head. The men ran after, standing now, and in an hour they came back to where Ukwane and I were waiting, lying on our stomachs under the jeep to be in shade, saying that they had killed it. We drove to the spot where the gemsbok, a female, lay and brought her with us, a present to offer the other Bushmen.

We drove for several hours and at last we came to a wide plain, grown over heavily with small trees of slender trunks, with a few short branches sprouting leaves, like fence posts. Gai directed us to one of the smaller trees in the center of the plain and told us to stop. He climbed down and looked around over the veld, then bent and picked up a small pipe, a piece of the leg bone of an antelope. He asked us for a match, lit his pipe, and smoked it.

At last we noticed on the other side of the tree two shallow depressions scooped in the sand and lined with grass, like the shallow, scooped nests of shore birds on a beach—the homes of the families, where the people could lie curled up just below the surface of the plain to let the cold night wind which blows across the veld pass over them.

Other than the depressions, except for a small pile of

brown, twisted bean shells, no sign would show that people lived there. Later we saw another scooped pit and a stick thrust upright in the ground beside it, right at our feet, which was Gai's place; the stick was to mark the spot, although Gai could have found his shallow pit at any time of the day or night.

Nobody was there; everyone had run away. We sat down and waited while Gai put his hands to his mouth and shouted, trying to summon the people back again. When nobody came or even answered him, he flung his pipe to the ground and marched off to find them among the bushes, alternately shouting to his hidden relatives and muttering to himself, for they might be far away and the day was getting warm.

We sat in the middle ground between the depressions so that we wouldn't risk stepping on or crushing anybody's hidden things, for, without knowing it, a European can in a moment trample through a Bushman's cache, breaking the delicate bone or wooden objects, bending the reed arrows, or crushing eggshell beads. Also, among certain groups of Bushmen, every fire has a man's side and a woman's side, determined by the position of the fire as you face the doorway of the scherm, the man's side being on the right, the woman's on the left. If a man sits on the woman's side, or where a woman has been sitting, he will become impotent and will also lose his power to hunt, and if a woman sits where a man has been sitting, she will get a disease in her vagina. Something intangible, invisible, but dangerously powerful, remains on the ground. We did not know which side was which of this werf's fires, or even for sure where the fires were; we did not even know that the Gikwe had this custom, for we had learned it from Kung Bushmen, but we knew that if they did they would not welcome our contaminating their ground. We would have liked to look around, but the best thing we could do was to keep our big boots and our bodies away from their delicate, fragile, almost invisible community.

In a short time we heard a rustle in the veld, and a young woman who seemed to be in her early twenties stepped from the bushes. She was, Ukwane said, Gai's wife, and on her hip she carried a baby, a naked three-year-old who looked at us from his wide eyes fearlessly, then, realizing that we were strangers, buried his face in his mother's arm. His mother stroked him calmly and came toward us smiling and nodding her head graciously, although a little pulse was hammering in the V of her throat. We learned later that she had been sitting in the bushes very near us, and when she had seen her husband go by she had assumed that everything was all right and had come to greet us, not bothering to answer his cries.

She was a short, sturdy woman with round arms, long thighs, and short calves. She had a rather large belly and square, strong shoulders, and she wore a very tattered cape or kaross over her back, with a small leather apron around her hips. She had no ornaments except a row of blue scars over her eyes, a decoration, and she had allowed her hair to become disheveled, long, and a little tangled, hanging down over her ears in tight spirals, instead of having shaved it off as most Bushman women do. All this gave her a very matter-of-fact air, which was not deceiving, for she saw in a glance that we were harmless and, looking us over, sat down at once beside me.

Her baby pulled, twisted, and tugged at her, and from the way he behaved I judged that he kept her too busy to be forever cutting her hair or making bead ornaments. Besides, she told us later, if she wore ornaments, the baby pulled them off. She had her row of scars, though, delicate and arching over her brow, making her eyes seem wider; as well as a row of striped scars along her thighs. These, say Bushmen, are made to imitate the beauty of zebras, and many women wear them, having been decorated when they were still young. It is a painful procedure. The cuts are made on the thighs and forehead with a knife or ax blade, then charcoal is rubbed in, but the woman told us later that in her case it had been worth the pain and trouble because, she said, she was extremely ugly and had been made more beautiful.

Her baby's name was Nhwakwe, she told me, and after that we were at a loss for conversation. I offered her a cigarette, which she declined, indicating that it made her cough. I was surprised, for she was the only Bushman I had ever met, man, woman, or child, who did not smoke.

Presently she smiled, pressed her hand to her chest, and said: "Tsetchwe." It was her name.

"Elizabeth," I said, pointing to myself.

"Nisabe," she answered, pronouncing after me and inclining her head graciously. She looked me over carefully without really staring, which to Bushmen is rude. Then, having surely suspected that I was a woman, she put her hand on my breast gravely, and, finding that I was, she gravely touched her own breast. Many Bushmen do this; to them all Europeans look the same.

"*Tsau si*" (women), she said.

Then after a moment's pause, Tsetchwe began to teach me a few words, the names of a few objects around us, grass, rock, bean shell, so that we could have a conversation later. As she talked she took a handful of the beans out of her kaross, broke them open, and began to eat them. This is a wonderful, bitter bean, shaped like a lima bean, which grows on tiny bushes in patches throughout the Kalahari. When you eat these beans they burn your tongue, throat, and stomach, but they take away hunger and thirst. Besides the beans in her kaross, Tsetchwe, who began unloading, brought out a large, edible root which she had dug up— she must have been gathering food before we came—and put it in the shade of a bush beside her fireplace. Also, she brought out six round green melons which are called *tsama* melons, and which, during the autumn, provide the only liquid available for all the Bushmen in the desert, and for all the game antelope besides. Under the green rind a tsama is very like a watermelon, filled with small oval seeds and very watery in texture, but is itself pale green and smaller, the size of a small cantaloupe. Tsetchwe placed one between her feet and, gripping it firmly with her strong toes, chopped a hole in the top of it with her digging-stick; then, lifting the cap away like the lid of a jack-o'-lantern, she mashed the pulp inside until it was liquid. She put the melon to her mouth and, tipping her head back, drank from it, using her long digging-stick to help push the pulp into her mouth, working it like an enormous chopstick, making a watery noise as she sucked. When Tsetchwe had collected a mouthful of seeds she put the melon down, took an old, dry tsama melon rind from her kaross, and spat the seeds into it to save them, for they can be roasted and eaten like nuts when they are dry. Tsetchwe drank all the liquid in the rind and seemed refreshed as she cast the empty rind over her shoulder and brushed off her mouth and hands.

At last Gai strode back into the werf, followed at a distance by a group of three small boys and, much farther, by three old women who stood waist-deep in bushes, close together like three antelope, craning their necks to see us.

When they noticed Tsetchwe and Ukwane, they came forward with more confidence, accepted tobacco, and, squatting immediately, began to smoke. It had been months, Ukwane said, since they had used their last tobacco, had been reduced to smoking leaves, and they were very happy to have the tobacco we had given them. Bushmen love to smoke. They say that tobacco, as well as the wild beans, takes away hunger and thirst, and, besides that, it makes their hearts glad. One of the old women, Dasina, who was Tsetchwe's mother, inhaled too deeply and began to faint. Tsetchwe half turned her mother so that everyone would not see her, and, putting an arm around her for support, let the old woman lean on her shoulder. Our interpreter laughed, and Tsetchwe turned to glare. Tsetchwe's back was exactly like her mother's, broad but curved in at the waist, the old woman's a little bloated but Tsetchwe's young and strong.

Another old woman was smoking, too, puffing on a short, wide pipe cut from a leg bone of some large antelope, so big that she had to stuff one end with grass to keep the tobacco inside. She almost unhinged her jaw each time she puffed. She would inhale and spit, cough, and inhale again without a sign of dizziness, and when she saw Dasina faint she too laughed out loudly. Her name, she told us, was Twikwe.

Twikwe was skinny and tall as a man, with long, lanky arms that she flung about in the air, gesturing, and long legs that jerked when she walked. She wore only a short piece of leather that reached from her waist to her thighs, and we could see that she was wrinkled from head to foot, her skin hanging in long, vertical wrinkles down her thighs and belly, like an old apple that has dried. She talked incessantly and loudly, always opening and closing her mouth, and she joked, for Ukwane and the young boys near her laughed at everything she said. She was telling how her husband had outdistanced her as they were running away and was surely running still. Every now and then she stopped her talk to shout out to him, jeering, saying that he was depriving himself of tobacco and should come back; then everyone would listen, but no sound came from him, no answer. He never did come back, and in the weeks we were there we never saw him. Perhaps he was running away from Twikwe, for we later learned that he was living in a valley with his other wife.

The third old woman was Ukwane's wife, and her name was Kutera. She was the oldest of the four women by many years, and much the frailest; her arms and legs were spindly, and she was so thin that her slender bones stuck out. She moved slowly, feebly, and spoke in a high, thin voice like the piping of a little bird. She didn't even have the big belly that Bushmen usually have; instead, her belly clung to her backbone and she looked like a little, dry bird skeleton, ready to splinter or be blown away.

The other members of the group were the three young boys. One, Giamakwe, about eleven years old, was the son of Ukwane's old age, and the other two, Wite and Witabe, about ten and fourteen, were the sons of Twikwe and the man who ran away. All were extremely thin, with arms and legs like matchsticks, and each wore a tiny rag of a loincloth that had been cast off by someone else and cut down to their sizes—just tokens of modesty, as the boys were not covered up at all. But they were very gay and active; their shyness of us vanished immediately and was replaced by excitement; they whirled and spun like dervishes when they saw the gemsbok, played leapfrog, jounced each other, and ran circles around the werf, followed by the baby, Nhwakwe, who chased them like a puppy and could not keep up. He would tire from time to time, fall into his mother's lap to nurse, and then, refreshed, would rush headlong after the three boys again. He never did catch them, but this did not make him angry or make him cry.

When everyone was present, looking hungrily at the gemsbok on the jeep with a swarm of redheaded flies already at its mouth, Gai and Ukwane got their knives and rolled the gemsbok to the ground. She fell with a hard bounce, a thump as her legs or her long horns struck, and a huff as gas rushed from her open mouth. She lay stiffly, looking awkward with her hind leg raised, looking wild with her cocoa-colored mane that stood stiff and straight along the bowed crest of her neck, wild with her great horns sharp enough to prick your finger, and her pale, half-open eyes.

Gai squatted beside her and began to stroke her udder. He squeezed a teat and milk squirted into his palm, and as he licked it off, Ukwane squatted beside him. The gemsbok was big enough for both men to squat at her udder milking, Ukwane under her lifted thigh. I was told that when the men had first followed her, they had come upon a gemsbok calf wedged high up in the fork of a tree. A leopard had killed it and left it there, and as the men tried to climb the tree to pull it down, robbing the leopard, the mother gemsbok had reappeared and challenged them, so they had killed her instead. That is why her udder was filled with milk. Her beige hide, we noticed, had been raked by the leopard's claws.

Almost everyone came by with a palm outstretched for a squirt of milk. Ukwane called for me to come, too, and, stroking the milk veins in her udder the way one does when milking a cow, he milked a white stream into my palm which I licked away. The milk was strong and rank and gamy, not at all like the mild, sweet-tasting milk of cows. It smelled like the intestines, too, perhaps because the animal was dead, perhaps because the odor of intestines and the milk both came from the strong, harsh grass of the country. Yet it was liquid, and the Bushmen milked her dry.

Afterward, Gai and Ukwane butchered her, Gai preparing himself by casually sharpening his knife on her narrow, heart-shaped hoof. Always working so that her wounded side was up, they cut her skin free, not spilling a drop of blood. Near the carcass they dug a shallow pit, which they lined with the skin, hair side down, and as blood would well up into the cuts they made butchering, they would collect it and place it in this bowl. The carcass itself, now red and pink and white, they rolled onto a bed of leaves and branches to keep it clean and cut off the front and hind legs of the upper side, forming a bowl of the carcass so that no liquid would escape. They pulled out the intestine, cleaning each length carefully, first squeezing out all fecal matter, then turning the intestine inside out over a stick and scraping it clean. A lot of liquid ran from the intestines, which was saved with the blood in the bowl of the body.

Next, the two men removed the rumen, the first stomach of ruminant animals, where the grass they bolt hurriedly is kept in quantities to be coughed up and chewed thoroughly when the animal is lying in the shade. Ukwane lifted the rumen out carefully, like a great water sack that might burst suddenly, and hurried with it to the pit lined with the skin. There he slit it and water gushed out, every drop saved by the skin. Ukwane and Gai removed handfuls of the contents, a yellow, pulpy mass of partially digested grass, and they squeezed each handful dry into bowls, tsama-melon rinds, and ostrich-egg water containers that the women had brought forward. They did not mind two great white worms that were discovered living in the rumen, for as soon as enough water was collected, the people all had a long, satisfying drink. Some was pressed on me by Tsetchwe; I could not bring myself to drink it, but I did taste it and found that it was not too unpleasant, although it also tasted strongly as intestines smell. It was fresh, however, it was only the liquid from grass, and I thought that if I had no other water I too could drink the water of rumen.

Also, the people drank the blood, scooping it out in handfuls to their faces. Soon they were stained with it; the three old women looked very savage, and Gishe, our interpreter, asked Ukwane for some, which Ukwane gave him. Gishe said: "I have been living among Europeans for a long time, but I remember now who I am."

From the body of that gemsbok the Bushmen bailed out

several bucketfuls of liquid, enough to supply them for almost a week. They cut the meat into strips which they would dry in the sun and use as they needed them, also enough for a week or perhaps even longer, as there were only a few people and the gemsbok was almost as big as a cow.

Tsetchwe had built a tiny fire beneath a tsama melon, an empty melon with the top cut away, and when she received her share of the meat—for any animal is divided at once by a rigid system of rules, some meat given to each person rather than kept as a communal supply or portioned to families—she cut a small piece and stuffed it into the melon, where melon juice, heated through the rind, was boiling now. It cooked like meat in a stew, and when it was done Tsetchwe emptied the melon into a bowl, fanned it to cool it, and then ate some, putting a strip of meat into her mouth and hacking off a bite with her husband's knife. She was ravenously hungry and she ate almost all, while her baby, lying in her lap, nursed from her breast. The last piece she saved for him; she put one end of it into his mouth and, as he bit down, flashed the great knife under his nose to cut him a small enough morsel.

The gemsbok had vanished. All that remained from the butchering was the pile of squeezed, dry grass from the rumen and a few lumps of feces that the redheaded flies buzzed over. The meat, bones, head, hide, and brushlike tail all now belonged to people, and all the people had carried their portions away. Gai owned two hind legs and a front leg, Tsetchwe had meat from the back, Ukwane had the other front leg, his wife had one of the feet and the stomach, the young boys had lengths of intestine. Twikwe had received the head and Dasina the udder.

It seems very unequal when you watch Bushmen divide a kill, yet it is their system, and in the end no person eats more than any other. That day Ukwane gave Gai still another piece because Gai was his relation, Gai gave meat to Dasina because she was his wife's mother. After the meat had been divided again in this way and cooked, the cooked food was shared. No one, of course, contested Gai's large share, because he had been the hunter and by their law that much belonged to him. No one doubted that he would share his large amount with others, and they were not wrong, of course; he did. It is not the amount eaten by any person but the formal ownership of every part that matters to Bushmen.

It was already evening and the sun sat on the flat veld like an enormous, flaming mountain. It sank, and its orange color was echoed in the three families' fires as the people warmed themselves and cooked their meat.

- - -

The following day the three young boys, feeling vigorous with all the meat they had eaten, went out to play in the veld and came back at noon with a tortoise, a lizard, and a tiny rabbit, a baby one that they had been able to run down. The young boys would have had to divide any substantial game with the adults, but since these animals were so small the boys were allowed to keep them. Small animals are divided among the children and cooked for them by one of their parents.

Wite carried in the rabbit, still alive, across his shoulders, pretending that it was very heavy and that he was tired and worn, as though he were a hunter carrying home a buck. When he threw the rabbit down, a soft ball of gray fur with the innocent eyes of a baby and pretty, drop-shaped ears that were pink inside, it rushed at him and bit his finger. A dire fate awaited it; Ukwane caught it and pinched its throat.

The tortoise was given to Nhwakwe, the baby, as the spoils of a hunt are always shared, and Gai, his father, took it to roast it for him.

First, Gai scooped a shallow pit in the sand in front of his sleeping-place, which he filled with burning sticks. Beside him, old Twikwe held the tortoise on its back, but the tortoise urinated brown urine and Twikwe let it stand up. It stood looking at the flames, blinking its hard black eyes, then started to walk away. But Twikwe caught it again and held it, idly turning it over and over while she talked with Gai about other things, about smoke they had noticed on the southern horizon which Gai said was Bushmen's smoke. Gai said he planned to go to see the people some day soon, and as he spoke he took the tortoise from Twikwe and laid it on its back, where it rested with its feet out and its neck bent, in the position that would be correct if it were standing. Gai took a burning stick from the fire and set it against the tortoise's belly. The tortoise kicked violently and jerked its head, urinating profuse amounts of the brown urine which ran over Gai's hand, but the heat had its effect, the two hard, central plates on the shell of the belly peeled back, and Gai thrust his hand inside. The smoldering shell reeked and the tortoise struggled violently, but Gai slit the belly with his knife and pulled out the intestine.

The tortoise by now had retreated partway into its shell, trying to hide there, gazing out from between its front knees. Gai reached the heart, which was still beating, and flipped it onto the ground, where it jerked violently for a moment, almost jumping, then relaxed to a more spasmodic beating, all by itself and dusty, now ignored. Gai pinched the gall away from the yellow liver and threw that away, but he left the liver and the surrounding fat because he meant for that to be eaten.

The baby, Nhwakwe, who owned the tortoise, came to sit by his father, leaning on Gai's leg and watching, looking smiling into the belly of the tortoise. A tortoise is such a slow, tough creature that its body can function although its heart is gone. Nhwakwe put his wrists to his forehead to imitate in a most charming manner the way in which the tortoise was trying to hide. Nhwakwe looked just like the tortoise.

Gai frowned with concentration and worked with his mouth open, pulled down at the corners. When the intestines were removed, Gai stuffed the cavity with green leaves of the kind that "make your gums numb," say the Bushmen, added for flavor, I believe. The tortoise at this retreated far into its shell with its legs pulled in tightly, and Gai heated the doors again to curl them down. Then he packed the opening with grass and the tortoise's dung, capped it with a tsama-melon cap, and put the tortoise into the oven that was prepared for it like a shallow little grave which the tortoise just fitted, a final agony, for the tortoise once more kicked and struggled as Gai raked hot coals over it. The steam escaping from the moist flesh caused the ashes to bubble and boil, and it was over; the meat was in the pot.

Gai flung the intestines away and sat down near his wife to smoke, and I, who wished that they could at least have killed the tortoise first, thought of the story of Pishiboro and one of his wives, an elephant. Pishiboro is one of the names of God.

One night, when Pishiboro and his younger brother were sleeping, the elephant wife took them both and rolled them between her thighs, which caused them great discomfort. The younger brother said to Pishiboro: "Let us go away now while it is dark. This wife of yours may want to kill us with her attention." So they got up and slipped away. Next morning, when they were far away from Pishiboro's house, the younger brother looked back and saw the elephant wife coming after them. "Run on," he said to Pishiboro, "and I will stay behind and talk with her." So Pishiboro ran on and the younger brother waited. When the elephant wife came up, the younger brother said to her: "I see that you have a big louse in your flesh there. Let me take it out for you." The elephant wife agreed to let him, and Pishiboro's younger brother took a long thorn and pricked the elephant wife on her chest, right under her beads.

"Oh, you are hurting me," said the elephant wife.

"Don't flinch," said Pishiboro's younger brother. "This louse is very deep in your flesh." With that the younger brother pierced her heart and she fell dead.

The younger brother then built a fire, cut off the breast of the elephant wife, and roasted it. When it was cooked he sat up on the body of the elephant wife to eat it, and it was there that Pishiboro, returning to see what had happened, noticed him sitting way up over the tops of the bushes. "Ah, can it be," thought Pishiboro, "that my younger brother has killed my wife and is sitting on her body?" When Pishiboro ran forward he found that his worst suspicion was absolutely true.

Pishiboro was wildly angry, but his younger brother handed him some of the roasted breast, which presently Pishiboro ate. The younger brother looked down at Pishiboro and said in a voice filled with scorn: "Oh, you fool. You lazy man. You were married to meat and you thought it was a wife." Pishiboro saw that this was true, so he sharpened his knife and helped his younger brother with the skinning.

- - -

The Bushmen as well as the gods ignore the suffering of animals. When they opened the pit and took out the tortoise several hours later it did look delicious, and the meat, which came easily off the small, thick bones, smelled delicious brewed in the green leaves, and the thin young boys smiled happily and brought their tsama rinds to be filled from the mortar where Gai put the pieces he had picked off and had pounded to make them even and small.

While there was gemsbok meat and tortoise meat, the

rabbit was not worth eating, and it hung from the tree, where it dried, like a little husk, to be moistened again and eaten when nothing else was left. It swung in the breeze like a leaf, like a tiny, eerie ornament.

The lizard was eaten that evening by the three young boys, who built a fire of their own, where they sat like hunters back from a hunt; with the red light of the fire on their thin faces, making their eyes bright, they roasted the lizard in the coals and ate it, and pulled its tiny bones out of their teeth.

CHAPTER FOUR

- -

The Fire

AFTER A LONG talk with Gai and Ukwane we found that, because of a shortage of melons and roots, they did not like to live at the place where we had found them, which was called Gu Nu, and they were planning to move. We asked them if they would mind our coming with them when they did move, and they, with great aplomb, showing no surprise at what must have seemed a strange request, said politely that they would not mind at all. We had good relations with them by that time and had already been living near them for several days.

As we would be asking them to spend time talking with us, we agreed to give them food, water, and firewood to make up for what they might gather if we were not taking their time, as well as salt and tobacco to make their hearts glad. It seemed to be a good arrangement, and they were as pleased as we.

Soon after that, when Ukwane had decided where to go, we packed up our camp, they packed up theirs, and we put everything on the trucks and drove away. The Bushmen all rode with us except the two oldest women, Kutera and Dasina, who said they were too tired to ride and preferred to walk. They did, too, taking with them all their possessions as well as great loads of melons, all of which we offered again and again to carry for them, but because, they said, they might want to stop for the night or just refresh themselves along the way, they would not part with their bundles.

The place we went to was called Ai a ha'o; it was the pan where we had seen the lion. It took us almost all day to drive there, and shortly after we arrived Dasina and Kutera joined us, having traveled almost as fast as we. Those two old women must have walked at four or five miles an hour all the way, over veld so rough that the trucks couldn't go much faster.

Before dark, the Bushman women had built a werf, a clearing of grass for each family with a shallow pit to sleep in and a place for the fire, all four clearings under the branches of a single tree which would give them shade in the daytime. On the branches each person hung whatever there was to hang, quivers, skin bags, or aprons, and these things swung in the cold wind. The women gathered firewood and lit their fires, and Dasina asked Twikwe to stand on her stomach because she was tired from her long walk and wanted a massage. Before they went to sleep the men and the three young boys walked to our camp, about fifty feet away, to say good-night, but the women stayed at home because at night all Bushman women stay at home. A woman does not even leave her fire to go to her neighbor's fire three feet away because people will say that she doesn't like to stay home; she speaks loudly to her neighbor instead. Bushmen are conservative people who keep their own rules.

- - -

The smoke in the west that Gai had seen when he roasted the tortoise intrigued him very much. Again and again he said that it was people's smoke, and one morning he said he wanted to go over to it, to look for the man who was Witabe's father, Twikwe's husband, the man who had run away for good when we had come. Gai and Ukwane both believed that he could be found, and as they regretted his missing the meat, the salt, the tobacco, and the water that they themselves were enjoying, they suggested that we look for him in a certain omaramba—a shallow valley like a dry river bed—called the Okwa Omaramba.

One morning John, Bob, William, Gai, Witabe, and I set out in the jeep to find him. We were loaded heavily because we were planning to stay the night, the Okwa being far and the terrain rough. All three little boys wanted terribly to go, but Gai felt that they would be a nuisance and chose only Witabe since we were going for his father. Wite pointed out that the man was his father, too, but Gai didn't listen. As we were leaving, the two boys ran beside us, using the last minute to beg to come, but Gai still would not listen or weaken, and the two boys saw that it was no use, lost heart, and dropped behind.

It was a fearfully hot day, with lots of dust and sticking grass seeds, the jeep was overcrowded and overloaded, and I had to hold the rifle between my knees and the camera in my arms to cradle them from banging against each other and on the sides of the jeep. My head cracked against the knees of the people behind me, and everyone was sticky, hot, and very uncomfortable.

We drove until we came to plains that only Gai had

seen before, and there the terrain was so rough that Gai and Witabe decided to get out and walk in front to find the easiest way. We would all gladly have done this, but some of us had to stay in the jeep to protect our possessions. Soon Gai and Witabe were far ahead, and we crept behind them for most of the day.

Gai walked first, Witabe behind him, as Bushmen always walk in single file, and they seemed very small, naked, and far away under the burned, pure sky, moving toward some remote destination where they hoped to find a man who had been walking away from them for almost a month, perhaps at some nameless little pan lost somewhere in the countryside, perhaps in a nameless bend of the omaramba. As they walked they zigzagged, avoiding small obstacles such as stones or thorn bushes, very incongruous with the enormity of the sky and the plains. The bow on Gai's shoulder made a bold upward curve.

A tree appeared on the horizon, and they veered toward it. When they reached it they sat in its shade, two shadows in the yellow grass, and a puff of smoke rose as they lit their pipes. We caught up to them and found Gai digging for a *torabe* vegetable. He reached into the hole he had made and dragged it from its roots, brushed the dirt away, and chopped it into six pieces, giving one to each of us. We ate that for lunch. It was bitter and moist, firm as an apple and pleasant because it was wet. As we sat there we noticed the smoke of three veld fires which had suddenly risen, perhaps stirred by the wind far away, two small ones in the north and east, one large one in the south, its smoke reaching up to the sky first in little tendrils, then billowing in great clouds like the clouds in the sky but browner.

Gai and Witabe stood up, brushing sand from their legs, and walked into the sunlight again, turning toward the larger fire. Bushmen often set the veld alight to signal to each other, but they do not send messages; a fire simply shows other people where they are, and even this is vague, as fires are sometimes set by natural causes.

After traveling several hours over the plains, we came to a little forest in a valley. A fire had been through there and had burned all the yellow grass from the ground, leaving black ashes and little black, charred thorn bushes, but the flames had not touched the leaves on the trees. These remained yellow-green, orange, and silver, tangled and confused above the black, breaking away from the branches when the wind blew and falling like autumn leaves in New England. The whole valley would have been very like New England except that there were leopards in the forest; as we looked around we found a leopard's tracks. We rested in the shade on the side of the valley, and as we sat quietly we heard the sound of hoofs in the valley below, and we saw through the bushes the dark backs of a herd of wildebeest, walking along in single file, first the cows, then the larger bulls, their curved cow horns making them look for all the world like a herd of small, dark cattle.

Gai was on his feet in an instant, his bow in his hand, and, like a leopard springing, he jumped past us and ran, silent and half crouching, through the bushes beside them, but he had no arrow, and when he got near enough to shoot he had to stand up and shoot a grass blade after them, partly for practice, as a Bushman hunter will never miss a chance to practice his aim, but partly because Gai was still too young to be able to resist making them run. They threw up their heads, snorting like horses, and galloped away, leaving behind them a great cloud of dust. Gai ran after, his heels pounding, and was gone in a few great perfect strides, as if a hawk had left us with a few stiff beats of its wings.

Witabe, too, was completely absorbed. Although he did not run after the wildebeests, he got to his feet and gazed

after them, unconsciously making a gesture with his hand
representing the head and horns of a wildebeest. He moved
his hand in time with their running, saying softly: "Huh,
huh, boo. Huh, huh, boo," the sound of their breath and
grunting as they ran.

Later Gai came walking back and we went on toward
the fire. We were going, said Gai, to a place where there
was a big rock in the Okwa Omaramba, the place where
he was born. On the way the ground was smoother, and
Gai and Witabe rode in the jeep, and as we went the smoke
got thicker, and at the end of the afternoon we saw orange
flames above the tops of the bushes. Gai said that we were
almost there, and all the men got out of the jeep to walk to
the veld fire, leaving me to drive through alone. We were
very near. We could feel the heat, and judged that the fire
was larger than we had expected. Suddenly the bushes in
front of us were caught by the fire and flamed up like tinder,
causing me to drive the jeep away and causing the men to
step back suddenly, but while I retreated they simply
waited for the fire to reach some low grass, and when it did
they stepped over it calmly and went on. I found a place
where the fire was out, where the jeep could pass, and went
safely onto the burned area. Witabe came to find me and
showed me a knoll that had not burned and was not sooty,
where the others had decided to camp. We left our jeep on
some bare sand and unrolled our blankets under the trees.

From our knoll we saw that all the omaramba was in
flames. From a fire which had started somewhere to the
east of us, a great ring had spread and was now burning
around us in an enormous circle. The gap where we had
entered had closed again, and the fire surrounded us on our
hilltop like a wall, with flames higher than our heads.

The bushes and grass had been consumed at once, but
in its path the fire had left great trees in flames, with fires

in the trunks that echoed like great chimneys, or fires in the upper branches that flamed like crowns of burning hair. As the trunks burned through, the trees would fall.

The orange sun set into the orange fire, hanging above the flames for a moment like a flame itself, then slipping down behind the fire, made the rising smoke a great, soft, purple cloud. As the sky darkened, the flames around us seemed brighter and more yellow, and farther away we saw a thousand smaller fires burning, each in a tuft of grass or in a tree.

After we had eaten we sat watching our burning wall move away from us, listening to the cries of birds, day birds chased from their branches by the fire, night birds flying through the smoke to catch insects that were trying to escape. All the air stank with an oily odor given off by the burning trees—not at all the pleasant smell of burning wood but a deathly odor, the smell of a forest being destroyed.

When we lay down in our blankets to sleep we found that even the ground was warm, and as soot and ashes drifted over us we lay awake and listened. Once during the night we heard something large run past us. A little later, farther away, we heard the sharp roar of a lion who must have tried to cross a patch of burned ground and had singed his soft paws. We heard his slow footsteps as he tested the earth carefully, then a grunt as he was scorched again. It made him cross, for he walked in a huge half-circle around us with a growl running steadily in his throat. I had thought that the Bushmen were asleep, but they had also heard him and they laughed. Now and then, during the night, the burned trees crashed around us, and as our fiery wall moved slowly away, the rising smoke was gray in its yellow light, the stars were all obscured.

- - -

Before dawn the crescent of the new moon rose, the tiniest sliver in the chilly air, followed by the salmon band of light, redder than usual because of the smoke. The wind must have blown a good deal of the fire back on itself because much of it was out, leaving a cloud of smoke hanging above the earth in a layer. We were crouching at a fire we had built, warming our hands against the cold, when the sun came up. We heard birds singing in the fresh air as if nothing had happened, then the sound of faint pounding far away, a mortar being struck with a pestle. Soon we heard a second mortar join the first as another woman began breakfast for her family, and we knew that two women meant perhaps six people, therefore a band.

Gai stood up and stretched his legs, then took a tiny coal from our fire between his thumb and finger and dropped it into his pipe, inhaling deeply and holding the smoke in his lungs while he handed the pipe to Witabe, who also puffed and returned the pipe, when at last Gai exhaled, spat, and scooped the pipe through the sand, extinguishing the fire and saving the rest of the tobacco. He stuck the pipe in his belt, flung his great kaross over his chest to warm his belly, and strode off in the direction of the sound, the ragged edges of his great cape swinging at his ankles as his strong feet carried him away. He walked under a burned log that had partly fallen and was braced up by another tree, and as he did the white ashes blew from it and the light of dawn shone through the ash like light through a flurry of snow.

Later in the day, when we had eaten cornmeal for breakfast, while we waited for Gai to come back, we went down to the flats below our hilltop to inspect the damage of the fire. The land below our camp was in utter desolation, startling and ruined, a desert of ash. We found only the orange sand and black ashes still in the shape of the grass blades that made them, black ashes below burned bushes still in the shape of the leaves that made them, and, on the ground, flat, perfect skeletons of vines, just in the shape of the vines that made them but black, in powder, disintegrating into dust when the wind touched them. All around us lay the smoldering great carcasses of fallen trees, some with the leaves on the top still green, that were filling the air with the smell of their wood burning. The ground was still warm to walk on, but all the bushes, all the little succulents, all the vines that marked the water roots were gone; no snake or lizard or animal was there, all were burned or had gone; we saw only animal tracks half filled with ashes, and a few birds come to eat dead insects. We saw a pair of secretary birds and later a pair of paouw, huge gray birds that walk more than they fly, wandering through the ruins looking for dead reptiles.

As we walked, fine black powder rose to dust our legs, and now and then, off through the standing tree trunks and between the fallen trees' great upflung roots, little whirlwinds crossed back and forth, raising the dust in spiraled pillars. Bushmen say that whirlwinds show the presence of the spirits of the dead.

Witabe's eyes searched over the ground, and when he saw a small mound of earth he walked up to it and punctured it with his toe. Out rushed a horde of ants, which had been safe in their tunnels when the fire passed and now began at once to repair their damaged mound. Witabe crouched among them and began to pick and eat them, selecting the soldier ants, ones with large heads and heavy jaws. He bit off the abdomens, tossing the heads away. Presently he offered some to us, as I had feared he would; as everyone else ate one, I did also, and found that it was not too unpleasant but sour and very watery, very like a blackberry before it is ripe. The workers, I am told, are tasteless, but the fighters are considered a near-delicacy; mine opened her jaws wide to fight my thumb before I ate her.

Later in the day, when the sun in the sky, the still burning trees, and the fire-warmed sand made the air on the flats unbearably hot, we turned back to camp for the shade of our trees, and on our way we found a path where before there had been none. We followed it, it led to camp, and at its end we found Gai and eighteen other Bushmen, whose feet as they had walked in single file had worn a track. As we approached, the eighteen strangers drew back and together, the women behind the men, babies in their arms, and watched us hostilely. Gai persuaded them to sit down, which they did, all together, and when we asked them if they were hungry they said yes, so we gave them a drink of water and set a big pot of cornmeal to cook on our fire. We gave them each tobacco, which they smoked while they waited for the cornmeal to cook.

In that band there were six men, five of them in their thirties, five women who seemed much younger, and one woman who was very old. There were also three young boys and three babies, two girls and a boy. We guessed from the looks of the people—and later found that we were right—that the band was a small extended family. The old woman seemed to be the key figure of the band, for with her were her two sons and three daughters, their wives and husbands, and their children. The sixth man—a boy, really—did not seem to belong in this tightly woven group, for he was not married, being too young; he seemed too young to be the child of the old woman, though too old to be her grandchild, and I wondered who he was. Witabe's father was not there, and on that trip we did not find him.

The three sisters of the band were all arrestingly beautiful. They looked alike, with very fine faces, slender features, large eyes, and they all wore handsome white bead ornaments. Heavy eyelids, set off by the pronounced, delicate bones of their faces, made them look of uncertain race, or like houris, and their slender bodies with skins slightly wrinkled made them seem of uncertain age. Perhaps the sun had made the wrinkles, perhaps they were older than they seemed. They glared coldly at us with jealous, narrowed eyes and held their heads back like three cobras, quite unlike their brothers' wives, young girls, unmistakably Bushman, who did not look at us at all.

The men seemed very big and heavy, with a lot of muscle and fat on their bones for Bushmen. Gai came right out and asked them how it was they looked so well, and they answered with the usual Bushman pessimism: "We have some meat here but we have no water. We may look well, but we are hungry."

Gai sat down beside them with his back to them, and as he talked he pulled his breakfast, which was a biscuit that we had brought with us, out of his hunting bag. He took a big bite, causing the eyes of all the newcomers to open. "Gai is a great captain now," said William, the interpreter, in Afrikaans. "There he is eating European food." The man who sat next to Gai and who seemed to be the oldest began to laugh a hard, humorless laugh, stretching out his hand at once for the biscuit. Gai sighed and went on eating indifferently, but the man, who could hardly contain his envy, laughed his long, dry laugh again, edging crablike closer to Gai until his outstretched hand was almost at Gai's mouth. Gai broke off the largest part of the biscuit at last and handed it inconspicuously under his left arm to the man, who had a bite, passed it to the other men, who also had a bite and in turn gave it finally to the women, who each ate a morsel very suspiciously. The man beside Gai laughed on and on, watching Gai from half-closed eyes, but Gai, who had a great deal of self-possession, did not seem disturbed.

Presently the smell of the cornmeal cooking filled the air, and the sound of its bubbling in the pot caused the man to stop his laughing and everyone else to talk pleasantly at last. The young, unmarried man took a small musical instrument out of his hunting bag, borrowed a dry tsama rind from one of the women, and, setting the instrument on the hollow rind, began to play. He filled the air with sweet, soft music, full of resonance and open, minor chords, even of rhythm and timbre as a music box would be.

The instrument itself was made of a small, flat piece of wood four or five inches square, with eleven metal prongs attached to it, arranged in two rows across two bridges. The melon rind acted as a resonator for the prongs, which were of different sizes and, when plucked, vibrated and rang like bells, in a scale which was not the octave and which I have never heard before. The name of the instrument is *te k'na*, and I believe that it is not native to Bushmen but traded from the Bantu people. Many Bushmen have them, though: Bushmen like music of any kind.

Soon the cornmeal was ready and we served it to the visitors on pieces of bark, in bowls formed from halves of tortoise shells, in tsama rinds. Bushmen have very little liquid food that does not come in its own natural container, and therefore they do not provide themselves with bowls. The bowls they do have, carved from wood—an art learned from the Bantu people—are constantly in use as containers for small, loose objects, such as seeds or unstrung beads. Since the cornmeal was hot and runny, the people had some difficulty eating it with their fingers, but they got it down, the women hesitating a long time, watching the men, before they dared to try it. I think they were afraid it would harm them, as I have heard many Bushman stories of strangers who poison tobacco or food. When they had eaten their servings and found that they did not die, they had more, a morsel at a time. We might have presented the pot to let the people help themselves, but by now we knew better. Bushmen expect each other to share, yet in strange situations they sometimes distrust each other, and it was always better for us to assume the blame for any inequality, real or fancied, than to make people quarrel. Bushmen are very quick to blame; yet also in their hearts they want everything to work out smoothly, and are therefore also quick to forgive, especially strangers who know no better.

Although he was hungry, Gai refused to eat, preferring to play the te k'na instrument while watching the food vanish into the mouths of others rather than arouse more jealousy. That day he ate nothing but the bite of biscuit in the morning and a root at night. When the pot was empty, the man who had been laughing seized it and scraped its sides with a stick, eating and dividing the burned, hard crust. The newcomers acted badly, but this would not have been so if Gai had not arrived with us.

The sun was in the zenith, and we felt we had to go in order to be in camp before night. We were faced with the problem of what to tell the newcomers. They would surely want to come with us, but our supplies would not sustain eighteen more people, and if they came they would disrupt the harmony with their jealousies. Ukwane and Gai would be forced to share what we gave them, which was only enough for themselves and their families. No one would have enough, yet no one would leave; so before we left we explained to the newcomers that we could not take them with us because we did not have enough food to feed them or enough water for them to drink. "We hear you," they said.

We were about to leave when Gai came forward with his arm around the shoulder of the young, unmarried man and said that we had to bring this boy with us. We said that we would. "Because he is my son," Gai added.

We were very surprised, for they seemed to be almost the same age, yet we learned later that it was so. We asked the boy to come into the jeep, which he did, watched by the others. We gave everyone a present of a large handful of tobacco, and drove over the burned grass, more crowded even than we had been before.

On the way home we saw and shot a springbok, as there was no meat left in camp. The bullet hit the springbok in the stomach and partly eviscerated him, causing him to jump and kick before he finally died. The Bushmen thought that this was terribly funny and they laughed, slapping their thighs and kicking their heels to imitate the springbok, showing no pity at all, but then they regard animals with great detachment. When the springbok died we tied him to the front of the jeep and drove on. The radiator boiled all the way, causing the body to decompose. Drops of blood and drops of moisture from the springbok blew back over us, mixed with the reek of decay and with a cloud of flies which we drove too slowly to escape, and which, spattered as we were, became very attracted to us. Only the Bushmen remained in good spirits, as they were pleased to see the meat and pleased with the amusement the springbok had given them.

On the way we saw an enormous hole in the earth, dug by an aardvark months ago. We stopped, and the Bushmen on their hands and knees crawled into it until all three were out of sight. After a while they backed out, one by one, reported that it was a very big hole indeed, and got back into the jeep. But before we could drive away Witabe jumped out again. He had noticed a mound of grass which looked like a haystack, it was so big, as high as a man's knees and as broad as it was tall. It was, said Gai, built by a mouse, a kind of nest, and at Witabe's request he got on top of it and jumped up and down to frighten out whatever lived inside. He was right: presently a mouse did come rushing out to vanish immediately down a hole. Gai continued treading in the halfhearted hope of another mouse, with a disappointed, intent expression on his face because the first had escaped him. Witabe, on the jeep, suddenly thought the whole performance so funny that he burst into laughter and laughed until he didn't make a sound, until tears ran out of his eyes and onto his belly, until he could hardly breathe, all to see Gai, the sole support of eleven people, the great hunter and provider, treading on top of a straw pile to chase away a mouse.

Gai was a little abashed and he stopped treading, but he did put his hand into the nest and pulled out the mouse's bed, a little ball of finer grass mixed with the mouse's own fur. Gai pulled it apart to show how it was made. We saw the mouse again when Witabe poked it out of the hole with a stick, but it ran back in at once, this time for good, so we went on, leaving the mouse with his home in a shambles and his soft bed gone.

We got back to camp late in the afternoon, and Tsetchwe was so glad to see us that she threw her arms around me and held up her baby for me to kiss. She and I were the only young women for miles around, so there was a bond between us. She often gave me her baby to mind— not an easy job because Nhwakwe was as innocent as he was bold, and I had once taken him from under the wheels of a truck that was about to move. I had carried him to the werf for safety, but he hadn't stayed long; in a short time we had seen the grass moving at the edge of camp and Nhwakwe had appeared once more, this time dragging a toy, having walked the long distance all by himself and having navigated purely by a sense of direction, for the thick grass was high above his head.

Tsetchwe did not kiss her husband or even greet him, as Bushmen are accustomed to short absences from each other and it is not the custom for men and women to kiss. They show affection openly only to people of the same sex and to their children. Tsetchwe looked at Gai, though, and she smiled.

Twikwe greeted us by smiling her wry smile and saying: "So."

The springbok was thrown to the ground, but before

it could go into the pot, Bill Donnellan, the doctor, came over to the werf to dissect it, this being an opportunity to find what the Bushmen thought about the systems of the body and what they knew about anatomy.

Gai agreed to tell what he knew, so the springbok was dragged to a sandy spot and a small fire was built—just two crossed sticks with one or two coals and a tiny flame, yet it warmed us, as the evening was becoming very cold. All the people sat around to watch as Bill opened the belly of the springbok and rolled it onto its back. He pointed to the diaphragm and asked what it was. Gai told him the name. "What is it for?" Bill asked.

"We eat it."

"Is it for anything else?"

"We don't know. We just eat it."

"What about the liver?"

"We eat the liver."

"Does the liver do anything for the springbok?"

"It stays there and then we kill him and eat it."

"And what about the stomach?"

"We Bushmen eat the stomach, too, and all the things in the springbok."

"Doesn't the stomach do anything for the springbok?"

"Yes, he eats grass which goes in there and makes him fat, and then we eat the fat."

Unwilling to give up easily, Bill passed on to the urogenital system, which is, after all, exterior and which anyone should know, but Gai became embarrassed and said gravely that Pishiboro put that system there for reproduction and he alone knew how it worked.

Ukwane then said that he would explain instead, because he was an old man. Gai could not speak of sex in front of women because it was both improper and dangerous and would weaken his power to hunt, but Ukwane was too old for hunting and, besides, was past the age when many of the taboos concerning sex applied to him. Old Bushmen understand everything better anyway, young Bushmen say.

Ukwane knew a great deal. He named every major part inside and out, of the animal, even naming the major veins and arteries that lead to and from the heart. We were not surprised to find that Bushmen, who prefer to be specific rather than general when dealing with minute things, distinguish more exterior parts of the body than we do. They have names, for example, for the inside of the elbow and the back of the knee. The *leg* of an animal means the hind leg, the front leg is the *arm*, and these are called by the same names as the arm and leg of human beings. Birds, too, fly with their arms and land on their legs, but I never could discover what insects do.

Ukwane went on to explain the various systems of the body, saying in the case of the urogenital system that liquid, which was "the little springboks," ran from the testicles into the kidneys, then down again and out the penis. He stuck to this version, too, even when Bill suggested that it might be otherwise. This does not mean that Bushmen think that urine causes conception, for they recognize the role of semen, believing that it unites with the menstrual blood of the mother to form a child.

Ukwane understood the course of food and water through the digestive system, but said that food and water spread out like sweat to all the body. He did not understand what the lungs did, or that air went into them, or that air went through the trachea. Breathing, said Ukwane, is air going down into the stomach, where it makes belches. Ukwane did not know about the circulation of the blood, believing that blood ebbs and flows, nor did he recognize pulses in the body except the pulse at the V of the throat, noticeable in people who wear little clothing, which is known as "the place of the heart."

The cold night had come, and Ukwane in the frosty

grass was shivering, yet he sat for an hour keeping his patience, putting his hands into the cold blood of the springbok to trace veins to their source, prefacing all his answers with positive, qualifying remarks. "I am an old man," he would say, "and I know that the diaphragm separates the heart and lungs from the stomach," or "I am Ukwane, and I know that when the heart is gone the animal cannot live, or a person either, because the heart is that animal's life."

- - -

As the dissection and the conversation went on, the three young boys, joined occasionally by Nhwakwe, the baby, played games all the time, creeping in between the adults to warm themselves by the fire and by the heat of bodies when they could stand the cold no longer. If you wear no clothing your skin is sensitive to very slight changes of temperature, and even the warmth of someone sitting beside you or the heat radiated by a few coals makes a lot of difference. When the young boys were thawed they would again leap into the darkness to play some more. They played a game of horse and rider, in which one boy would leap astride another boy and ride without holding on while the other boy would stagger forward as fast as he could. In a moment, both would fall, jump up again, hitch up their loincloths, and resume the game, only this time the horse would jump on the back of the rider. Sometimes two boys would make the horse, one boy holding the wrists of another boy in front of him while a third boy would ride, and these horses, reinforced, were much more successful, traveling farther at faster speeds. Now and then, as we talked by the fire, one of these little phantom creatures would rush silently by us in the dark, its dark rider in silhouette against the sky.

As we talked, we heard music, very sweet, sad music, as though a music box were playing, coming to us from a little distance away. It was Gai's older son, the boy who had come back with us, playing the te k'na to himself. Thus we discovered that Gai had not fared as badly as it had seemed he did in his meeting with the strange Bushmen, for the te k'na had belonged to the man who had laughed at him. All the Bushmen at the fire, who loved music, stopped their talk to listen, and even the young boys were charmed from their game, for they moved silently toward him and crouched in the cold grass to listen, too. Soon they stood up to dance, a usual Bushman dance of men, taking small, pounding steps, moving in a circle. They danced very well, with freedom and with great precision, but they were too excited to dance for long and instead began to play a dancing game called Ostrich, performed by two boys dancing forward to face each other. As one either crouches or bends double from the hips, the other, who in the game is called the ostrich, swings his leg over the first boy's back without missing a beat in the rhythm. The boy who bent jumps backward as another boy steps in to take his place. This is repeated again and again, accompanied by spoken, rhythmic sounds: he he *hi*, hehe he *hi*, and the whole game is very fast and vigorous, requiring great practice and co-ordination, as the body movements, which often include the slapping of the elbows against the ribs, are sometimes at counterpoint to the spoken rhythm. The game represents ostriches, perhaps ostriches fighting or mating.

The game was intoxicating. The boys danced so fast, so perfectly, and made their rhythm so vigorous and free, that Gai, who had been sitting quietly listening to Ukwane, could stand it no longer. Throwing his great cape around himself, he suddenly leaped to his feet and sprang among the little boys, scattering them like a hawk among sparrows, towering over their heads as he began to dance. He stamped, bent, straightened, and swung his long leg over the little boys' backs, dancing with far more abandon, not as precisely as they, but madly; he took our breath away.

He wore his great kaross backward, flung across his chest, and when he stood still waiting for his turn to leap forward and crouch he was as motionless and dignified as a tribune standing, and when he danced the great wings of his kaross swung like the cape of a bullfighter, masculine, open, and free. He was a wonderful sight, and the old people watching him smiled, and the little boys dancing under his long legs and under the wings of his cape looked up at him and laughed with pleasure because he was playing their game.

Gai was a man of great dignity and for him the dance was not altogether a success, for when the young boys tried to swing their legs over his back they generally kicked him in the rear or in the face. Soon he tired of it and came back to the fire to sit by Ukwane, but he was too excited to stay quiet long and in a moment he tore off his cape and, calling Ukwane and his oldest son, he began another rhythmic game, called Kaross. This is played by several men or boys who rub the kaross between their hands in the way that they rub it to soften or cure it, only they rub more vigorously and accompany themselves with several very rhythmic, very gay fast songs, sung in falsetto to imitate the falsetto singing of women because, say the men, women's voices are admirably beautiful.

Twikwe and Tsetchwe sat side by side, their legs straight out in front of them, the soles of their feet lit by the fire. They sang gaily and clapped their hands while the baby Nhwakwe walked up and down on Tsetchwe's leg, balancing himself like a child who is walking on a railing, then climbed to her shoulder and stood there triumphantly without holding on, gazing around like a child on a hill. He looked utterly astonished when Tsetchwe suddenly swept him to the ground and, flinging off her cape, jumped to her feet and began to dance. Everyone was astonished. Women almost never dance, although they are quite welcome to, but least of all Tsetchwe, a very conscientious mother and wife.

Tsetchwe's dance was extremely lively and extremely gay, and everyone except Nhwakwe looked up at her happily. She sang and waved her arms with great abandon, and danced her gay dance right behind the men, just for once flinging motherhood to the four winds and dancing right over her baby, who came trotting sadly after her, holding up his arms to be carried. In a moment the baby gave up and went to the lap of his grandmother, frowning as his mother danced happily by him again. When Tsetchwe finally got tired and flung herself down on the ground he ran to her and nursed immediately to reassure himself. She held him loosely in one arm as she coughed from exertion and laughed, with a pleased, shy expression on her face that said: This is what I used to do when I was younger.

- - -

When the people were tired of dancing they still seemed to feel like talking, and as the moon was down and the stars showed clearly we asked Ukwane to tell us something about the sky, and we pointed to several stars to learn their names. But Ukwane said that he had been talking and singing all evening and his voice was hoarse from telling about the inside of the springbok (which by now was partly cooked and eaten). He was, in fact, too hoarse to answer questions and would rather tell a story if he had to talk. We said that we would like to hear a story, and the Bushmen said that they would also like to hear some stories, so Ukwane told the last part of the story of Pishiboro and his elephant wife.

In the morning, after the elephant wife had frightened Pishiboro and his younger brother, before she had followed them away, she had told her elephant parents that she had married a man whose people might eat her, and that they should give up hope of ever seeing her again. Pishiboro knew that she had spoken with her parents, and while he was sitting upon her body with his brother, eating the breast, he looked around anxiously for he knew not what. Soon some elephant beetles came up to eat the uterus, for the elephant wife was pregnant, and when Pishiboro saw this he became very alarmed that the fetus would be eaten and he asked his brother to chase the beetles away. But the brother did not, and when Pishiboro was looking the other way, seeming to have forgotten, the brother cut open the womb, and the fetus came out.

"Oh, you foolish man," said Pishiboro. "I told you not to do that. You are lazy and stupid, and now the fetus will go to the elephant's parents and say what we have done."

Pishiboro then asked his brother to dig a hole to catch the fluid from the womb, but when the brother went to do this the fluid flowed past him. Pishiboro scrambled to dig another hole, but the fluid flowed past him, too, and only a little was caught. Pishiboro and his brother drank it.

The large part of the fluid went on until it came to the scherm of the elephant's father. It went in the front and out the back, and then came to the scherm of the elephant's brother, and when the father and mother of the elephant saw the fluid they knew it was from the womb of their daughter, and all the elephants gathered together to go and kill the people.

Meanwhile, Pishiboro's brother thought until he thought of a plan. He then went off alone and, finding an anthill, asked the anthill to open itself, which it did. He prepared many anthills in this way, and then returned to Pishiboro, who was cutting up the meat, but told him nothing of his plans.

After a while the brother, who had been watching the direction taken by the fluid very carefully, saw the elephants coming, and he told Pishiboro to go to the anthill which he had prepared, but when Pishiboro got there and asked the anthill to open, it did not, and presently, when the elephants were very near, the brother found Pishiboro standing there helplessly. The brother then said to the anthill: "Please open, so that this fool can go inside," and the anthill opened and Pishiboro went inside. The brother waited for the elephants alone.

When the elephants came, two of them tried to stab Pishiboro's brother with a knife, but the brother flew up onto their shoulders and they fell dead. In this way he killed them all, all except one old, old elephant which he did not want to kill because it was so old and useless. Instead, he asked the anthill to open again so that Pishiboro could come out and kill it for him. Pishiboro came out and farted on the elephant three times and the old elephant was not affected, but when the brother farted once, the elephant fell dead.

Then Pishiboro's brother sang this song:

My brother is older, but he kills only little things.
I am younger, but I kill big things.

And that was the end of the story. Everyone asked Ukwane to tell more, so he told many. One of them interested us particularly because of its vague similarity to one of our own. It is the story of how carnal knowledge came to Pishiboro, for although he had two human wives (or perhaps goddesses, as he himself was god), he did not know what to do with them.

Pishiboro was digging a hole. When he had finished he told his wives to go to look at it while he went hunting in a different direction, but instead the two wives went to get tsama melons. They found one melon, brought it home, and, taking out the seeds, were grinding them to powder when Pishiboro arrived. The two wives had taken their own genital organs and had mixed these with the melon seeds which they were grinding. Pishiboro ate the mixture, which he thought was very nice, and he jumped to his feet and asked his wives where they got such nice meat.

"Oh," they said, "we told you when you left that you were going in the wrong direction. You should have come to the hole with us because when we got there, we found a baby giraffe inside, but we could not get it out, so we cut pieces off its feet, and this was the meat you found so good."

They slept, and the next day they all went to the hole. The two wives had, in the meantime, defecated into the hole until it was full. When Pishiboro leaned over to look for the giraffe, they toppled him in; then, laughing and shrieking, they ran away and climbed into a camel-thorn tree.

From the depth of his hole, Pishiboro looked up at his wives in the tree, and as he looked, it came to him what wives were for, and he climbed up the tree and possessed them, and they conceived, and when the children were born they dropped from the tree like fruit.

Then the whole family came down, and as they were walking away Pishiboro found a night adder's home. Only the baby snakes were there; the parents had gone out. The Pishiboro family laughed at the baby snakes because they had such ugly faces, and when they had laughed all they could they went home to their scherm. That night the baby snakes told their mother what had happened, and in the morning, when Pishiboro returned for another laugh, the baby snakes were dancing and the mother snake was hiding in a little hole she had made. Pishiboro, too, began to dance, and when he danced by the hole the mother snake jumped out and bit him, and although he ran away, the poison was working in him, and soon he was ill and in great pain.

The omarambas, the dry valleys in the land, are furrows that Pishiboro made on his way home because he suffered so much, and the hills at the sides of the omarambas were made by his kicking feet.

Pishiboro died from the snake bite, and now all the water that flows in the rivers in the north, all the rain, and all the water that collects in pools is the rottenness of Pishiboro, liquid made as his dead body began to decay.

- - -

After that, Ukwane stopped telling stories. He brightened the fire by adding a stick, and the light showed everyone's face. Firelight does not dispel darkness. It just shows things in the darkness while the darkness is still there. Behind Ukwane's back we saw the shapes of the young boys bending over something, and we asked Ukwane what they were about. He told us that they were setting a snare for a mouse, a mouse which had troubled the people greatly by chewing their karosses and biting holes in their melons, which made the melons dry.

We looked at the snare. It was made of a tiny sinew cord tied to the bending branch of a bush with a noose on the free end spread open with tiny sticks pushed in a circle into the ground, one of which was a trigger, baited with a melon seed. The ground was swept clean, and melon seeds were scattered around alluringly.

The young boys then went back to the werf and lay down on the ground, naked in the frost, as the older people lay nearer the fires. Tsetchwe and Gai lay side by side, the baby in Tsetchwe's arms, and everyone went to sleep for the night, and we went home.

In the morning, even before the sun rose, we went back to the werf to see if the mouse had been captured. We found the young boys already at the snare, standing in the cold grass with their arms hugged against their chests for warmth. They looked discouraged, and we saw that the snare was dangling helpless and empty. The cord was bitten through, all the tsama seeds were gone, and the earth was printed confidently with the prints of the mouse's feet.

CHAPTER FIVE

GAI and UKWANE

AT OUR CAMP in Ai a ha'o I had a small tent not high enough to stand in, tied to a very small thorn tree. The tent was made of ragged waterproof fabric which billowed in and out when the wind blew, and when lit from the inside by a candle at night looked luminous, pale green, like an aquarium or a lantern on the moon. The tent was a shade from the blazing sun at noon and a shelter from the wind, and through the thin canvas I could hear the creatures that passed at night—hares and small buck that made the long grass rustle, and occasionally small predatory animals, such as jackals, whose footsteps make a sound and which sometimes call "*tsa, tsa,*" their sad, loud cry that means in Gikwe "water, water."

Whenever an animal called, someone would surely answer it. People do this for fun, a hobby, answering every animal except the lion. In the Kalahari it is considered safer to let the lion have the last word.

I had luckily pitched my tent in the sun, and during the long cold period that followed our arrival at Ai a ha'o I was the only person who was warm because the tent kept out the wind and held the sun-warmed air inside itself like an oven. The three young Bushman boys found this out quickly, and early in the morning when the sun came up they would crouch outside, shivering and naked, and whisper "Nisabe, Nisabe" until I opened the door to let them in. The four of us filled the tent entirely, but when I would leave for breakfast they would stay behind, looking in my mirror and leafing through my notes. I gave them crayons and paper and asked them to draw, but they wrote instead, wiggly little lines that looked for all the world like handwriting, complete with dotted *i*'s. Once, when I looked in to see if they had drawn anything, they showed me a page of my notes which had a smudge and a tiny rip in one corner. They had not torn it, for they were more careful and precise than cats—in fact, I had done it myself—but they were upset over the destruction of property, and when I told them it was nothing important, perfectly all right, they were not pleased. I seemed to them lavish and wanton; I should have repaired it or at least shown that I was sad.

One morning in early July they came to my tent before sunrise and I woke up when I heard their teeth chattering. Before I had the door completely open they had all popped in, and when I went outside, wearing a sweater, a coat, and mittens, I found that it was surely the coldest day of the year. A strong south wind was blowing, straight from the Antarctic, scattering our fire, whose smoke and heat blew down the wind, and even standing in the smoke we could not get warm. In our pails the water was frozen into solid ice, and we saw our breath in clouds around our heads.

We went to the werf through grass white with frost to see how the Bushmen were faring and found them all awake, crouched over the coals of their little fires. Tsetchwe and Gai sat side by side, Gai all wrapped in his big kaross which covered him entirely so that only his head and toes were showing, Tsetchwe in her small, ragged kaross which covered only her back, leaving her legs, belly, and shoulders bare. Near them sat Ukwane and Kutera, bundled up together in Ukwane's tattered kaross in front of a handful of embers on a small pile of white ash, Kutera having been too tired to gather much firewood the night before. Dasina sat by herself at another very small fire with the baby, stark naked, standing on her lap. He alone did not seem to mind the cold, for he smiled at us cheerfully when we came by. The others hardly looked up.

They had burned all their firewood the night before, and now it was too cold to go for more, or even to go for food, so they sat cold, hungry, thirsty, and even tired, since they had been too cold to sleep during the night. They were waiting, as they had waited all night, with infinite patience, infinite endurance, for noonday, when the sun would give a little warmth; but the sky was overcast, and even at noon the sun would still be far away.

Twikwe stood up to poke her fire and the Antarctic wind howled along the ground, blowing her little kaross back from her shoulders and leaving her naked except for her apron whipping around her legs, and her string of beads. The icy wind made the branches over her head rattle, made her breath blow back like smoke and her eyes stream with tears. She sat down again, downwind from the fire, wiped her eyes, and, wrapping her lanky arms around her legs, put her head on her knees and waited. It was six o'clock in the morning; they had six hours to go.

A little later I crossed the flat pan of Ai a ha'o to look for firewood in the plains on the opposite side. When I got there I saw a hawk in a tree, a hawk with a fine red beak and handsome gray feathers. He had gnarled, stalky legs and he stood on his branch with the legs wide apart, bracing himself against the wind. When I got near he dropped from his branch and let the wind carry him away, and I saw that he had been watching a colony of ground squirrels close by which had not seen him and did not see me. They, too, were miserable with the cold, for they walked around slowly as they looked for seeds to eat. I sat down to watch them, which they noticed, and some of them stood up to watch me. Their fur was oddly greenish and it blew in the wind showing little patches of white. They had long fat bellies, long heavy thighs, and little feet, and when they stood up they, too, kept their legs wide apart and braced. As they peered at me I heard on the wind almost inaudibly high, soft whistles, their cries of warning to each other. They decided I was dangerous and vanished down their holes.

I came back to the werf with some wood, which I gave to the Bushmen. They reached out their hands for it and put it on their fires, but they didn't say a word. Later, in our camp, we put all the wood we had on one great fire, where the Bushmen joined us and where we spent the morning making and drinking cocoa. We even put up a white canvas, and, lying between it and the fire, we were fairly warm.

Ukwane used that occasion to tell us something about his life and his relatives, his former wives, the children he had fathered and where they lived. Most of this centered around melon rights, or who could live in which areas, for if a person is born in a certain area he or she has a right to eat the melons that grow there and all the veld food. It is perhaps this factor that explains in part why the Gikwe bands are composed the way they are; a man may eat the melons wherever his wife can and wherever his father and mother could, so that every Bushman has in this way some kind of rights in many places. Gai, for example, ate melons at Ai a ha'o because his wife's mother was born there, as well as at his own birthplace, the Okwa Omaramba, where we had found the eighteen Bushmen, who after all were not strangers but closely related to Gai and Ukwane and an extension of Ukwane's band.

Ukwane himself had had three wives, and he and his first wife had been divorced, which Bushmen do by announcing the divorce and separating. There is no ceremony connected with divorce, and no difficulty, as there is no ceremony connected with any marriage but the first. After a divorce a Bushman man may take up residence with another woman whom he prefers.

Without the visible evidence of ceremonies, however, it is hard for non-Bushmen to recognize what is happening, as occasionally Bushmen live together for short periods without being married, or commit adultery. But in cases such as these there is someone who does not want the union to be permanent, either the man or the woman, or perhaps his or her children; perhaps even the man and woman are taboo relatives, and unless everyone concerned is more or less in accord, the union does not take place. Among Bushmen, incest and adultery are strongly condemned.

Once, among Kung Bushmen we lived with, a woman ran away from her husband to take up with another man. She had considered marrying him, and they ran off one night to his family to live permanently. When her husband found out, he got so wildly angry, taking up his spear and sharpening it, that the headman of the band set off after the elopers to preserve the peace. My brother and I went with him, and at noon we found the lovers resting in the shade.

The headman talked with the elopers and told them how they were bringing shame on both their families, and how the woman's husband was violently upset. By this time the woman had begun to regret her act, and as her children, whom she had brought with her, were crying for their father, she agreed to return. She then explained her reason for leaving; her husband, who had until recently been a serf Bushman, could not hunt well and was not able to clothe her. She was a handsome woman, but her kaross showed that what she said was true—the only garment that she had had to wear on the day of her elopement was tattered and old. She also explained how she and her lover had passed the night, she sleeping on one side of the fire, he on the other, with the children between. She put straws on the ground, a straw for each person, to show how it was, and we believed her.

The whole affair seemed to center itself around raiment, for though the woman was poorly dressed with what her husband had given her, the beads and ornaments that she had made for herself were fine and white. Her children, too, were poorly clothed with leather, but they also wore white beads, and her lover, the man who had attracted her so much that she committed an unconscionable act, was dressed beautifully in a soft new leather loincloth, sewed finely and worked with white beads. I myself was adorned with the story, for when we came upon the spot where the lovers were resting I found that I had a pen but no paper and so wrote everything that happened on my arms and legs.

When we got home, the woman's husband took her back and was very glad to have her. No one ever mentioned the affair again.

In the same band there was another man, about forty

years old, who took a beautiful young girl not yet twenty as his second wife. His first wife, also forty and the mother of three, was very jealous and bothered the beautiful girl until the girl, who did not love the husband anyway, ran away from him and back to her parents. The husband was enraged and set off after her, but when he finally found her his anger had been replaced by longing and he pleaded with her, reasoned with her parents, and plied them with the meat of an entire eland he had shot, asking for her to return. But she would not, her parents would not make her, and finally she drove him away with these words: "I don't want an old husband like you, you man with a big black belly."

Thereafter, the marriage was recognized by everyone as dissolved. The husband was sadly disappointed, but the two women, at least, were pleased.

Both Kung and Gikwe Bushmen permit divorce, condemn adultery. We saw very little marital strife among the Kung with whom we lived for over a year, and none among the Gikwe. Even so, many Bushmen over thirty years old in both groups had previously been widowed or divorced. Death and strife take too many people; a Bushman cannot really expect his first marriage to last him all his life.

Ukwane's second wife had been a widow, the mother of Twikwe, and when that woman had died Twikwe had lived on with Ukwane. His third wife was Kutera, and their only living child was Giamakwe. Ukwane had another son still living at Chukudu, the Bakalahari settlement, who was surely one of the Bushmen servants in that long procession of Bakalahari villagers we had seen moving to winter quarters. We told Ukwane about this migration and Ukwane said he was sorry to hear it because he had hoped very much to see his son again before he died and many seasons might pass now before the son would come.

Kutera herself had been married twice before, once to a Bakalahari, once to a Bushman named Gainaho, and last to Ukwane, to whom she had been married about fifteen years.

Even Gai had been married once before, when he was in his teens, to a wife not yet eleven, as most Bushmen marry at a very early age. A Bushman girl can be betrothed before she is weaned, while she still lies on her back and waves her tiny feet. When she is eight or nine she marries and her young husband, who is probably in his late teens, comes to live all or part of the time with her family. He will not have intercourse with her until she reaches puberty—she must pass her first menstruation and her breasts must show. They then live together as man and wife, always with her family, as Bushmen are matrilocal until the couple has borne three children, the sign of adulthood, or, if they are not so blessed, until they reach the age when most people have three children. Then, if they wish, they may live with the husband's family.

It is said that when a man raises his wife, feeds her, and cares for her, the two enjoy their youth together, she is the more his, and a more stable marriage results than if she were allowed to grow up wild and free and perhaps make a hasty choice of too young a husband (one of her own age) in the passion of her adolescence. An early marriage also ensures that the girl will be a first wife, a more desirable and authoritative position than that of a second, or co-wife. The girl's parents benefit from an early union as well, for the young man hunts for them and the meat he kills goes to their band.

This system may be good for women, but it is hard on young men, who often must endure desire for years and years, waiting all through their teens and early twenties before they can possess their wives. One young man among the Kung Bushmen had been thirty when his wife had died, and he had found no one else to marry except an infant girl. When we knew him he had been waiting five years for his wife to grow up, and at that time she was only about seven (younger than his son, who was about eleven); and when he thought that he would have to wait at least four years more for her, he would get into such a passion of desire that he would have to send his wife away for a time, lest he forget himself and break one of the most stringent rules. Bushmen believe that it harms a girl terribly to be possessed before she is mature. It might even drive her mad.

Bushmen have no real solution for this problem, as there are no prostitutes and only in a few bands are there promiscuous women. Homosexuality is not permitted either; the young men just have to get used to being tempted constantly but never gratified.

Gai had raised his young wife, and when she reached puberty he had possessed her and she had borne him a son. This was the young man Gai had found at Okwa. Shortly after that his young wife had died and Gai then had married Tsetchwe, whose young fiancé had been taken away by a farmer to work on a farm. Gai and Tsetchwe had borne two children. Only one was still alive; this was Nhwakwe.

When we asked about the residence and about the parents of Gai, an argument arose. Gai lived with Ukwane because his wife wanted to live with her mother, Dasina, and Dasina lived with Ukwane because she and Ukwane were relatives, sharing a common grandparent. Gai himself, said Ukwane, was conceived by a Bushman mother and a Bushman father named Gwena, but Gwena had died while Gai was still in the womb. When that had happened, Gai's mother had gone to Chukudu to marry a Bakalahari man. She and the Bakalahari had then moved to the big rock in the Okwa Omaramba, where Gai was born. This was Ukwane's side of the story.

Gai had been listening, and when Ukwane had finished, Gai raised himself on his elbow to say that Ukwane was quite mistaken, for the Bakalahari was his real father. An argument dragged on, the old people insisting that Ukwane was right, saying that Gai may have *thought* the Bakalahari was his real father, but that Ukwane knew better. I expect that Ukwane was right at that, for Gai certainly looked like a Bushman.

But whether father or stepfather, Gai said, the Bakalahari kept sending messages to Gai with Bushmen who might be passing through Ai a ha'o telling him to come back to Chukudu (probably to work), but Gai never did. Gai was too clever.

- - -

At noon the sun had warmed the air a little, although there was still an edge of frost, and the women got up and walked off together into the veld to search for wood. In an hour or so they came back heavily loaded, Tsetchwe with her kaross bulging with melons, perhaps twenty in all, a great load of wood on top of them piled higher than her head, and Nhwakwe riding on top of it all. Even in the cold air she perspired, and as her load must have weighed almost a hundred pounds, she walked leaning forward.

By night the cold had deepened. The Bushman boys came out of my tent and went home for dinner, then lay by the fires to sleep when the adults curled up in the shallow pits. The moon rose, a frosty circle, hard as a coin, and before we went to sleep that night we heard a jackal calling "tsa," out on the plains.

"Tsa," called one of the Bushmen, answering him.

"Tsa!" the jackal replied.

- - -

In the morning we were very pleased to find that the cold had broken. We woke up to find the sun just rising, and on the other edge the moon just sinking down, lustrous and pale in a current of balmy air coming warm from the equator. In the east, only the planets showed of all the stars; one of them, "Walks-Before-the-Sun," was just starting its

journey across the sky. This planet, which we call the morning star and which is a different one from time to time, rises
just before the sun and walks all day across the sky looking
for shade. Every day, say Bushmen, the sun overtakes it
and scorches it, and though people walking can cut branches
from trees to put up over their heads as parasols, the poor
star finds no branches in the sky.

Over the moon the Firewood Star was sinking too. This
is a real star, the star by which the Bushmen, when they
see it rising, can tell if they have enough firewood to last
the night.

When the sun was up, when the moon and all the stars
were gone, we went as usual to the werf, where we found
Ukwane curing fox skins with urine, the only liquid he had.
It was not fresh urine either; it was rank, saved for days
by all the people, collected in tsama rinds. We had noticed
a stench, but we had not known what it was. To be certain,
we asked Ukwane, and he said: "Water."

"What water?" we asked, knowing there was none.

"The water that all the people in the Kalahari have to
use."

"Is it urine?"

"Yes, it is," he said.

The skins were from five Delalandes or long-eared foxes
which Ukwane had snared three seasons ago. He had
stretched and scraped the skins but had not cured them
because until now he had not had the time. A few days ago
he had told his people to begin saving urine so that he could
cure and soften the hides. They had, and he now poured
urine onto each skin, letting it soak, then rubbed the skin
hard between his hands. He repeated this process again and
again, working one skin at a time, and before long the skins
were moist all through, and when they were dry they were
as soft as chamois. Ukwane said that he was going to trade
the soft skins with Bakalahari people for tobacco when we

had gone and when the tobacco we had given him had all been used. We asked how much he would get and he measured an imaginary pile in the palm of his hand—not much for four or five days' work, although the skins of Delalandes foxes are quite small.

There were Delalandes foxes living not far from Ai a ha'o, a colony of them, for they always live together. I saw them often and they were charming creatures, fuzzy with huge ears and black stockings. I have always admired them, for although they have no defenses, can neither run fast nor fight, they are not afraid to go mousing far from their burrows. Then, when they are surprised by a menace, they have to run home, and they start off all together and run and run, humping on and on at an even pace, neither speeding nor slacking, until long after you first saw them they disappear into their holes. They are humble creatures, but persistent and brave. One member of our expedition hunted them for months with rifle and shotgun, trying to get a specimen for a museum in the United States, but I am glad to say he never succeeded. Ukwane caught them, though, the easy way. He set five snares for them at five mouse-runs in the grass; five foxes strangled in the snares, and Ukwane came around the following day to gather them up.

We filmed Ukwane working the skins. Then we found the shoulder blade of the gemsbok we had shot weeks ago still lying in the werf and we asked Gai to make an arrowhead out of it so we could film that, too. It was the right kind of bone, the kind that Bushmen use. The small antelope and even some of the larger ones, such as springbok and wildebeest, have bones which are too fragile to penetrate another antelope's heavy hide. Gai agreed to make the arrow; he broke off the scapular spine and pushed it into a fresh tsama melon to let it soak. When it was moist all the way through he called to us and we then filmed him making the arrow.

We took a long time setting up the cameras, reading light meters, focusing the lenses, and finally took a picture with the still camera. To our astonishment, when the shutter clicked Gai let out a great huff of breath. One of the interpreters must have told him at some time to be absolutely still, and he had begun holding his breath when he had first seen the camera. We thanked him and told him he need never do it again, but we laughed and he was embarrassed.

Always, Bushmen were wonderful people to film. They were totally unselfconscious, never looked at the camera, and, furthermore, had infinite patience. They would stop what they were doing, wait, start again and repeat what they had done before, making each repeated action seem miraculously as if it were being done for the first time. But on this occasion Gai got bored. He had a quiverful of arrows anyway, and while he waited for us to load the camera the arrow he was working got brittle and dry. When this happened he had to suck it until it was moist again, then whittle some more.

He made the foreshaft of the arrow first, chopping with his knife to hack the rough shape of it, pausing occasionally to hone the knife blade on the tough sole of his foot, then cocking his head and squinting down the blade to see the edge. He then carefully whittled the head, leaving a tiny spine up the middle for strength but shaving the edges so thin that you could see light through them. As he worked, though, he yawned and sighed with boredom and now and then he would pause to sing a nonsense song, "bibibi di bo," by flapping his lower lip with his finger.

When the arrowhead was finished he fitted it into a reed shaft exactly the right size and bound it in place with a bit of fine sinew which he had also sucked to moisten. Then he turned the arrow over and over, sighting down its length to see if it was straight. It was.

Gai then surprised us somewhat by taking from his hunting bag twelve round nutlike tiny shells which we recognized as the cocoons or pupa cases of the poison grubs, the source of poison for the Bushmen's deadly little arrows. Gai said he would poison his arrow, a process which he seemed to find more interesting than making it, and we said we would be very glad to see. We wondered where he got the grubs, for he and Ukwane had both told us that there were no poison grubs anywhere near Ai a ha'o, and he said he had received them from the people whom we had met in the Okwa Omaramba, as they had plenty there.

We regretted very much that we had never seen a tree or shrub that houses the poison grubs of the Gikwe, and that we had never been able to catch one of the adults of the beetle that in its pupa stage is poisonous. Gai said that his grubs came from between the roots of a bush, called in Gikwe simply a poison bush. We do not know if the grubs are the same as the grubs used by Kung Bushmen, which live among the roots of a tree, called by the Kung a poison tree, called by us marula kaffra. The grubs of the Kung are from the beetle *Diamphidia simplex*, which lays its eggs on the leaves of the tree. Once, all in one afternoon at a single tree of Kung Bushmen, I was shown by a young hunter the yellow eggs on a leaf, the young larvae just hatched, which the hunter said crawl down the tree under the bark to pupate in the earth among the roots, and the pupae of this beetle.

It has always amazed me that the Bushmen ever discovered these beetles, which are only one species among thousands in South Africa, and which the Bushmen say are poisonous only in their pupa stage. The pupae themselves are enclosed in the tiny brown pupa casings with brittle shells like eggshells, exactly the color of the earth around them, and are found only among the roots of certain trees and bushes. Nothing edible grows among the roots, and although the marula kaffra has edible nuts that drop and are gathered from the surface of the ground, there would be no likely reason for Bushmen to be digging there. Bushmen do eat certain beetles, certain ants, and certain caterpillars, which, they say, are sweet as honey, but even if a Bushman were to eat a poison beetle he would not die (unless he had a cracked lip or an ulcer) because the poison works only in the bloodstream, and even the black meat of an antelope taken from the site of the arrow wound can be eaten with impunity.

Only people who pay the closest attention to every tiny object and who investigate all its possibilities could ever have discovered a thing like this.

I not only do not know if the beetles used by the Kung are the same kind as those used by the Gikwe, but also do not know if the Kung use only one kind, for I have seen Kung Bushmen take two kinds of pupa from the roots of the same tree, from cocoons that appeared to be exactly alike. Even the Kung do not know, when they see a cocoon, which kind it is. One kind of pupa is small and pure yellow with a black head, a thorax, an abdomen, and six small legs. The other kind is larger, fatter, and orange, with no noticeable body sections such as thorax and abdomen, but more like a caterpillar, the same all the way down. The yellow pupae, the Bushmen say, are males, with sacks of poison only under their front legs. To get the poison Bushmen pull off a leg and squeeze out a single drop, discarding the rest of the body. The orange pupae are said to be females, with poison throughout the entire body. To get poison from these, Bushmen tap the grub all over to mash the insides, then pull off the head and squeeze the insides out like toothpaste from a tube. Both kinds of poison are equally good, they say.

Perhaps the two types of pupae are the pupae of two different kinds of beetles. Perhaps they are from the same beetle but in different stages of development. Perhaps they really are males and females, as Bushmen are often scientifically accurate, but, as Bushmen also have male and female rain clouds, perhaps not.

Kung Bushmen, who use metal arrows obtained by trading animal skins for wire with the Bantus, have a complicated system of poisoning in which they use several ingredients for the poison paste. One of these is a binding fluid, used because the pure poison squeezed from the grub will not adhere well to metal but must be made binding and sticky. The binding material comes from the bark of a tree. They chew the bark thoroughly and spit the mash into a little mortar made from the knee bone of an antelope, a nice little cup, into which the Bushmen have squeezed the milky juice of sansevieria plants, got by wringing the heavy, thick leaves. This juice has an irritating effect when it is dissolved in a wound and causes the antelope to rub and scratch its wounded spot against a tree, which stimulates circulation in the area, which carries the poison more quickly through the body, which hastens death.

The paste in the mortar is thoroughly mixed, then smeared with a straw on the foreshaft of arrows, never on the head, for if the sharp edges of the head were poisoned any child might accidentally nick himself and die. When the arrow is poisoned it is propped up by a fire and the poison is allowed to dry into a shiny dark paste, to be melted again by the moisture and warmth of an antelope's flank.

Gai had stored his poison cocoons in a tiny bag inside his hunting bag, and when he came to poison his arrow he took them all out and felt them, shook them, to see if they were fresh. Then he took his arrow, his cocoons, and a scrap of leather he had been saving which was so thin and ragged it had very little use, and, moving all these things to a place in the grass far away from the werf, he sat down to work. He did not work in the werf because a drop of poison might be spilled and months later would still be dangerous.

Gai first spread out his rag as a worktable and arranged his cocoons upon it. Then he called Witabe, who was watching from the werf, and asked for a fire, which Witabe brought in the form of a few sticks in one hand and a live coal from one of the werf fires in the bare palm of his other hand.

At last Gai was ready and his fire burning. After inspecting his fingers carefully for cracks in the skin and telling us to sit upwind from him so that no drops of poison would blow on us, he scratched open one of the cocoons. The shell was as brittle as a little seed pod. It opened easily and Gai fished inside carefully with a straw, digging out the grub, which struggled feebly with one slight, almost imperceptible convulsion and then lay alive but motionless, curled in a U on the palm of Gai's hand. The cocoon was small and the grub must have filled it entirely, for, once outside, the grub seemed twice as large as its casing. It was a yellow one, like the kind the Kung call males, but I cannot say for certain that it was exactly the same.

Gai laid it across his thumbnail and tapped it gently, mixing the insides. Then he twisted off the head, squeezed the body, forced the paste inside onto the shaft of his arrow, and smeared it evenly with his straw. Gikwe Bushmen do not have to use a binding fluid, for their bone arrows hold the poison very well.

After the foreshaft was coated evenly all around with the poison of several grubs, Gai dried the arrow by the fire, then coated the foreshaft again. In all, he used ten grubs, all that he had except two which were found to be shriveled and dead. The last coating he did not smear; pulling off the grub's head, he dotted the arrow with little spots of poison. He did not poison the arrowhead but only the foreshaft.

When the arrow was finished and the poison dried to

lacquer on the shaft, Gai carefully collected all the cocoons and all the grub skins and burned them in the fire, keeping out of the smoke. He then called for a fresh tsama melon, which Witabe brought him and which he used to wash his hands. At last he put his arrow in his quiver and lit his pipe. He was through.

While we were there with the camera set up and loaded we asked Gai to demonstrate for us the way he would shoot a bow, which he did, and we were surprised to see that the Gikwe, who use bows of the same size and shape and arrows of the same size as the Kung's, have a different arrow release. The Kung grip the arrow between the thumb and the side of the forefinger as they draw back on the string, but Gai gripped it between the first two fingers, holding his thumb back. He said that all other Gikwe do the same.

Ukwane called to us from the werf and said that since we were here he would show us how a Gikwe Bushman makes a string. We went over to him, and he did make a string for us by pulling the tough fibers out of aloes and rolling them together on his thigh, leaving just enough fiber unwound at the end to splice with the next rolled section. The string was so strong that when he jerked it between his hands it neither broke nor raveled. It took him only a few minutes to make it, and he said that when he had many such strings he would tie them together to make himself a net.

As he worked, for the sake of efficiency, he held the fibers in a fold of his belly and held the finished end of the cord between his toes. Then, as he finished a section, he would pull with his toe, moving the cord into a new position while with his hand he removed a new tuft of fibers from his belly. It was very efficient. The cord almost finished itself. It seemed to me then that this use of a belly fold might once have given someone the idea of a vise or clamp, or the pulling foot the idea of a pedal.

The day turned out to be a very eventful one. In the afternoon someone discovered that a large snake had occupied a hole right next to our camp. We all went to see the track, and found it so fresh and so enormous that we shook the Bushmen from their afternoon naps to tell us what we had found. Ukwane came alone, saying that he would know as well as anyone, and after looking at the track for a moment and following it out into the veld a way, he returned to say that the snake was still in the hole.

From the size of the track, which was as wide as the rut of a cartwheel, we could see for ourselves that the snake was about fourteen feet long, and from the straightness of the track, from the fact that it had no parallel scratches on its sides which would mark it as the track of a python, Ukwane could tell that it was made by a mamba, the deadliest snake in all Africa, second-deadliest in all the world, a snake that can travel almost as fast as a horse can run and whose poison will kill an adult human being in ten minutes or so.

The snake had come only that morning, perhaps attracted by a colony of bushy little rats that lived around our camp, and induced to move by the warm sun, which must have set his great length in motion out on the veld somewhere.

The members of our expedition felt that something should be done, so while my father brought a shotgun, Ledimo, the interpreter, lit a fire near the hole, then lit gasoline-soaked rags in the fire and pushed them burning into the back door of the burrow, hoping to drive the snake out the front. Nothing happened, and the tension naturally rose; and as the snake was fourteen feet long, everyone began to edge backward.

At that moment Gai arrived on the scene, still sleepy from his nap, balancing his spear over his shoulder. The sun shone on the blade. Gai walked through the circle of people straight up to the hole and, crouching, pushed the spear inside. "What are you going to do with him?" we asked. Gai looked back over his shoulder.

"Eat him," he said.

But though Gai worked his spear in the front door of the burrow, then in the back door, for almost twenty minutes, he never felt the snake and we never saw it. Soon Gai gave up and walked away, disgusted and cheated of his meal, followed by Ukwane, and for the rest of the afternoon we avoided going near the hole. But in the evening, when we returned to inspect it, we found another wide track winding out into the veld. The snake, disturbed, had gone.

That night we all stayed close to our fires, in our circles of light, and kept out of the dark veld where the snake might be mousing, lying quiet in the grass where one of us might step on him.

- - -

Quite late that night, while we were still sitting quietly enjoying the warm air, we heard the growl of a large, deep-throated creature right next to our camp, answered in a moment by the growl of a second creature very near the first. The growl rose into a sort of cry, higher and higher, and broke with a sighing, tentative role. It was a hyena crying to another hyena, a female and a male. The night air was moonless, close and tropical, and their crying made a ghostly sound as they answered each other, two specters in the veld, their green eyes searching, and presently they were close together, growling now and panting, snapping their long teeth. They closed, each one's growls muffled in the other's dark fur, and we heard the male hyena's growling quiver as he shook the female, the sound of a dog worrying a bird. They were so occupied with each other that they did not notice or did not mind being very near our camp; if there had been a moon we could have seen them easily, but the sky was overcast and black. We heard their footsteps shuffle in the dry grass and presently we heard them move away. They must have gone in different directions, for one of them, a little later, called alone, was not answered, and called again; we heard the other calling finally, a hesitant, tentative crying, faint and far away.

CHAPTER SIX

Veld Food

WITH THE WARM air came a series of long, fat clouds sailing from the north like slow dirigibles, some of them showering down a few drops of rain. We were amazed to see rain in winter, the dry season, something we had not seen before, and we asked Ukwane about it. He said that it was not unusual for rain to come in the wintertime but very hard on the people of the desert, as it fools the wild vegetables from which the Bushmen get their water.

There are many kinds of wild roots which can be eaten in winter, and each is marked among the grass blades by an almost invisible dry thread of a vine. The roots are swollen with liquid by which the plants preserve their life during the drought. When the plants feel the onset of spring, warm air and raindrops, the dry vines suck moisture out of the watery roots, turn green, and put out tiny leaves, and in this way, if the false spring lasts, the roots are soon sucked dry entirely. Bushmen cannot get enough water from eating the vines and leaves. The plants do not bear fruit until summer; the spring-season vegetables, such as little onions, pods like pea pods, and leafy green vegetables that taste like rhubarb, have not grown in yet; and so the Bushmen must go thirsty. People have died of thirst in these false seasons.

Gathering veld food is the work of Bushman women, and I used to go with them quite often on their trips. We sometimes stayed in the veld all day eating roots instead of drinking water. One day my brother came along to film the gathering of veld food, and as we were getting ready to leave, Gai also joined us. It is customary for Bushmen never to let a group of their women go anywhere with a Bantu or a European man unless a Bushman man goes with them to protect them. Gai sauntered along behind us in his role of guardian, quite unhampered, as he had nothing with him but his loincloth. Dasina, Twikwe, and Tsetchwe walked in front, each with a digging-stick thrust in her belt like an enormous knife, each wearing a heavy cape, and Tsetchwe carrying her baby, who rode, carefree and swinging his feet, on her shoulder. John and I walked in the middle of the procession, and at the end came the three young boys, who did not stay in single file but ran all over the veld, ran circles around us, and shouted to each other happily.

We walked across the pan of Ai a ha'o through the fine, soft grass, which left tiny, barbed seeds sticking to our legs. We walked through the brush on the opposite side and then over a wide plain, where we saw a herd of wildebeest. No one was armed, and when the wildebeest saw us, put down their heads, and ran, we could only watch helplessly as all that meat galloped away.

We walked until we came to a patch of tsama melons, perhaps twenty of them lying together, shiny, smooth, and green in the grass. The vine that once had nourished them had dried away and already some of the melons were turning yellow, overripe, ready to open and release their seeds.

The women stopped and began to gather up the green melons, Twikwe picking them with a mechanical, stereotyped gesture. She first slipped her hand under a melon; then, twisting her elbow, she lifted the melon and held it pinched between the heel of her hand and her forearm, and with a scoop slipped it into the pocket of her kaross on the side. In a moment the side of her kaross was full, and she stood erect for an instant, looked at the sky, shifted her weight, and suddenly the melons rolled to the back of her kaross, leaving the side free for more. She was very efficient. In a moment she had a load. I was a little surprised at her, however, for now she would have to carry the melons with her all day, whereas she might have gathered them on the way home. But Bushman women do not seem to mind this.

The women left behind the yellow melons which would have been bitter and rotten, touching them disappointedly with their toes instead. The false spring was hastening the time when all the melons would be gone, forcing the Bushmen to eat roots as a staple diet, not as desirable because of the uses that tsama melons have. Melons are eaten as both food and water, their pulp is added to meat which needs liquid for boiling, their seeds are roasted and eaten or ground into powder and used as flour, their rinds serve as mixing bowls, as containers for small, loose objects, as cooking pots with or without the pulp inside, as urine containers for curing hides, as targets for the children's shooting practice, as children's drums, as resonators for musical instruments, and all this amounts to a serious loss for Bushmen when the melons rot or dry.

We went on until we were about two miles from camp.

We were going to an almost imperceptible small hill, a place, said Twikwe, where a great deal of veld food grew. On the way a moving shadow caught our attention, and we looked up to see a white-breasted, black-winged vulture sailing not far above our heads, not stirring himself but riding the drafts and currents of the air. He was looking at us with hard eyes, his red face turned to look down, and suddenly he closed his great wings under his body, sweeping them down so far that the long wing feathers brushed together four feet under his belly. Then his wings swept up again and bore him on. I had never seen a vulture do that before. He did it only once, then made a circle all around us, looking down at us, his eyes cool in their red wrinkles; he rose higher and higher and soon he was gone. All over Africa the sky is full of vultures, but so high that you can seldom see them; any time you look up with binoculars, however, you will probably be able to see one sailing, waiting up there for a disaster.

We were going particularly to look for *bi*, a fibrous, watery root that is the mainstay of the Bushmen's diet during the hot season when the melons are gone. From the end of August, when the spring begins, the heat increases in intensity until December and January, when the rains come, relieving the drought. During this hot, dry season the sand reflects the sun until the air all over the veld shudders and dances, until human beings and animals alike gasp for air and water. This is the hardest season of all for the Bushmen, yet most of them remain alive by going into the veld early in the morning in the cooler light of dawn to gather bi. The bi they find is brought back to the werf before the sun is hot; it is scraped, and the scrapings are squeezed dry. The people drink the juice they squeeze. Then they dig shallow pits like graves for themselves in the shade. They urinate on the bi scrapings and line the pits with the now moist pulp, then lie in the pits and spend the day letting the moisture evaporating from the urine preserve the moisture in their bodies. They lie still all day and at dusk go into the veld again to gather food, perhaps a few roots or cucumbers, returning to their werf before it is utterly dark, for in the hot season the big snakes, too, move only at night, the mambas and the cobras out of their holes.

By the end of the season the Gikwe are emaciated from hunger and thirst, and it is because of this season that the Gikwe hear the jackals on the plains cry "Water, water."

When we reached the little hill Twikwe had mentioned we found no bi root, but we found other kinds of veld food: a bush with red berries, several kinds of roots, and a spiny cucumber not three inches long, round and bristling with its spines like a sea urchin, handsome in its light-brown, yellow-striped skin. The young boys found five of these cucumbers lying in a crooked row on the sand, all put there by a vine which had mostly dried and shriveled away. We picked them and ate them. They have a watery green flesh which looks just like the flesh of a cucumber as we know it but which is sweet.

Witabe, noting the direction of the vine by the way it had deposited its cucumbers, traced it to its source and found a bit of it left above the ground, below the branches of a white-thorn bush. He said there would be an edible root there, and when he dug, there was.

Meanwhile, Gai had found a solid, stiff vine like a stalk among the roots of a gray bush which was the home of a small flock of birds. Just for fun, Gai chased the birds out; they would have gone anyway, but, frightened by him, they flew like little pellets in every direction, leaving behind a pale, soft grass nest blowing in the wind. Gai sat down facing the bush with the branch shadows all over him and dug with a digging-stick in the sand between his legs. The branches around his head got in his way, tickling his ears, causing him to slash impatiently at them with his digging-stick, and when this did no good he endured the nuisance for a moment, then flung himself down on his back, put up his long legs like a fighting cock, and kicked the branches down.

He dug out a great deal of earth, throwing it behind him, and finally uncovered a *ga* root, big and dark with a warty surface all covered with lumps like a toad or a stone; a fascinating thing, for although it was large and nonde-script, brownish gray in brown-gray sand, marked only by an old dry vine, it was life itself to Bushmen, bitter but quite moist even in the hottest season. Tsetchwe put the root in her kaross and we went off, Gai generously carrying the baby, taking him from Tsetchwe by the forearm and swinging him up to his shoulder. The baby rode astride Gai's neck with the soft kaross he wore draped over Gai's head. From the rear they were an apparition, as this made the baby's head, not much higher than Gai's, look like a tiny head on a man's tall, slender body.

We wanted very much to find a bi root, and while Gai, the baby, and my brother went off to look for one I waited behind with the women. We rested in a small circle in the dim shade of the grass, which, when we were sitting, came high above our heads so that all we could see was a circle of sky and, in the circle, the ragged, waxing moon. It had risen luxuriously in the daytime and was a pale, large cres-cent, pearl-colored in the sun. The moon is a root with a climbing stalk, a vine. It can be eaten.

Gaimakwe began to urinate right in our midst, crouch-ing and pulling his loincloth aside. Although the adults are slightly inhibited about this, the children are not, sometimes simply turning aside to urinate as one might turn aside to cough. Presently the young boys got up and ran away, and when they did Tsetchwe herself got to her feet, stepped aside, and urinated also, standing up but leaning forward. Bushman women sometimes do this, but Bushman men crouch to urinate. "It is our law," they say.

While the women rested they had refreshed themselves with one of Twikwe's melons, which Twikwe chopped for them by holding the melon between the soles of both feet and mashing its pulp with her digging-stick, which she held in both hands. Then they got up from their grass nest, sharpened their digging-sticks with Twikwe's knife, and set out to begin the search for food. They each chose a different direction and soon they were out of sight. I followed Twikwe to see what she would find, hurrying to keep up as she trampled ahead of me on those spindly, awkward legs of hers, which she kicked out with each step in a walk like the walk of a clown. She kept her back straight, for it was still early and the load in her kaross was light.

As I could not speak many words of Gikwe, she didn't even try to talk, but paused from time to time instead to show me things. Once she crouched among the branches of a thorn bush and beckoned to me to show me a tiny vine winding around the bush's trunk. I nodded. It marked an edible root. She pinched the base of the vine where there was a faint touch of green, then, grasping her digging-stick, began to dig. The ground was quite hard, but she dug rapidly, her slender back curved as she squatted over the hole and the muscles of her thin arms swelling. After a long time she threw down her digging-stick and tugged at something in the bottom of the hole. She sat back, and in her hands was a huge stone, which she heaved aside.

"Look," she said, and I crawled beside her into the bush. She had made a hole three feet deep, a foot across, and at the bottom, dim in shadow, lay an immense gray root wedged securely between two stones. "*Ga,*" she said. She ripped the severed vine from the bush it clung to and tossed it into the sunlight. "Look," she said again, assuming that I would now recognize a ga vine when I saw one; but although I examined it closely, it still looked like any other vine to me.

Again she bent over the hole, leaning over so far that her head came between her knees, and grasped the huge root with both hands. She tugged so hard that I heard her joints crack, but the root was wedged and she couldn't move it. She took up her digging-stick again, panting now, and struck the rocks, and the point of her digging-stick splintered.

"Ai," she said, exasperated, sitting back on her heels to carve a new point with her knife. She bent again, pried at the rocks, pried at the root, but it was useless, she couldn't move it. Then she relaxed, resting for a moment as she rubbed her sore shoulders before she got to her feet and walked away, beckoning with her head for me to follow. We would leave it.

We wandered about haphazardly for a time, looking for a vine, and presently I saw one twisted around some grass blades, binding them together in a tuft. I pointed it out to her, but she smiled and shook her head, turning her hands palm upward in the gesture for nothing. She meant that it was a useless species of vine, marking nothing below. Later, as we walked along, she laughed. Twikwe was charmed by the mistakes the members of our expedition made, for they were always elementary and, to her, very diverting.

Keeping her eyes on the ground, Twikwe noticed a tiny crack in the sand. She scooped at it with the point of her digging-stick, tipped out a truffle, and picked it up almost without stopping. As we walked on she broke it in half, put half in her kaross, and offered half to me. I ate it. It was light brown and had a delicious, salty flavor. Truffles grow an inch or so below hard-surfaced ground and have no leaf nor stalk nor vine to show where they are, only the tiny crack made by the truffle swelling, which the Bushmen notice.

We had crossed a barren stretch of plain where only grass was growing and were in another patch of low bushes where veld food also grew. The great plains of the Kalahari may seem undiversified, but really they are divided into countless little patches, some barren, some fertile, depending probably on the soil. In this veld-food patch Twikwe found another vine tangled in the lower branches of a thorn bush and she crawled in after it and began to dig. The thorns around her head, all smooth and shining white like jewels, were tickling her, but, unlike Gai, she delicately put up just one hand and picked off the very thorns that pricked her.

She resumed her digging and after perhaps twenty minutes as she followed down the vine she uncovered another ga root also wedged among stones. This ga was not as large as the other one, nor was it wedged as tightly, and when she grasped it, arched her back, and tugged, clenching her teeth and straining her thin arms, the rocks suddenly gave way and the ga flew loose, sending Twikwe crashing back among the thorns. She wiped the perspiration from her forehead with her thumb before she crawled out of the bush, dragging her root and her digging-stick. I noticed that the root was very wrinkled, as if it had shrunk. Twikwe struck at it with the point of her digging-stick, chipping out a fragment, which she put in her mouth. Then she spat, stood up, and walked away from it. When I, too, tasted it to see what was the matter I found that it was flaccid, dry, and very bitter, quite inedible. I looked inside the bush and saw that its vine had begun to turn a little green.

We went on, and passed a few dry melons on our way, yellow and empty, perhaps bitten by an antelope some time ago. I kicked at one of them and a gray lizard ran out, straight and fast as an arrow. Then it turned around and ran back in again, having no place else to go.

Soon Twikwe found a third root and, after digging it out and tasting it, found it quite acceptable; putting it in her kaross, she went on to find a fourth. We found old, dry holes where Bushman women had dug out roots seasons ago, a few dry vines with bitter, useless roots below, and three more roots that proved to be edible, as well as two more melons, a few spiny cucumbers, a handful of berries from a tiny bush, and one more truffle. This would feed Twikwe and her two sons for one or two days, or perhaps would be shared with Ukwane and Kutera because Kutera, that day, had not felt well enough to gather food of her own. Bushmen help each other, each Bushman woman contributing to the support of her own family and perhaps to the well-being of some very old people as well.

When Twikwe considered that she had enough, we turned back to find the others, and presently we came to the plain where we had left them. Twikwe called, and was answered by three or four voices very nearby. Then, right in front of us as if from nowhere, the three boys, Tsetchwe, and Dasina appeared standing, having been crouching in the long grass. Twikwe and I joined them, and the Bushmen passed Twikwe's pipe, the short, wide antelope bone stuffed with tobacco. When it was passed to me I puffed it, too, but it was so strong and rank that it made me dizzy.

Soon we heard a wail, a sad crying out in the veld, and it was Gai and John returning with Nhwakwe, who had begun to miss his mother or want to go home. Gai looked cross and walked rapidly with his little burden riding on his shoulder, and even John seemed somewhat annoyed because of the noise and because they had not found a bi root. When they came up to us Gai swung Nhwakwe down, danging him by the arm as he handed him to Tsetchwe, who took him at once and let him nurse. Bushman babies do not like to go for veld food because the sun is hot, there is nothing to eat except the raw roots, and there is nobody to play with, yet they do not like to be left at home alone either. This is a constant and insoluble problem for Bushman mothers.

After asking Gai more questions and, at his suggestion, roaming from one point to another over the veld in search of a bi, it came to John and me that he did not want to show us where one was growing. We understood this, for the bi roots of the veld are naturally limited and if we took one when the Bushmen did not need it, it would not be there when they did. We assured Gai that we did not want to eat it, only to see its vine, and at last he remembered, he said, where one was, far out in the veld and on the way to Okwa. But we were not discouraged and set off in that direction, and after a while we found it far away but not as far as Gai had said. It took us an hour to reach it, but we had traveled slowly because the women had stopped to gather melons along the way.

When we came to the center of an enormous plain with no tree or bush to mark the place, Gai stopped and, glancing around for a moment, pointed suddenly with his toe. After trying hard to see, we noticed a tiny shred of a vine wound around a grass blade; no part of the vine still touched the ground, as the vine had dried and parts of it had blown away. Gai had known where the bi was, he told us, because he had walked by it months ago in the last rainy season when the vine was still green, and he had remembered. He had assumed that it was still there because only his own people used the territory around it and if one of them had taken it he would have heard. Bushmen talk all the time about such things. He had had it in his mind to come back and get it when the tsama melons were gone, but now, perhaps when he saw its vine there and thought about it under the ground, he changed his mind. Squatting near the vine and digging with his hands, he soon had exposed it, two feet down and dark in shadow. He seized it and tore it from the earth.

It was shaped like a monstrous beet, with its vine coming from the top like a little stalk and its root bristling from the bottom like a tassel. It had a hard, barklike crust and it was gray and hairy. Gai held it daintily by its vine, and, as dirt was still dropping off it he slapped and brushed it to clean it; then he held it high above the big cavity it had filled, looked at it with a rather satisfied smile, and said what nice water it would be.

We went home then, walking again in single file in a straight course over the veld, veering only once toward a fallen tree, where the women stopped to gather firewood. The women, walking first, were heavily loaded now with melons, roots, and firewood, Tsetchwe loaded most heavily of all because the baby rode on her shoulder. The women used their digging-sticks as canes because their knees were bending, and walked quickly, trying to get home as soon as possible. After the women came the young boys carrying nothing, and last of all came Gai, holding his bi by its tassel of root. Before long he hurried and caught up to Tsetchwe, and once again he took a turn with Nhwakwe, swinging him from Tsetchwe's shoulders to his own, where Nhwakwe rode happily, his tiny hands pressed over his father's eyes.

CHAPTER SEVEN

Mood Songs

WHEN WE CAME to the pan of Ai a ha'o we found a small veld fire burning just at its edge on the opposite side and we noticed someone standing near it, partly obscured by the smoke. We called out to see who it was and a cracked voice answered: "Ukwane." He came over to us and told us he was looking for the piece of string that he had made which must have dropped out of his hunting bag. He had been searching patiently over the ground all afternoon, but I did not see how he could hope to find it with all the smoke and with his hazy eyes that were almost blind. He decided to go home with us and fell in step beside us. We were hurrying because of the women's heavy loads and because of the fire, which by now was putting up a cloud of boiling, brown smoke that streaked out with the wind, making a long pathway above us that reached from the fire to the sun. Birds were being chased from the bushes, still singing because they always sing in the afternoon, and insects from the grass.

We went past the fire and soon it crossed our track behind us and went harmlessly into the west. As we walked, Ukwane told us that during the afternoon the band of seventeen Bushmen whom we had met at Okwa had arrived and were planning to live beside us, as life at Okwa was getting very hard. The veld, said Ukwane, was beginning to dry, a condition that we had noticed, which was showing itself in the scarcity of roots and in the rotten, bitter melons. But we suspected that jealousy as much as anything else had brought the seventeen people to Ai a ha'o, the fear that Ukwane's band was feasting while they were being deprived.

At camp we found only three men of the visiting band, as the others were waiting somewhere in the veld, and the members of our expedition, who were trying to find a place for the visitors to camp. The three men were looking stonily around, seeing nothing that seemed agreeable. They had first been offered a grove of trees right by our camp, but they had refused this because of the mamba which they had heard about from Ukwane and which they believed might still be near. One spot after another failed to suit them, and finally they dropped their skin bags of belongings under a pair of small trees very close to Ukwane's werf. Ukwane welcomed them, of course, but I think he felt that difficulties would arise with them living so close and always watching.

One of the men went to summon the others of his band, who had been resting in a patch of heavy thorn bushes not far from our camp, and they came, carrying their youngest children and their bags of belongings, followed by their children old enough to walk by themselves. One of these was a toddling youngster who hadn't been walking long and who surely had been carried most of the journey. The others were three young boys of about the same ages as the boys of Ukwane's band; when they saw where they were going to be living, they abandoned their parents with a great shout and, running to Ukwane's werf, started a game of horse and rider with the three boys of Ukwane's band. The Gikwe bands do not meet very often, and when they do the children play together day and night. All the young boys were extremely happy to see each other and expressed their joy by starting their game at once, wasting neither time nor breath to say hello. Before the adults of the visiting band had set their bundles on the ground two little horses with their riders had run past, the riders trying to unseat each other.

They played all afternoon and into the evening while the adults went about the business of setting up a camp. I went to the new werf to watch and found that the women had stored away their belongings, stuffing some of their bundles among the tree roots, hanging others from the branches, and were now clearing grass, each woman clearing a small circle for her family. Soon five circles were formed, not quite touching, all sheltered by the branches and all in the space of a few square feet. I helped one woman pull grass, for she was clearing it tuft by tuft, pulling it up with her hands, and as I did this I felt something cold and firm in the grass I was holding, and, looking down, I saw that I was holding an asp. I dropped it, one of the Bushman men ran up to kill it, and one of the women lifted it between her fingers and placed it in her kaross. Later it would be cooked and eaten by a child.

- - -

That same afternoon, some of the members of our expedition went hunting and shot a gemsbok, which was brought back to camp and given to Ukwane to divide. This was, perhaps, a great mistake on our part, for Ukwane gave the entire carcass to the newcomers except for the head, one foot, and a little of the liquid from the rumen, which he kept for his own people. Twikwe dug a pit in the veld and roasted the head in it, and that night, while the newcomers were still butchering, drying, and cooking their larger share, the members of Ukwane's band cut little strips from the cheeks of the gemsbok and sustained themselves with that.

An atmosphere of tension and strain pervaded the whole werf. The Okwa people had arrived primed with jealousy, and had surely accused Ukwane of selfishness; the false spring, the dry conditions at Okwa had surely given their jealousy momentum. By giving most of the gemsbok to the newcomers, Ukwane had done all he could, for he had shown with his immediate generosity, and with the magnitude of his gesture, that they had nothing to fear from him. Of course, the members of his own band were as jealous of the newcomers as the newcomers were of them, but Ukwane surely felt that the internal struggles of his own band, easier to cope with, would be forgotten sooner.

The tension showed itself in struggles over food. Twikwe made a soup from a bone of the foot, mixing it in the rind of one of the melons she had gathered, and when it was cooked she drank it herself out of the tsama rind, watched all the time by her son Wite. When she could stand his hungry eyes no longer, she put her bowl on the ground so that both of them could scoop up the broth with tortoise shells. After they had eaten part of it, Twikwe decided that it was time to pass the bowl to Kutera, who sat a little distance from them, eating nothing, looking very scrawny and trying not to watch. Twikwe started to do so; then, remembering her son, who was still hungry, she reached behind her for a second tsama rind, a little one, which she would fill for him. In this way she would, of course, have none left for herself, but she preferred to share. Adults are used to hunger, and it seems that the older Bushmen become, the less they mind deprivation. Children are different, and as their needs are considered more pressing than the adults', they are accustomed to receiving more. Twikwe herself had among her possessions a fiber string, which, she said, she kept to wind around her belly when she was very hungry for the purpose of warding the hunger away.

Wite was tired and cross, and his patience was worn thin by hunger, and when he saw what his mother was doing he realized that he would have less food than he had expected. He lost his temper, shrieked at Twikwe, and tried to keep her from reaching the little rind so that she would have no container to give him a smaller share in—a very Bushmanlike thing to do, instead of trying to snatch the large, full rind, perhaps—and the two of them struggled, each tugging at the little rind and each exclaiming wildly. The old woman won the struggle and filled the rind with soup, using her tortoise shell as a spoon, hindered once again by Wite, who snatched the spoon away, still trying to prevent her filling the small rind for him. Twikwe struggled for the spoon, and, seeing that he was going to lose it, Wite quickly ladled an extra spoonful into the little rind and sat back resigned while Twikwe thrust the little rind toward him. He took it finally and sat sulkily, not eating, but with his lips pressed against the side of the rind, his eyes hard and shining, staring at nothing over the top. Twikwe handed the larger share to Kutera, who pretended not to have noticed the struggle and who thanked Twikwe in an ingratiating way.

There was another struggle over food that evening, started as a malicious joke by Gai. When Gai saw Wite with a strip of meat from the gemsbok's cheek he snatched it out of Wite's hand and pretended to eat it. When Wite, tried beyond endurance, burst into tears and flew at Gai, Gai ran away and really did eat the meat, chewing as he ran, keeping just out of Wite's reach. The chase ended under a tree, where Gai, seizing a branch, grappled Wite with his legs and swung him off the ground. Wite did not resist, but swung limp and resigned, and when Gai released him he started to walk away. Gai had eaten all the meat except one morsel, and this he tossed to Wite, who picked it up from the ground and ate it apathetically.

Only the baby set a good example. I had picked him up and was carrying him when the three young boys of Ukwane's band noticed that he was mouthing something and holding something else in his hand. For a joke they extended their palms, telling him to share what he had in his hand, and he gave it readily. It was only the crackly skin that flakes off bones when they are roasted, quite flavorless, impossible to chew; Nhwakwe was only playing with it and the boys only pretended to take a bite, then threw it away. But either the baby didn't see them reject it or didn't care because in a moment he made them another present, the meat that he had been holding in his mouth. The young boys didn't see where he got it and they were about to eat it when Nhwakwe opened his mouth to smile and they noticed. They threw it down, but the baby spat some onto his finger and offered it to them anyway, and when they didn't take it he smeared it on their chests.

After the unhappy hour of eating, the people of Ukwane's band, their appetites dulled even though their bellies were not full, seemed more relaxed and the young boys went off to join the boys from the visiting band. The youngsters were always friends. The tensions suffered by all the members of both the bands did not affect their enjoyment of each other.

That evening the boys sat down near one of the fires to talk, and they told each other all the things that had happened since they last had met, perhaps a year before. Most of the incidents had happened fairly recently and most amounted to anecdotes about the other members of the bands, who at the time were barely out of earshot. One story concerned Dasina, how she had fainted from smoking too much the day we had come, and to show exactly what had happened, Wite and Witabe acted the scene, Wite taking the part of Dasina and fainting on Witabe's shoulder while the other boys laughed. Bushmen's jokes and stories are usually funny at the expense of a person, an animal, or the god Pishiboro, maliciousness being one way in which Bushmen rid themselves of their resentments.

Somewhat later Wite and Giamakwe acted for the others the scene of the hyena's mating, as they imagined it or knew it to be, for the night it had happened only the sound had reached us and the hyenas had not been seen. Giamakwe took the part of the male hyena, Wite took the part of the female. First they walked together on all fours and rubbed faces, and then Giamakwe climbed on Wite's back, emitting a lonesome howl just like the howl we had heard. It was not meant to be funny, and the other boys watched it calmly, treating the mating of hyenas as a matter of course. All in all, it was a majestic imitation, with snarls and growls, then mounting and pretending to copulate with shivering and ecstasy, then more growls, until finally the male fell away exhausted and curled up on his side, whereupon the female attacked him. It took a long time from start to finish, the Bushman boys being so literal that they not only gave a precise rendition of the event but took exactly the amount of time that the hyenas had taken.

The adults had not watched the children but were visiting quietly with each other, some of the men from the Okwa band having come to Ukwane's werf to sit at the fires. Very late at night, when the Firewood Star was rising and the Zebra Stars of Orion were just setting foot upon the earth, the visitors got up to go.

We had stayed up to watch the children's games and also to observe Orion setting, for the Bushmen tell a story of the stars in Orion which takes place in the sky every night at certain seasons and we wanted to see it for ourselves. The story is simply that the god, who at the time the story takes place is standing on one of the Magellan clouds, shoots an arrow at three zebras. The arrow is Orion's sword, the zebras are the three stars of Orion's belt, the star in the center being a male zebra and the two stars flanking him his wives. The arrow falls short, as one can see, and presently, as the constellation touches the horizon, the zebras step upon the earth, first a female, then the male, then the other female. It is slow and deliberate, and that night we saw it plainly. The zebras vanished into the brush at the horizon, but the arrow was still there.

When the constellation had gone, when many of the people were asleep and we were about to leave the werf, Ukwane took out his hunting bow and, setting one tip on a dry melon shell, he began to tap the string with a reed, making a sound. Soon he played a song, humming a melody and playing an accompaniment on his bow.

He sat alone at his fire, his wife a tiny heap under her kaross and fast asleep some distance away. He was squatting, his eyes on the embers of his fire, holding one end of the bow with his toes. With the fingers of one hand he touched the string, making different notes, and when he wanted to change the pitch he turned his head slightly, catching the other end of the string with his chin.

His song was a mood piece, as are all Bushman songs except the medicine songs. It was a song of pure music without words, a song composed to express a feeling the composer had had, a mood, or an emotion. The mood songs do have names or titles, but these only tell the subject of the piece, the minute incident that may have inspired the composition. Ukwane had composed this song himself, and from time to time he sang the words "bitter melons."

We stopped to listen, caught in the net of music which Ukwane had cast into the air, for it was a soft, sad song that he hummed and played, a song in a minor key to wring your heart, to make you think of places far away and make you feel like crying. Ukwane was so dark that he could hardly be seen against the black veld, and all that showed clearly was the yellow reed tapping and his filmed blue eyes. When he finished the song he put down his bow. We asked him what the song was about and he told us: "If you are walking in the veld, and you remember where a field of melons was growing and you go there and find them but when you taste them they are bitter, so you can't eat them, you leave them, that is what this song is about."

We asked him to play another song and he obliged, playing a shorter, rhythmic one called "Pass on the Other Side," a song Ukwane had composed when he had been humiliated, beautiful to our ears but not as beautiful as "Bitter Melons." He had come into a werf where the people were sitting in a circle taking turns smoking a pipe, and Ukwane, who had wanted to smoke very badly, had seated himself beside the person who was smoking, hoping to be next in turn, but that person passed the pipe by Ukwane, and Ukwane did not receive it until all the others had smoked first. He had felt so badly to be treated in this way that he had gone for a walk in the veld, and while walking he had composed the song.

He sang one more song, which was called "A Song of Shouting," a song about his wife's brother who had lost his way in the veld near Ukwane's werf, and had shouted, expecting someone in the werf to answer him, to give him the direction, but no one had bothered to call to him. That night Ukwane had asked his wife if her brother had returned. She had answered "Yes," and Ukwane had composed the song about it out of guilt and sorrow.

"A Song of Shouting" was beautiful, too. When Ukwane had explained it to us and we had asked him to sing some more, he smiled at us and said that he was tired. But the day of jealousies, the fact that he had not found his piece of string, and the subject of his songs had put him in a mood, and presently he began to tell us what was in his heart.

He said that he was old and blind, and that he and his wife could no longer support one another but had to depend on Tsetchwe and Gai. Even Twikwe and Dasina were old and would not be strong much longer, and if Gai should leave them, perhaps to go to his Bakalahari father, the old people would perish surely.

Hearing Ukwane's cracked voice saying these sad things, his wife got up from her bed and sat beside him in silence. Soon Twikwe and Dasina joined him, too, so all the old people were there, crouching near the fire, their eyes gazing over its light out into the darkness.

Presently Dasina said: "It is bad to die because when you die you are all alone," and after being silent for a moment Ukwane told us how various members of his band, once a large one, had died, reducing their number to the hardy few who lived with him now. Both his father and his mother had died of thirst, and his children, his young nieces and nephews, and his grandchildren had all died in an epidemic of smallpox three years before. That had been a horrifying season, and in the hottest time, when the sun was drying them all and the ground was too hot to walk on, the smallpox had come, and pox had got into people's mouths so that they could not eat, and the children had all died one morning and their young mothers had died before night.

The old people, the survivors, had not expected to out-live their children and grandchildren, and then they had to bury them; they had scooped shallow graves for them and had placed their bodies inside, then had covered the graves with branches. The old people had then lived by the graves for months to mourn and to protect the corpses from ma-rauding animals. It had been a ghastly season, a season of carnage, and the old people did not like to think about it even now. We watched their sad faces when they spoke of it and saw that these old people themselves felt death very near, foreseeing the day when Gai would leave them, when the melons would dry, when they would starve.

Suddenly, unnoticed into the midst of this discussion came the baby Nhwakwe, having been awakened by the voices, his eyes still filled with sleep, to put an empty veg-etable husk on the head of his grandmother, Dasina. She was too depressed to notice, though, and presently the husk fell off and Nhwakwe stumbled back to his sleeping place, secure between his father and his mother, as though perhaps he had not fully awakened at all.

Dasina was speaking. She said again: "To die is bad, but in the end we all die anyway," and Ukwane said he did not expect to live another season. Then he asked us when we would have to leave. We told him that we were leaving in a very few days, and he said he was sorry to hear it, but if we liked he would come back to our country with us to tell us everything he knew about the customs of the Gikwe. We told him sadly that this would not be possible, and he said that in that case he would live out his life beside our track, waiting for the day when we would return. We told him not to do even that, for European farmers would surely follow our tracks into the desert looking for Bushmen to take as servants. "I hear you," said Ukwane, "but I would still like to go with you to your country."

We told him then that we lived so far away and over so much water that if he went there he could never get back, and we said that even if he did go he might find that the longing to be back among his own people would be worse to suffer, harder to bear, than even hunger and thirst. "That is true," he said. "Perhaps."

- - -

That night we had, of course, not wanted to ask about the customs and beliefs of Gikwe Bushmen concerning death; we wanted very much to know, but that night the people were grieved and with Bushmen death is always a bad subject. Another day, however, Ukwane and Dasina did tell us their funeral customs, which were similar to those of the Kung, though not as elaborate. We learned that the Gikwe dig a grave with digging-sticks, then bind the body with the arms crossed over the chest, the knees raised and bound, the ankles tied together, and the head resting on the fists, which are drawn up to the chin. The body is then wrapped in an old kaross and placed in a sitting position in the grave, braced upright by a forked stick. Each person present throws a handful of earth into the grave to "make the person remember them" and also to make the spirit go peacefully away. The grave is then filled up and covered with thorn branches to protect the dead person from wild animals, for a hyena will sometimes unearth a corpse.

While performing a funeral, and from the time of the funeral on, the Bushmen always stay upwind from a grave, for after death the spirit blows down the wind and will be harmful to the living. Gikwe Bushmen remain by a grave for at least three months—three moons, or longer—before they move away because they cannot bear to leave the dead person, because they want to make sure that animals do not spoil his body, and because, said Ukwane, "He is our person, whom we love. We do not want to leave until we have given up hope."

We learned one other thing, and that was that the Gikwe put a medicine power, a fragrant powder made of an herb called *sasa*, in the nostrils of the dead person, and sprinkle his body with sasa before the burial. This, said Ukwane, is done to ensure heavy rain in the rainy season, but also it may well have to do with protecting the living from the spirit of the dead. We did not learn more about this because Bushmen will talk about any subject you may name except the subject of the spirits of the dead. The Kung respect and fear spirits more than any other thing, and only after a year of trying did we learn about them; the Gikwe seem to feel the same way, and for that reason we did not expect to learn very much. We did find, however, that the spirits of the dead are called, at least sometimes, the *kwe be ha ki* (person who is not here), and that these spirits travel in the wind—not in open, blowing wind, but in whirlwinds; that is why the Gikwe Bushmen avoid whirlwinds, because a spirit might be there to carry them away. Once a whirlwind passing through our camp uprooted a tent and carried it spinning to the sky. Possibly, explained the Bushmen, a spirit of the dead thought that there was a person inside, although sometimes the spirits cause only mischief.

With the Kung, the funeral customs are very much the same as those of the Gikwe. The body is folded into a sitting position and bound, but the head is bowed down to the knees. Beads and a kaross ornament the body, which is also lowered into the grave and buried upright, but thereafter the custom differs from that of the Gikwe. The Kung, after filling in the grave and protecting it with stones or thorn branches, break the scherm of the dead person down over the grave, shatter all or most of his possessions, and strew the fragments over the grave together with sasa powder.

Last, they kindle a fire in front of the now destroyed scherm and bend a reed, which they thrust into the ground, so that the grave, the fire, and the pointing reed make a line toward the place where the person who is now dead was born.

The Kung then abandon the grave immediately and forever, for when darkness falls the spirit blows down the wind and remains near its grave for an indefinite time. Whenever the Kung pass near the grave they blow sasa toward it to ensure their safety.

The Kung are so afraid of the spirits of the dead that they do not feel it necessary to remain as guardians of the grave, or even until they have "given up hope." Occasionally their custom proves unfortunate, as it has happened that the buried person rose from his grave and followed his people to their new camp. We ourselves knew a Kung Bushman who had died, been buried, and was resurrected; he clambered out of his grave at night, followed his band to their new camp, and rejoined his family to live out a happy life. It must happen rather often that people are mistaken for dead and buried accidentally—often enough, at least, to necessitate a word in the language, for those people who do revive and manage to dig out of their shallow graves are called the *twi*.

The spirit that does not become a twi does not remain alone by the grave forever, but is found by the great god in his wanderings over the veld and is taken to his home in the east. There it is hung in a tree and smoked in a medicine smoke until it becomes a *gaua*, a spirit of the dead, and can serve the great god as a messenger to bring disease and death to people, or to lead them to game and honey, depending on the great god's whim.

The Kung do not consider the gauas to be either happy or sad in their roles after life, but lonely and neutral, roaming above the veld either singly or in twos, on little paths of theirs, little invisible threads like spider webs, that run through the air. Whenever Bushmen have their great night-time medicine dances, the gauas are present, just out of sight in the dark among the trees, and whenever there is a ring around the moon the Bushmen know that the gauas themselves are dancing, for the moon is their dance fire, the ring is the circle made by their dancing feet.

The aloes and the spiny plants of the desert. Far away, on the horizon, two baobab trees are showing.

TOP: *Gai was afraid of us at first. He listened carefully to everything we said, but he would not speak.*
BOTTOM: *Gai's wife, Tsetchwe, and their baby Nhwakwe.*

Ukwane eats a tsama melon, the source of food and all water for Bushmen during the drought.

*Tsama melons on their vines are almost hidden in the yellow grass,
but Dasina and Twikwe find them.*

TOP: *Twikwe.*
BOTTOM: *This is Gai's house, this bare sand under the branch of a tree.*

He climbed to her shoulder and stood there triumphantly without holding on, gazing around like a child on a hill.

The jealous men from Okwa.

The people from Okwa camped right beside Ukwane; the two groups were shaded by the same little tree.

CHAPTER EIGHT

The Dancers

WHEN BUSHMEN DANCE their medicine dances, the medicine begins to work in the bodies of the medicine men. Medicine is warmed to potency as the exercise of dancing warms the shaman's body, and by the heat of the fire that the shaman dances around. The medicine purges evil and cures a sickness that is known to the Gikwe as "star sickness," a mysterious magic sickness that has no tangible symptoms but together with evil is brought to people by the spirits of the dead. You can tell that powerful curing medicine is at work during one of these dances because the medicine men fall into trance, shudder and shriek and roll their eyes up into their heads, fall into the fire or wash their faces with flaming coals and are not burned, and when they rub their fire-warmed hands on you to cure you their hands are hot and dry and flutter like moths, and presently the star sickness leaves you, enters the bodies of the medicine men, and is shrieked into the air, hurled back to the spirits of the dead who brought it.

There are many types of medicine at work in the Kalahari, and every band among the Gikwe, Kung, or any Bushman nation possesses certain of these. Some bands, for instance, have the giraffe, rain, and gemsbok medicine. Others might have the ratel, fire, and gemsbok medicine. Ukwane's band had the sun, dove, and gemsbok medicine. Almost every band has the gemsbok medicine, for magically the gemsbok are very important animals, obvious from the black medicine markings on a gemsbok's face.

The medicine songs are songs without words and are given to both Kung and Gikwe Bushmen by the great god who sends his messengers, the spirits of the dead, to a sleeping person. The spirits of the dead teach the person a medicine song in a dream, and when the person awakens he teaches the song to the other members of his band.

At dances, women sing the medicine songs, men dance and use the medicine to cure people, for almost all men are made medicine men when they are in their late teens, after they have been initiated into manhood, having shot their first buck. They are made medicine men by older medicine men, and although any Bushman man may become a medicine man, only certain of them find that they have strong healing power, and these are the ones who practice, who fall into trance at dances and chase evil from their people. Ukwane himself had been one of these. None of the people he cured ever died, he said, but as he grew old his powers seemed to leave him, so now he did not practice anymore. In his band Gai became the strong healer.

Of course, a medicine dance is a great affair, for it

usually takes place at night and lasts all night into the morning. Everyone in the band takes part, every young boy old
enough to walk may dance, every young girl may sing with
the women, and women themselves may dance if they feel
inclined. People talk, eat, and smoke between dances, or
go off to bed to sleep for a while, so, all in all, dances are
social affairs as well as important curing ceremonies and
might be called informal rituals, for everyone has a good
time.

Underlying the gaiety and informality of a dance, however, is deep magic, taken very seriously by everyone, for
using this magic is the way in which the Bushmen protect
themselves from the dark forces in themselves and their
country, the only way in which they can protect their lives
from the evil of dissension, from thirst and starvation, from
disease and death. In their dances the Bushmen defy the
great god himself and his ominous messengers, the spirits
of the dead.

To have a dance, the women sit in a circle with their
babies asleep on their backs and sing the medicine songs in
several parts with falsetto voices, clapping their hands in a
sharp, staccato rhythm at counterpoint to the rhythm of
their voices. Behind their backs the men dance one behind
the other, circling slowly around, taking very short, pounding steps which are again at counterpoint to both the
rhythms of the singing and the clapping. Now and then
the men sing, too, in their deeper voices, and their dance
rattles—rattles made from dry cocoons strung together with
sinew cords and tied to their legs—add a sharp, high clatter
like the sound of shaken gourds, very well timed because
the men step accurately. A Bushman dance is an infinitely
complicated pattern of voices and rhythm, an orchestra of
bodies, making music that is infinitely varied and always
precise.

It is with great care and effort that this perfection is

achieved, for the people learn the songs and dances when they are children and work for perfection in skill and timing all their lives. Even the dance rattles are carefully tended, hung from tree branches to preserve their dryness, their sharp sound, and a great deal of labor goes into their making. Gai's pair of rattles, which swung in the wind from the branch that shaded his dwelling, had about sixty cocoons on each rattle of the pair, and in each cocoon, from which the pupa had been carefully extracted and the cocoon closed up again, there were from ten to twenty fragments of ostrich eggshell, each fragment chipped to a uniform size and round. Each pair of rattles is expected to last a lifetime and more, and I'm sure that Gai's rattles were older than he.

The day before we left, Ukwane's band and the visitors from Okwa decided that since they were all together and in sufficient number, they would hold a dance. Perhaps it would purge the bad season or relieve the strain of jealousies they felt toward each other. Dances are usually held at night, but this time, out of consideration for us, they agreed to hold it during the day so that we could film it. We found a place which would be suitable for filming, helped gather sufficient wood because there would have to be a fire, no matter how hot the day was, and as we did all this the six young boys got more and more excited, tried on dance rattles, danced tight little circles around each other and tugged at the elbows of the adults, urging them to start.

Some of the women wanted to sing, others felt too hot, too tired, but the men walked among them encouraging them all. A dance is long, hot work for women, the pleasure of dancing being mostly for the men. At last Twikwe and Dasina went to the spot chosen for the dance and, sitting side by side at the fire, their backs to everybody, sang a few bars and began to talk, then sang a little more, joined now by Tsetchwé, who sat beside them and began to sing in earnest. All three of them looked so small down in the grass and set up such a loud noise singing—for in order to interest the other women they were shrieking the song at the top of their voices—that they seemed like three tree frogs or three cicadas, hard to notice in the landscape but putting forth earsplitting songs.

At last a few more women joined the singers and the singing mounted, the voices took on several parts. At last the men began to join, dancing toward the circle in twos and threes, moaning the song in their throats, leaning on long staffs, their coming heralded by the dry, loud staccato of their rattles.

The men came from different directions, and they stood so tall and danced so strongly, with their muscles standing out on their necks, that their coming was like the coming of bull antelope, they were so radiant of strength and tension, they were so lithe and male. They came together out of the trees and, without the slightest change of pace, arranged themselves around the dance circle, wheeling slowly, one after the other, and the dance began.

The air was hot, the sun was shining strongly, the fire was sending a shuddering cloud of heat around the dancers, and as the dancers moved almost imperceptibly faster and faster, Gai suddenly flung his arms into the air and with a piercing shriek crashed to the ground. He landed stiffly with a bounce, his head cracking. On the ground he writhed and groaned, and Ukwane pulled him by the arms to remove his body from the dance circle.

Gai was in deep trance. Ukwane was ministering to Gai's body because Gai's spirit had rushed away.

Bushmen say that when the medicine in a medicine man becomes stimulated by a dance, warmed by the fire and by the heat of the man's body, the man's spirit may leave him, causing his body to fall because there is nothing there to hold it up, and fly into the veld, where it seeks out the evil that is troubling people. Some medicine men in this way have seen the spirits of the dead, some have seen the great god. At another dance we once attended, one man's spirit rushed into the veld, where it came upon a pride of lions that had been troubling the people by their constant presence and by their deafening roars at night. The man's spirit spoke with the lions, defied them, and ordered them away, and the lions did go; they troubled the people no longer.

When the spirit returns, the medicine man comes to himself, as Gai did presently. He stood up and ran into the veld, gaining speed as he went. Far out in the veld he screamed, a shriek of defiance, then turned and charged back toward the dance fire. He passed through the dance like a wind through dry leaves; the people ducked aside and shrank away from his feet, then settled together when he had gone by. Gai shrieked again, turned himself, and rushed back, charging bull-like toward the fire again; this time Ukwane seized his arms and though Gai plowed forward, Ukwane hung on, dragging behind with all his weight, until at last Gai fell headlong into the dance fire and his hair burst into flames.

Ukwane snatched him out and slapped out the fire in his hair, and Gai, his mouth open and his eyes quite wild, sparks still falling from his head like stars, strained against Ukwane's hands. At last he broke away.

In a moment he bent slowly over the fire and washed his hands in the flames, then went to one of the women in the circle of singers and, placing one hand on her chest, the other on her back, shuddered and groaned as he sucked the evil from her, then straightened suddenly and shrieked the evil into the air. In this way Gai cured all the people, followed as he went by Ukwane, who now held Gai's arm to keep him upright. Before long, Gai had fallen again exhausted and was dragged by the ankles to a place in the shade.

I looked at him and saw that his eyes were closed, his

eyelids puffed, and thought he seemed unconscious. His breath came rasping through his mouth and nose, and his pulse, showing in "the heart's place," seemed very quick. But he was all right; no one paid any attention to him as they would have had he not been well. His baby came to watch him, though, and gazed down into his swollen face.

It was very hot. The dancers and the women singing steamed with perspiration, first becoming gold in color, then ash white as dust stuck to them. Soon the women felt that they had sung enough, their feelings showing clearly in the diminished vigor of their songs, until finally the singing faded out entirely and the dance stopped. The men complained, but the women would sing no more and presently everyone had drifted away, leaving only the children wheeling slowly around the track worn by the dancers' feet, dancing soberly, carefully, without music, and Gai, who now lay prone and forgotten in the dust, in the shade of a little tree.

Hours later, when even the children had wandered back to the werfs and had joined their parents, who were tired from the exercise and were taking afternoon naps, Gai came to himself once more; he sat up and wiped his face, got slowly to his feet, and walked slowly home to sleep, next to his wife beside their fire.

- - -

All the Bushmen were asleep but Twikwe. Some people lay on their backs with their arms shading their eyes, their mouths open, some on their bellies, their arms and legs sprawled. All the young boys except Giamakwe lay like puppies, tangled together in a knot of arms and legs, for even in sleep they would not be parted. Giamakwe slept at a little distance from the others on his side with his body bent backward into a U, his head almost touching his buttocks, as limp and supple as a young snake or a young cat that drapes over your hand. Even Nhwakwe was fast asleep, lying on his belly and using as his couch his father's body, his head on his father's chest. Both were deep in slumber, Nhwakwe snoring a loud baby snore, saliva from his open mouth moistening Gai's dark skin, but Gai absolutely silent in the fast, still sleep of a hunter. Only Twikwe was not sleeping. She lay on her belly with her chin propped up with one hand as she built a precarious little toy hut out of strips of bark, carefully, the way one builds a card house. When I came by to look at the people she looked at me with her amused, wise-woman's eyes.

In the afternoon the young boys naturally woke up first, as they were so entwined that the movement of one was bound to wake the others, and began sleepily to delouse each other, taking turns in pairs, one lying with his head in his partner's lap while his partner searched through his hair, catching and biting the lice he found. Then they cut each other's hair with a razor blade they had got from someone in our expedition, cutting away certain tufts of hair and leaving certain others until patterns on each head were formed, ranging from scalplocks to rather fine designs. One boy had only two tufts left on his entire scalp, one on each side, like a pair of horns; another boy had an egg-shaped pattern of tufts but with two holes of bare scalp showing so that when he bent his head he accidentally presented an oval face with a pair of staring eyes. All the patterns were supposed to be geometric, never intentionally having fantastic or representative designs. Wite's head was shaved entirely, his partner having shown no imagination at all; and his bare head made his ears seem even larger and more pointed, his face more elfin even than before.

It was a gray, hazy afternoon. Below the fine overcast were clusters of little white clouds all grouped together like white flowers. In the west a great cloudbank was gathering, an ominous sign.

Later, when the young boys had dispersed to play horse

and rider, Ukwane took his bow and played a few songs. He played "Bitter Melons" again, and "A Song of Shouting," and one other song about Kutera, his wife. Both the last song and its subject were very simple, the song itself having only three or four notes and a gentle rhythm. It was composed by Ukwane one chilly night because he had asked Kutera to gather firewood during the afternoon, but she had refused. That night Ukwane had been cold because there was no fire.

Ukwane sang and played in the shade of a tree, and over his head the birds in the branches were also singing. Everything seemed very peaceful, very quiet under the hazy sky; the west wind moved the grass, yellow as young wheat, and blew the sounds of people speaking, the sounds of the young boys playing, and the fragrance of the great veld over us. The strain among the people seemed to have gone; they had held a dance together, their children were playing calmly; there was, for a time, enough to eat, as the gemsbok had not yet been quite devoured; and all these things seemed to relax the people, allowing them to see each other in more favorable lights. Their naps and their soft singing showed their relaxation, and we were glad, for we had become so fond of Ukwane and his people that we did not like to think of them abandoned by the Okwa people or involved in strife.

We were loading our trucks because we planned to leave before dawn. At the end of the afternoon all the Bushmen had drifted into our camp to watch us, and Tsetchwe helped me pack. I cut my finger on the sharp edge of a box and when she saw me trying to wipe the blood away she told me to wait, so I did, and when the blood was dry she scratched it all off with a stick.

We gave her presents, and presents to all the people there. We gave blankets to the people in Ukwane's band, long strings of white beads to everyone, metal to make knives or spearheads, tobacco and pipes, salt and candy and all the water their containers would hold, all they could drink, and even enough water to wash in, for we had enough to take us to a waterhole a few hundred miles away where we could fill our drums. They did wash. Gai washed his whole body and emerged a shining gold. The others washed their arms and faces, modesty preventing their washing the rest, leaving them with golden arms and oval golden masks.

Tsetchwe was pleased with her presents—she hung her white beads in her hair and wrapped herself in the blanket, which, she said, was far softer than leather and which would not get stiff in the rain—but she did not seem happy. She spent the evening sitting beside me, for though we could not talk much, we liked each other. "I will cry when you are gone," she said.

The two horses, formed by the six young boys, came prancing by, the riders riding loosely, the front feet of the horses galloping but the hind feet, because of the heavy load, trotting up and down. One horse disintegrated in front of us and the young boys who had formed it came forward slowly. The rider, a young boy from Okwa, seemed to want to ask me something. He was very shy, but finally he mustered his courage. "Are you a woman?" he said.

Ordinarily, he would have been too polite to ask a personal question, something which Bushmen almost never do because to them asking questions implies distrust, but it may be that on the day before our departure he had found his curiosity impossible to resist. Tsetchwe frowned at him, but I said: "Yes, I am."

The horse had been arguing with the rider, and the two boys who had been the front and hind legs seemed quite triumphant. "We told you so," one said.

A great thunderhead was rising in the west, which would probably disperse before morning, and the sun set into it, turning the whole horizon a pale and delicate rose. We built up our fires and at the werf the Bushmen built up their fires and when it was dark our fragment of the veld was rather gay with firelight. A huge star, Fomalhaut, appeared in the southeast, as it did every evening. Tonight it looked as big as the moon and blue in the haze, but very dim, getting smaller and brighter as it rose.

Ukwane played his songs for us and said again that he would wait for our return, living beside our track, and if his son should come to visit him he would wait no longer but would follow our track to find us again somewhere.

We told him that under no conditions should he do any of this, for he would never be able to find us and we would probably never come back. He nodded, and we believed that he would not wait, but then again perhaps he did.

- - -

We got up before dawn in the morning and stamped out our fires and threw our bedrolls on top of the trucks. When it came, it was the pinkest dawn that I have ever seen and when the morning wind rose we shivered. I found a few coals left in a fire and tried to warm my hands, and when Wite saw what I was doing he crouched beside me and showed me how to pick up just one coal, roll it between the palms, and then hold the warm palms against the face. I tried it and of course was burned, but Wite patiently did it again and again, hoping that I would learn. His palms were flat and calloused almost as thickly as the soles of his feet. Twikwe, Tsetchwe, and Nhwakwe came to sit beside us and we waited together in silence until the trucks were ready. When I got up to go they got up too and Twikwe shook my hand and kissed me with a great smack, doing at this moment what she had seen Europeans do, not what Bushmen do, for they just wave calmly at each other, if that. But Tsetchwe turned her back to me and would not say good-bye.

We climbed into our trucks and started the motors. Ukwane called out to us with great sincerity to wish us rain on our journey, a very generous wish, for though his people might suffer from it, it would cool the air and we might even be able to collect enough for a drink. We thanked him, of course, and he repeated his wish again. The trucks started to move and when they did Tsetchwe waved at last, and, lifting her baby to her hip, she waved his hand too, and so we left, and drove away in the direction opposite the one we had come from, over the plains, flatter and wider and longer here than we had ever seen, sloping miles and miles away to tiny trees on the horizon which were farther away than anything we had ever seen before except distant mountains, the earth from a plane, or stars. At noon, many miles from Ai a ha'o, we saw great herds of game, thousands of animals grazing together, and we regretted that the Bushmen were not near the game, or the game not near the Bushmen, for the people could have been feasting, and then we passed through the game into empty plains again, where we saw nothing but grass except once when we saw a plant very like a tumbleweed which leaped over the ground and then was caught by the wind and lifted higher and higher into the sky up against the clouds. It made us sad to see it flying there, the only moving thing in all the country. "It is the plane to America," the interpreter said.

In the evening when we camped, the sun set into a little dome of its own pink light, and in front of this minute sunset we saw whirlwinds crossing. Later, when the darkness came, we even saw a ring around the moon with red at its outer rim, and on the following day it did rain, something that happens only rarely in the month of July.

CHAPTER NINE

Peoples of the
Veld and Sky

AFTER MANY DAYS, during which we crossed the rest of the great central desert of Bechuanaland, we came to a strip of fertile country which is in both Bechuanaland and South-West Africa and is owned to a large extent by the Chuana people, who have great cattle ranches, vast areas of grazing land, and rather small villages. In this fertile land is Lake Ngami, a flat marsh or even a dry pan at most seasons, but when we saw it, it was filled with water, something that had not happened since Livingstone was there.

The country had changed greatly since we left the central desert. In the fertile land there were forests, thorn thickets, even little hills. At some places there were vast grasslands with grass higher than the hoods of our trucks, but in other places livestock had eaten away everything, cattle having devoured the grass, goats having chewed the leaves from the bushes. We saw five or six great herds of cattle grazing on the flat land surrounding Lake Ngami, where the grass was short and green and looked kept, like a park. There were perhaps a thousand cattle in each herd, and mixed with the cattle were herds of springbok, a few ostriches, and marabou storks. It was pastoral Africa, for the path we followed was marked with the hoofs and dung of the cattle, tracked by the huge ox-drawn, forked log sledges of the Chuana farmers, and now and then patterned with the footprints of a jackal, a hyena, or even a leopard or a lion, for although there are great herds, the country itself is wild.

Lake N'gami was an enormous, shining expanse of water a few square miles in area and very shallow everywhere. We got out of our trucks and went to the water to rest our eyes with so much luxury and we found that the water was warm, full of brown duckweed, and swarmed with innumerable tiny flies. Ducks and geese were swimming, storks and flamingos were wading at the edges, and while we were looking the largest herd of cattle that we had ever seen came to the lake to drink. There were hundreds upon hundreds of them drifting toward the lake, and the noise of their hoofs was like the sound of a tornado, a great waterfall, thunderous and mighty. A Chuana was riding among them and it took him nearly an hour, traveling in a straight line, to pass through the herd, the cattle parting a little as he came to let him by. He rode on and on, and when we left he was still riding, still among the cattle, and still not out of sight.

We left Lake Ngami and its vast pastoral lands and went on until we were away from the Bantu farmlands, over the border of Bechuanaland into the Kalahari Desert of South-

West Africa, which at that place is called the Nyae Nyae area. This country we knew very well, for it was here that we had lived a year among Kung Bushmen, and although it was a desert it was also totally unlike the great barren steppes of central Bechuanaland, as it was quite rolling, marked by large forests of small trees, by little rolling hills, by omarambas, and by pans, which in the rains were shallow lakes and in the drought were clay flats. The land was still very open and tilting, but the low hills and the forests veiled the great sweep of country, and the sun, the moon, and the horizons.

As soon as we were there we felt very familiar, very at home. We knew quite a lot about Kung Bushmen, who in ways are different from Gikwe Bushmen—as the country is not as harsh, the Kung are a little grander, living together in larger numbers because they have veld food more abundantly, a little more extravagant with their time and their possessions. They build themselves grass huts or scherms, at least during the rains, and though they know vast sections of their country perfectly, being quite sure of the whereabouts of game and certain of the whereabouts of different types of veld food, they do not have to memorize the whereabouts of each root individually and store this information in their minds for future seasons, as the Gikwe do. The Kung are diligent and powerful hunters, although in some respects their country is harder to hunt in than the land of the Gikwe, more overgrown with brush and trees. But the Kung have metal-tipped arrows and complicated poison, and the men make a point of hunting often and well because their people love meat.

We knew their rolling veld with its baobab trees and hidden waters, for in Nyae Nyae the people do not have to scrape roots and suck melons, but are the possessors of deep waterholes where they can drink clear water almost all year long. We knew which stalks among the grass blades marked edible roots, and where game antelope might be found.

We knew not only the veld but the beings that live in the sky above it, and knew the beings under the earth and in the four directions. We knew where the great god lives in the east with his tree and his medicine smoke with which he makes spirits of the dead from dead people. We knew his names, for besides his usual, everyday name, Gao Na—which means "Big Gao," Gao being simply a man's name—he has many other hidden, secret names that may never, never be spoken during the light of day but only at night and only then at dances. Some of these names are Haishi, Gao ha, Nao, and Gara, and if he hears one of these names being called he will come to see who called it. He does not like to be disturbed during the day, he does not like the hot sun, and if a person bothers him during the day he will make that person sick. He is called at dances and cursed for the things he does to people, and some medicine men have even seen him when they were in trance; he appeared once as a yellow mouse, once as a gray man the size of a mouse, and once as a cloud of mist, although these are not his usual forms; usually he is the size and shape of a man, but, the Bushmen say, because he is wild he is always seen far away.

We knew of his wife, whose name is Khoana, a Kung Bushman woman's name, but who is also called the "Mother of Bees," and we knew of the being who lives in the west, whose name is also Gao Na and who is both the namesake and the servant of the great god, bringing good and evil to people as the great god chooses. This god of the west can also do things to people on his own initiative, and people sometimes say that evil comes when the two gods disagree.

There is one more figure, another being who has no place, such as the east or west; another god whose relation to the gods of the east and west has not been formed. His name is Gaua; he is called by the same name as the gaua si, the spirits of the dead, and though to the Kung today his identity has become vague, we felt that he well might be an older, primal figure, a god whose being has been now infused with the gods of the east and west. Today the great god of the east is sometimes called Gaua, called by the old god's name, and when he is, it is because he has brought evil, sickness, catastrophe, or death.

The old god still exists, the Bushmen know him, but his presence is diffusing; he, the old power of evil, is becoming faint, his entity obscure.

In the west live the *kwa kwa kwara* (knee knee nothing), the people with no knees. These people have no knee joints, but must stand up always. At night when the sun sets, the people with no knees catch it and kill it, for the sun is meat. They put it in a pot, and when it is cooked they tell their children to run off and play, and when the children are gone the people with no knees eat it. When the children come back, the people with no knees pick their teeth and give what they remove to the children, and then the people with no knees take the shoulder blade of the sun and throw it back into the east again, where the new sun grows and rises in the morning. If a tall man throws it you are aware of nothing, but if a short man throws it you can hear it whirring overhead. We knew a Kung Bushman man who, said he, had been to the west and had visited the people with no knees. He had been very interested to see them and very curious to know how they slept at night, for he did not imagine that they could lie down, so when darkness came he had watched and waited, and, just as he had suspected, when they had finished the sun they did not lie down but leaned against forks of the trees, where they rested, propped.

In the north is a great river, the Okovango, and Bantu

people live there. In the south live the gemsbok people, who are not ordinary gemsbok but beings in gemsbok form. It was these beings who taught the Bushmen how to make ostrich-eggshell beads, for when making a bead the gemsbok people use their long horns to bore the hole in the center. The gemsbok people often wear strings of beads around their necks. The gemsbok people look just like gemsbok. When Bushmen are hunting they must be very careful not to mistake these people for ordinary gemsbok, because if a hunter should shoot a gemsbok person even by accident he would get very sick and die. But such accidents are rare, for if a group of gemsbok people are out grazing and notice that a Bushman hunter is drawing his bow at them, they will say to him: "Do not shoot us, we are not gemsbok," and the hunter will naturally leave them alone.

Under the world is another world just like this one, with trees and omarambas, hills and pans, a sun and a moon, Bushmen, Bantus, and Europeans just like the people here, and the bottom of our world is that world's sky. There is no other connection between our world and the lower world except possibly through certain deep waterholes, for it was through a waterhole that the great god climbed from that world when he first came here.

Over the world, of course, is the sky, and there is nothing above that. The sun, which is not only meat but a death-giving agent because it burns the veld and dries up the waterholes, is a male, and the moon when it is full is female. A crescent moon, called *nui ma ze* (moon small new), is male, and so are the great destructive thunderheads that bring hailstorms or electric storms which break down dwellings and flatten the grass. The soft gray clouds that carry land rains which blow like mists into the plants of the veld and make them grow are female. The rain of male and female clouds is itself male or female, depending on the cloud's gender or on whether the rain is creative or destructive, but if you can't tell from the rain as it falls you can tell from its footprints, for male rain leaves sharp, pierced marks in the dust and female rain leaves wide, soft splashes. And as for the stars, they are called by some the eyes of dead people and by others are said to be ant lions which at night rise from the bottoms of their little traps of sand.

Since we had lived a year in Nyae Nyae we knew the round of the seasons, which Kung Bushmen say are six in number. We came there in July, in winter and the start of the drought, the coldest season. August was bitterly cold and also dry, but in September the air began to get warmer and heralded the next season, called "little winds before the rain," a season of whirlwinds, drought, and clouds of dust. In October, suddenly and presenting a startling sight, a thorn tree near our camp turned quite green and the heat began to be intense. This was the start of the springtime, the dryest, hottest time of all the year and a time of starvation, for the water in the waterholes gets very low until only a little remains on the bottoms and the wild roots push sap into their vines so that the vines turn green and sprout but the roots themselves are shriveled. This was the worst season of the year for the people. Before this, during the winter, the large extended band that we had gone to visit was separated into little family groups that were scattered through the veld, living at little waterholes that did not keep their water all year long. During the dry season the water in these waterholes vanished, causing the small family bands to gather at the last sure waterhole of the area, a waterhole called Gautscha, which was beside a huge flat pan called Gautscha Pan.

There was one rather large band that always lived at Gautscha and numbered some forty people, who divided themselves into sometimes three, sometimes four family groups. They thought themselves lucky to live there, for Gautscha was considered to be a sort of paradise, where the waterhole was cool and deep, and (it was said) game gathered at all times to lick the salt, for Gautscha was a salt pan. It was the salt that made Gautscha most desirable, because salt is greatly esteemed and is gathered from the crust of the pan in moist balls. Bushmen sprinkle the surface with water in order to roll up just the first layer where the salt lies. When the salt balls dry, Bushmen crumble them into their food, preferring salt to all sweet things and honey. Once when we asked some of the Gautscha people what they called themselves they replied with this phrase: "We are a salty people, who come from a salty place."

In the dry season, two hundred people came to Gautscha and lived in the bushes at the edge of the pan. This was an enormous number for any area to support, but all had indisputable rights to be there, for either their parents had drunk at Gautscha or they had relatives whose parents had; by the rather complicated system, any Bushman may drink water and gather veld food wherever his parents had a right to do so, or may live with his parents, his brothers or sisters, or his wife at any place where the relative of his choice has rights. There was water but not much food at Gautscha, and all the people got thin and very hungry and sat around their fires at night with sweat pouring from their bodies but with nothing to eat; to make matters worse, one man coming for a visit proved to be ill and gave his disease to everyone. It was a disease that caused vomiting, high fevers, chest pains, and nosebleeds of great intensity—a woman whom I tried to cure bled all one morning with blood squirting from her nostrils, pouring down over her arms and hands and dripping from her elbows, making a dark pool on the ground. The disease struck all the people, from the youngest infants to the oldest grandparents, and all the people lay for days scattered all over the ground, too ill to move. We did everything we could, of course; we provided food and medicine, firewood and water, and took turns staying up all night to nurse the people. As it happened, everyone got better within fourteen days, although not all were completely cured; and many, feeling that their luck was very bad at Gautscha, decided to take their chances at other places in the veld where, although there was no water, there were watery roots that could be scraped for moisture. One day many of the people walked away in single file, taking their belongings and carrying on their backs their relatives still too sick to travel, leaving Gautscha Pan deserted except for the three small family bands who made their permanent home there.

One day when we were traveling in the veld, about twenty miles from Gautscha we came upon an old man lying on his face on the sand in an open place. He was a member of one of the bands at Gautscha that tried to escape bad luck, and, thinking he was hurt, we stopped at once. But he was not hurt; when we came near him he did not get up, but turned his face away from us and lay as if dazed, pressing one hand to his forehead. We knew him; he was the only Bushman of any nation we had ever met or even heard of who had never married, this because Bushman men must shoot a buck and undergo initiation before they can marry, which he had never done. Instead he lived with his sister, who took care of him and provided him with food, and who had been very ill during the plague at Gautscha. As we looked at him the headman of that band stepped out of the bushes and told us that the old man was not ill but grieving for his sister, who lay dead in a grove of thorn trees a little way beyond. The old man, who had been alone with his sister when she died, had been too weak from the illness to bury her, and had only been able to hide her body under a pile of stones. When the other members of the band had returned to the grove after a day or so of veld food-gathering, it had been too late, too dangerous because of the now roaming spirit, for them to assist the old man with a funeral, and they had had to abandon his sister's body as it was.

The headman lifted the old man from the ground and we saw that he had not been weeping but had only been lying inert and helpless, powerless now to keep himself erect. On our truck he lay just where we put him, motionless, prone, all the way back. We passed the grove where his sister lay, a grove of high white trees with red beans on their branches, and the old man did not turn his head to look.

After that, the situation for the people who remained at Gautscha got better because the summer came. Great cloudbanks like mountains formed at the horizon, dispersed themselves in brown haze, and formed again, getting larger day by day. Some of the bands who had left Gautscha began to return and once again the countryside was populous, the air filled with the murmur of voices and the smell of smoke from the many fires. Some of the men went hunting and shot a giraffe, so there was lots of meat for a while.

One day some of us went to a place called Kubi Pan to see a cheetah that was supposed to live there, but instead we saw a flock of guinea fowl walking single file as people do, raising a cloud of dust. Two of them began to fight because it was their mating season. When we got to Kubi it was evening and the clouds on the horizon were very thick, and just when the sun set into them the full moon rose on the other side, causing a balance of the two great bodies over the earth.

It seemed to be an auspicious night. On the way home we felt something electric in the air and when we got to Gautscha the moon had risen high and pale in the clouds and we found that the Bushmen were dancing the rain dance. Everyone was there, the women all singing and the men wheeling in a circle around the dance fire, the clouds of dust rising under their feet making them look like specters in the eerie light between the fire and the moon. The dance was very powerful. The men wheeled faster, the singing mounted in pitch. A medicine man coming from a far werf and singing as he came sprang among the dancers like a leopard, soft-footed and fine, and as he looked around him for a moment before beginning to dance, the moon behind his head filled a white ostrich feather in his hair with light. He smiled to himself, then, dancing suddenly, led the other dancers in a serpentine track through the circle of women, over the fire, and out the other side. The wind blew hard along the ground, and the smoke and fire streamed into the veld. The singing was very hard, very fast, and as the dancers swung around the circle dancing harder and faster, it suddenly began to rain.

It was like a miracle. It was the first rain of the year. First, there were just a few drops, but soon it was raining steadily in gusts behind the wind, causing the dancers to relax a little but continue dancing without paying attention to the fact that they were drenched. A bolt of lightning illuminated the veld for miles around with a blue-green light not of this world, showing all the trees and bushes stark and rain-lashed in the grass, then a blast of thunder as the light went out which struck us deaf as the lightning had struck us blind. For a moment it was black and still except for the lashing rain, and in the silence we heard a lion roaring far out in the veld, answered by another lion which was a little nearer, and then a peal of thunder shook them silent, drowning even their great voices.

The people had not danced to bring the rain; they had known that rain was coming and had danced to use its strong medicine. It rained all night, the rain so drenching and torrential that it put out the dance fire and drove the dancers into their scherms, and in the morning there was a lake of shining water on the pan and lilies growing everywhere, where only their dry leaves had been before.

After that the rain came often. Some weeks it rained a little every day, some weeks the rain became torrential and flattened the Bushmen's grass scherms, but it made the veld rich and green, with flowers everywhere and all kinds of fruit, which grew on trees and stalks and bushes. The pan became the home of shore birds, marabou storks and flamingos. Leopards and lions drank there, game antelope waded through it, leaving deep tracks in the mud, and the Bushman children sometimes danced in the shallows, their feet making flashing, rhythmic splashes, or bathed themselves until their skins were shining gold.

One night I went to the werf with a lantern and suddenly found myself beset by insects flying all around me, attracted by the light. It was the mating flight of white ants, which had come out of the ground in great numbers and now filled the air. The Bushman men were away on a hunting trip, unfortunately, but the women came to the light as quickly as the ants and began at once to catch them and stuff them into their mouths, saying *"gurico gum"* as they did so, *gurico* being the name of the ants and *gum* the word used for candy, for sweet gum that oozes from the trees, and for sweet caterpillars. Much faster than the women could eat, more and more ants came flying in a swarm as thick as a blizzard and already the ground was white with wings, for the ants, throwing themselves to the earth, would drop their wings instantly and begin to mate with each other in twos, in threes, even forming in great circles that turned as the ants ran scurrying to keep their positions, each one mounted with its forefeet on the back of the ant before it, pushed on by the ant behind. Sometimes an ant would fail to shed its wings and, finding that the great train's dragging hampered its mating, would twist and thrash and struggle, squeezing the wings between its thorax and abdomen, which did break off the wings but left the stubs. More and more ants were flying to the light and their circles were growing bigger and bigger until we couldn't move without stepping on them, but the women, getting more excited and moving very quickly, as if responding to the pace and the excitement of the ants, scooped them up and ate them as fast as they landed, spitting out the silver wings as one would spit out chaff. Over our heads a few night birds and many bats were flying, catching and eating the ants before they reached the ground, and around our feet huge pink hunting-spiders rushed in and out of the swarm, dragging the ants from their acts of copulation and carrying them away to eat them in the dark.

Before long the flight had ended. Only a few late-coming ants bumped against the light, the night birds and bats were gone, and the spiders had run away. Nothing was left but the white wings like petals all over the ground and the wings that were caught in people's throats or stuck to their faces. The women, quite composed now, brushed themselves off, and one of them sang a song:

> *Gurico gum, ah*
> *Ah, ah.*

I noticed that each woman had managed to save a little bag or vegetable husk full of ants for her husband. These they put away.

That was in the late spring, a fertile season full of promise, and when it was over the best season of the year began, called the Veld Food Season, which starts some time in March. The big rains have ended, the air is warm but not hot, the veld is filled with water, game, fruit, roots, and green-leafed vegetables, and sometimes many of the people of the large extended bands come together to live, to hold important ceremonies which require many people, and to enjoy each other's company. Sometimes they separate into very small bands because they can now go anywhere they wish, each family going to the part of the veld where the type of food grows that the family most enjoys. There is water everywhere, in small seasonal waterholes, in shallow salt pans, in hollow trees, and the people thrive and grow quite fat. One of their favorite foods, one that grows in great abundance at this season, is a ground nut called *tsi*, which grows on a trailing vine and has so much fat that if you leave a kernel of it on a piece of paper it will leave a greasy stain. Tsi is regarded by the Kung Bushmen as a very powerful food, one of the powerful veld foods in which there is a special essence, something mysterious and magic which gives them a life force all their own so that it would be dangerous to eat them during the year if this life force were not first subdued or not first integrated with the life force of the people. These foods are the mainstays of the Bushmen's diet, and contain fat; and every year people in their child-bearing years, when they consider themselves subject to harm, protect themselves against these foods by a ritual act.

The act of protection is called *choa*, and it is interesting because it differs from the protective rituals performed by agricultural peoples to save their crops or animals from harm, or to cause their increase. The Bushmen choa themselves not to protect their fertility, for decrease in the number of children is not a problem to them, but to make sure that they, the young adults and mainstays of the community, will not get thin and starve.

Those whom Bushmen call "old people," adults who have had three children, are expected to protect themselves and also to protect young people of the same sex. The choa ceremonies are performed in the Veld Food Season for each of the powerful veld foods as they ripen. The ceremony itself is simple; in order to choa tsi, for example, an old woman simply chews a mouthful of tsi with a few bites of a root called *shasha* if shasha is available or any one of certain other permissible roots if shasha is not, and spits the resulting paste into her palms. If she is choaing herself she washes her hands in the paste; if she is choaing a younger woman she rubs the paste on the young woman's arms and chest. It is an important ceremony, for no young person would think of eating tsi without it, but it is at the same time a casual, household ceremony, done without fuss or audience; more often than not, it will be performed in the morning before breakfast, say, or when the woman is resting for a moment in the veld, ceasing her digging to drink a sip of water. It is a powerful ceremony, though, for the woman choaed may then eat tsi in safety for a whole year, until the next season when it ripens again.

- - -

That year, in the Veld Food Season, there was a tragedy and also a wedding. The tragedy took place late one afternoon when a baby girl, playing house with a real fire, burned down her grandfather's grass scherm, thus destroying everything her grandparents owned, everything they had made over a lifetime. The two old people had been very industrious and the wife a prolific maker of ostrich-eggshell beads.

At the start of the blaze a great crowd of people gathered, arriving just in time to see the baby girl run out of the scherm as it collapsed in flames behind her. She ran straight to her mother and sat at her feet, ignoring the great crowd of people and placidly eating one of her grandfather's leather sandals which she had rescued from the fire and which, she found, had been cooked to a turn. No one was angry with the child, everyone was thankful that she had not been hurt. The people remarked at the size and the intensity of the fire and shook their heads at the destruction, each one telling someone else where he had been when he first had seen the blaze. They asked each other why no one put the fire out, as no one did, and soon the scherm was a heap of white ash and the old couple who owned it ruined materially, too old to start again.

A few weeks after that, two children were married. The groom was about sixteen and the bride was eight. It was considered to be an excellent match, as the bride was pretty and the groom was already becoming famous as a hunter. But even in these auspicious circumstances complications and involved negotiations arose, until, for a while, people began to think that no wedding would take place. The bride's aunt disliked the groom's mother, and recalled an old scandal that had shadowed the family for years. The groom's mother had divorced the groom's father long ago to marry her presesnt husband, which in itself was altogether usual, but it came out that the man and woman had maintained an adulterous relationship before the divorce and furthermore were taboo relatives, which made their union incestuous—not as severely so as marriage between parent and child or brother and sister, but incestuous nevertheless—and it caused a scandal that reverberated throughout all of Nyae Nyae. The two were middle-aged when they married, and they had clung solidly together through the storm of scandal and disapproval, for it was truly a marriage of love.

The little girl did not want to be a bride. When we asked her how she felt about her wedding she hid her face in her hands and said that she was still a young child, too young to get married.

All in all, only the groom's family showed patience and forbearance until at last the wedding took place. One day the young man killed a duiker and, according to custom, gave most of it to his bride's parents, thus proving that he hunted well and would provide for them and their daughter. With this the engagement was sealed. Shortly afterward the mothers of the bride and groom built a scherm for the young couple, which they furnished with wood and water and enlivened with a fire, kindled by brands from their own fires. Very early the following day the bride's mother adorned the bride, washing her, hanging white bead ornaments from her hair, rubbing her clothing with red, sweet-smelling powder, a symbol to Bushmen of beauty. Then, sitting her upon one large kaross, they covered her with another and left her to spend the day motionless, waiting for evening, when the union would take place.

It is common in Bushman ceremonies for a person at a transitional moment of life to be raised from the ground and hidden from the sun, as though suspended between earth and sky. Young people on the day of their first marriage are protected in this way; so are newborn babies, and so are girls on the day of their first menstruation. At a funeral, too, the body before burial is covered and raised from the ground, and perhaps all this is because a person is especially susceptible to damage at times of life when change is taking place, when, perhaps, a person is as delicate and fragile as a new moth emerged from a cocoon.

Because the sun brings death, no ceremony or part of any ceremony is performed when the sun is strong; but when evening came and the sun itself was dying, the groom was led to his new home by his three brothers, who took him by the hands and pulled him there, forced him, for custom demanded that he show reluctance. The bride, according to custom, refused to go to her husband and had to be picked up by another little girl and carried to him. In the drama of reluctance the bride struggled while the other girl caught her. She lifted the bride and carried her on her shoulders, not upright as a figure of triumph but wrapped in the kaross and motionless, like a dead little animal, then put her shrouded body on the floor of the new scherm and left her there to lie quietly while the wedding guests arrived. Again according to custom, the groom seemed to take no notice of his new bride; the people in the werf paid no attention, and, in fact, all the people went about their business in such a matter-of-fact way that an observer would think that nothing had happened although the young people were now married, the wedding had taken place.

The parents of the couple could not attend the wedding, for the young bride and groom were so taboo to them at this time that they could not even mention their names. In fact, no older person could attend, and the guests who came were all children, three-year-olds to teenagers, who sat by the young couple's fire decorously, the boys on the man's side, the girl's on the woman's, and talked quietly for twenty minutes or so, the youngest guests leaving when their bedtimes came. That was all. In the morning the little girl and her young husband were anointed with fat by their mothers, and they lived together from that day on.

A month later the bride's mother, who was herself a young woman, bore another child, her second daughter. We were at her werf at the time, sitting in the shade. That day the young woman had not gone out for veld food, but was lying propped up on her elbow in front of her scherm when suddenly, without telling anyone what was happening, she stood up and walked into the bushes, only to come back some time later with her baby in the fold of her kaross. We might not have known what had happened except that she was smiling a sure, sweet smile because she was pleased with herself. Her belly was flatter, and a tiny foot with a pink sole and curled toes stuck out from her kaross.

- - -

Day or night, whether or not the bush is dangerous with lions or with spirits of the dead, Bushman women give birth alone, crouching out in the veld somewhere. A woman will not tell anybody where she is going or ask anybody's help because it is the law of Bushmen never to do so, unless a girl is bearing her first child, in which case her mother may help her, or unless the birth is extremely difficult, in which case a woman may ask the help of her mother or another woman. The young woman was only fifty feet from the werf when she bore her daughter, but no one heard her because it is their law that a woman in labor may clench her teeth, may let her tears come or bite her hands until blood flows, but she may never cry out to show her agony. Bushmen say a woman must never show that she is afraid of pain or childbirth, and that is why a woman goes alone, or why a young girl goes only with her mother, for then if she shows her pain and fear, only her mother will know.

When labor starts, the woman does not say what is happening, but lies down quietly in the werf, her face arranged to show nothing, and waits until the pains are very strong and very close together, though not so strong that she will be unable to walk, and then she goes by herself to the veld, to a place she may have chosen ahead of time and perhaps prepared with a bed of grass. If she has not prepared a place, she gathers what grass she can find and, making a little mound of it, crouches above it so that the baby is born onto something soft. Unless the birth is very arduous and someone else is with the woman, the baby is not helped out or pulled, and when it comes the woman saws its cord off with a stick and wipes it clean with grass. Then the mother collects the stained grass, the placenta, and the bloody sand and covers them all with stones or branches, marking the spot with a tuft of grass stuck up in a bush so that no man will step on or over the place, for the ground where a child has been born is tainted with a power so strong that any man infected with it would lose an aspect of his masculinity, would lose his power to hunt. The woman does not bury the placenta, for if she did she would lose her ability to bear more children.

The moment of birth is a very important one for the

child and for the mother; it is at this moment that the child acquires a power, or an essence, over which he has no control, although he can make use of it. It will last him all his life; it is a supernatural essence that forever after connects the person born with certain forces in the world around him: with weather, with childbearing, with the great game antelope, and with death, and this essence is called the *now*.

There are two kinds of *now*, a rainy or cold one and a hot or dry one. If a person has a wet *now* and burns his hair in a fire or urinates in a fire, the person's *now* is said to make the weather turn cold (if it is the dry season) or to bring rain (if it is the rainy season). If a person has a dry *now* and burns hair or urinates in a fire, the *now* is said to stop a cold spell or a bad storm. When a person dies, too, the weather changes violently according to the person's *now*. After a death, scorching droughts or devastating storms are sure to follow.

We knew a Bushman woman at Gautscha whose young son was living not with her but far away with the family of his infant wife, and once, when a rainstorm came so violently that branches were splintered from the trees and water ran in torrents like waterfalls over the rocks beside the pan, the woman began to pine and grieve for her son, who, she felt sure, was dead. At last a visitor came from her son's band who assured her that her son was safe and well, and she knew then that the storm was not for his *now*, loose in the air, but possibly for the *now* of someone else, though when she heard the news it did not matter to her who might have died, for she was happy.

The effect of *now* is simple when a person dies, or when a person burns his hair or urinates to change the weather. With childbearing for women and with killing the great antelope for men (as the great antelope also have *now*, al-

Contagious Magic

though the small ones do not) the *now* has a larger, more complex effect. In these cases the *now* of the hunter interacts with the *now* of the antelope, the *now* of the woman interacts with the *now* of the child newly born, and when the blood of the antelope falls upon the ground as the antelope is killed, when the fluid of the womb falls upon the ground at the child's birth, the interaction of *nows* takes place, and this brings a change in the weather. In this way a mother may bring rain or drought when she bears a child, a hunter may bring rain or drought when he kills an antelope, no matter what kind of *now* the mother or the hunter may have. The mother or the hunter can only watch the weather to see what has taken place.

Now is intangible, mystic, and diffuse, and Bushmen themselves do not fully understand its workings. They do not know how or why *now* changes weather but only that it does. They watch the changes carefully, though, and by observing have discovered the limits of their own *nows*. When the fluid from a mother's womb falls upon the ground the child's *now* is determined, and it is partly for this reason that birth is such a mighty thing.

Birth is usually joyous. Bushmen of all ages adore their children and grandchildren, placing a child's health and wishes uppermost in their minds. Orphans are eagerly adopted by their aunts or grandparents, and a newborn baby is welcomed as though it were the first baby the werf had ever seen. Sometimes, though, a baby is born that cannot be supported, and if this happens the baby is destroyed. If a woman bears a child that is crippled or badly deformed, she is expected to destroy it, and if the season is very hard and she already has a baby under a year old depending on her milk, she is forced to kill her newborn child. Bushman women can hardly bear this, but they do.

If a woman knows that she must kill her baby, she braces

herself for this as best she can, and when the time comes to do it she must act immediately, must take advantage of the moment after birth before the infant has "come to life," that moment between the time the baby is born and the time her love for the baby wells up in her so that the act would be impossible forever after. She must think of the child she has already and act quickly, before she hears her infant's voice, before the baby moves or waves its feet; she must not look at it for long or hold it, but must have a shallow grave ready for it and must put it in at once and cover it and never think of it again. In times of extreme deprivation she can do this, or she can wait to watch both her children die. All this is very hard, and Bushmen, who have no mechanical form of contraception and know no way to cause miscarriage or abortion, prefer to abstain from intercourse for long periods rather than to suffer such pain.

We knew one woman who had been forced to destroy a baby to save an older child, and we knew one woman who had borne a crippled child and had been persuaded to destroy it by her mother, who had been present at the birth. Such things are very rare, though, and this is fortunate.

- - -

When the young woman came back to the werf with her baby she sat down and calmly washed the blood from her legs with water from an ostrich eggshell. Then she lay on her side to rest with her baby beside her, and covered the baby from the sun with a corner of her kaross. She put her nipple in the baby's mouth and let her try to nurse. The young woman still said nothing to anyone, but she did open her kaross to show the baby, and one by one we all came by to look at her, and she was not brown, not gold, but pink as a pink rose, and her head was shaped perfectly. At the bottom of her spine was a Mongolian Spot, dark and triangular, and her hair, which she shed later, was finely curled and soft as eiderdown.

The father had been away, but he came home a little later and sat stolidly down on the man's side of the fire, his hands on his knees. He pronounced the baby's name softly to himself. Later, when he had no audience, he slipped his finger into the baby's hand. Of course the baby grasped it strongly, and the father smiled.

CHAPTER TEN

BEAUTIFUL
UNGKA
and LAZY KWI

FOR TWO DAYS we drove our trucks through the scrub forests of Nyae Nyae and on the third day we came to a water pan not far from the village of Gam. In 1953 we had lived at Gam a short time; it was the cattle post of a very wealthy Chuana farmer. This farmer lived at Tsau, a large Bantu town several days' travel from Gam, but he had cattle posts with herders all through the country, keeping only fragments of his great herd at each one. Two Chuana families guarded his cattle at Gam. The village had once been the home of about a hundred Bushmen, but when the Chuanas had taken it, many of the Bushmen had been made

serfs and they and their families now worked for the Chuanas, tending the herds.

The little pan near Gam was full of blue water, and
was surrounded by yellow-leafed trees. We found two ostriches beside it. The ostriches stared mutely at us first,
very wide between the eyes and square at the jaw, until it
came to them that we were not ostriches; and with that
they rushed headlong away, flapping their ostrich-feathered
wings, working their naked thighs and knees like pistons,
wildly out of control. They had an air of old people with
tough, gray, varicose-veined legs, wearing nothing to hide
their nakedness but little feather boas around their waists,
which were the wings.

As we left the pan a boar got up from the grass where
he was lying and ran before us, a warthog with a heavy
neck and red bristle of a mane, with curved tusks and with
his tail stiff up in the air like a banner, trotting like a horse.
He held his head high and ran away proudly, and he was
old and very massive for a pig.

Not long after that we saw the two thatched rooftops
of the village of Gam. A feather of smoke was rising over
the rooftops, and soon we were there.

The people must have heard our trucks. A small crowd
was standing in the bushes, the people watching apprehen-
sively as we came up. Mostly they were Bushmen, naked
and smooth and brown, but here and there we saw a Bushman man wearing a ragged shirt or a woman in an old,
filthy dress. In the crowd, towering over the Bushmen, were
the Chuanas, a woman and a man, the woman dressed in
a turban and a long dress, the man in shorts and a jacket.
These two were the cattle-keepers. When our trucks
stopped, the woman recognized us and, clapping her hands
together, ran forward to meet us, followed at once by several
Bushmen who also recognized us, and after that the crowd

broke and all ran forward, the tense looks of apprehension gone, for if all the Bushmen had not known us they had heard of us and knew who we were. In a moment we found ourselves in the center of the crowd as all the Bushmen who knew us threw their gentle arms around us, touching us so lightly that it was like being embraced by moths. All those who did not know us crowded to look at our faces, and everyone talked at once until our ears rang. The Chuana couple, both more reserved, held back until the others had greeted us and then came forward to shake our hands.

When the excitement had died a little and everyone had a chance to look at everyone else and see who was there, we found among the Bushmen one entire band, six people, who once had lived at Gautscha. These were an old man, his two daughters, his son, his grandson, and his son-in-law, a man named Lazy Kwi. Because Kung Bushmen have relatively few names in use, resulting in the fact that many, many people have the same name—one man we knew had two wives named Kushe and two daughters named Xama, called after his mother, whose name was also Xama—they distinguish their various Xamas and Kwis with nicknames.

Lazy Kwi was a kind, warmhearted man, devoted to his family, and was named Lazy, an insulting name, only because he was not a good hunter. He was said to be heavy-footed, therefore noisy, and not an excellent shot; but he was a good trapper and got meat for his family by snaring birds and lizards. But because he did not hunt he never owned large shares of meat and ate only what came to him by the Bushmen's system of dividing, which put him in the role of poor relation and sometimes forced him to eat what others would not touch. Once he had suppressed his pride and eaten a badger. Although the other Bushmen had turned up their noses at this rank meat, he had said: "I am the badger-eating man," laughing off their scorn to hide his shame. He had eaten it sadly, and the sweet taste of it had sickened him and had made him vomit and retch for the rest of the day. Luckily for his family, his father-in-law made beautiful arrows and in the hunting system of Bush-men the man who gives or lends the arrow with which a buck is shot is automatically the owner of a large share of the meat. His father-in-law often lent arrows and often got meat. In fact, the old man had a dominant voice in the running of the family, for though old men may be aged and consumptive, those younger than they do what they say. Far from being derogatory, "old" is a term of respect. In his family, the old man decided where the band would live.

Lazy Kwi's sister-in-law was called "the old woman." Her name referred not to her age but to her bearing and her personality, for she was outspoken, positive, and sure, qualities that are seldom found in young Bushmen.

She was not at all surprised to see us. She took my ear to turn my head, and kissed me on the cheek. Lazy Kwi laughed when he greeted us, showing a gap in his mouth where a tooth was missing, and called me his wife, a joke among Bushman men, who pretend they will marry any woman who is not a taboo relative. His baby hugged my legs and showed a huge white smile, then held up his arms to be lifted. He had grown so that I could hardly get him off the ground.

Many Bushmen who greeted us had been at Gam when we had lived there, and among them was a young girl whose name was Ungka, a very common name; as she had no distinguishing nickname, we called her Beautiful Ungka, for so she was. She was probably the most beautiful girl in all Nyae Nyae, and even though she was only sixteen years old she already had a flaming past. When she was ten she was married to a man much older than herself, but, young as she was, she knew what she wanted, and because the old man filled her with loathing she cut off all her hair and all her ornaments, rubbed ashes on her face until she was filthy, and swore she would stay that way until her marriage was dissolved. Of course it wasn't long before her husband and her parents complied with her wishes and she became single once again.

When she was about thirteen she attracted the attention of another much older man who was already married but who became so inflamed by her beauty that he begged her parents to give her to him as a second wife. This time her parents consulted with her, entreating her to marry him as she was getting older every day and already developing a reputation for shrewishness, but Beautiful Ungka flatly refused. When her admirer heard of this he felt he could not live without her and he asked his wife to kidnap her for him, but his wife, far older than Beautiful Ungka and quite possibly jealous, would not, so nothing remained for her admirer but to kidnap her himself. This he did, planning carefully, and one night when everybody was asleep he stole quietly to Beautiful Ungka's scherm, lifted her bodily from the side of her grandmother, and bore her away on his shoulder. The grandmother awoke and set up an outcry; but Beautiful Ungka, a girl of remarkable self-possession and composure, didn't kick or struggle because she knew she wouldn't stay with her captor long. When her kidnapper reached home, masculine and forceful, he flung Beautiful Ungka down in the back of his scherm on the far side of his wife "to show," said the Bushmen, "that he wasn't afraid of his wife or anybody," and Beautiful Ungka lay still, as if subdued, until she heard that her captor and his wife were asleep. Then she got up, stepped over them, and walked home. That was the end of that episode.

Every day she became more beautiful. Her parents tried hard to marry her to a steady young man, and as she would have none of her suitors, they chose a second husband for her, this time a young and presentable man in his twenties who had quite a number of worldly goods got by working at Gam for the Chuanas. So Beautiful Ungka, now fourteen, was married again. By now she had menstruated and was old enough for intercourse, but although she lived with her young husband she wouldn't let him touch her and he was driven to despair. He did everything for her, requiring no work from her at all—his relatives helped feed him—and once he walked forty miles, from Gam, where he was living, to Gautscha, where we were, to ask for medicines from us that would relieve headaches that Beautiful Ungka had, then forty miles back again to bring her what we gave him. And yet she would not love him; she told him the medicine didn't help her at all (which was probably true) and she asked to go back to her parents. But her parents, wanting her to try harder to stay married, wouldn't rescue her, and her husband was pleased. After that her husband borrowed a donkey from the Chuanas to bring her to us at Gautscha, hoping that we could cure her with pills, not of her headaches but of her moods. She rode all the way while he walked leading the donkey, and when they arrived she said she would not live with him but with others of her relatives instead. Public opinion prevailed in this case and Beautiful Ungka was finally forced to stay with him. While he went the forty miles back to Gam to return the donkey, Beautiful Ungka got a relative of hers to build a scherm for them, and when her husband came back they lived in it together.

One night in this scherm, when Beautiful Ungka's husband was sleeping and she was lying reluctantly beside him, he must have dreamed of her, for he tried to possess her in his sleep. Beautiful Ungka, malicious girl that she was, sprang from her bed and rushed about the werf in the darkness screaming as loud as she was able, calling him dirty and filthy and at the same time telling all the startled people what had taken place. Her husband was ridiculed for days, and Beautiful Ungka used the event as an excuse to separate, for shortly after that her parents came to live with her, saddened and defeated, and her husband was sent away. But the young man loved her still and would walk miles to visit her, for they were still married, only to be sent back wherever he had come from as soon as he arrived.

All that can be said is that she was extremely handsome. When we met her at Gam we noticed that she had begun to walk like a beauty, proudly and aloof, but she was only sixteen and soon her reserve broke and she was very friendly, happy to see us, and we noticed then that her husband was not with her and was nowhere to be found. In fact, as we looked at all the faces, we saw that many people who should have been there were not. We asked for this person and that person, and the two Chuanas, instead of answering, invited us to their house where we could talk. My mother, my brother, myself, and Ledimo, the interpreter, who had been with us before and had been almost suffocated by the demonstration of affection he had received, walked to the village of Gam while the rest of the expedition went on to make camp.

The village of Gam was more peaceful than ever. We first went through a tiny gate in the high fence of cut thorn bushes which surrounded the village, put up to keep the cattle safe from the lions and other wild creatures at night, then past the ten or fifteen Bushman scherms that housed serf Bushmen, to the central part of the village where the Bantu houses were. There had been two; now there were three, but one was unfinished, and this was a large square dwelling with a window and a door. The other two houses—occupied by the two Chuana couples—were round, built of mud plaster, and had great thatched roofs but no windows, only doors. A thorn bush had been pulled into one of the doors, intended to keep the dogs and goats of the village from walking inside, a sign that the owners planned to be away for a long time. Gourds with milk in them hung from the roofpole of the other house; leaning

against the wall was a basket of souring *muhengo* grain. The
Chuana woman was brewing beer. A goat had been butchered and skinned and hung from a tree by one hind foot,
and the sunlight shone red through it like sunlight shining
through an ear.

The Chuana man went into the house and brought out
two chairs made of poles and thongs in imitation of European chairs but much smaller. He and my mother sat in
these while John, Ladimo, the Chuana woman, and I, being
young people, sat on the clay ground. Presently the Chuana
man began to speak, saying he hoped we had come well.

My mother asked for his cattle, how they were, and his
goats, if they had increased, how the rains and crops had
been, and if he had heard about the water in Lake Ngami,
which he had. My mother said: "Time must have stood still
here. No one looks a bit older."

"Yes," he said. "We get sick sometimes, but we have
not changed."

But things had changed; it came out that their son, the
other Chuana couple, two entire bands of Bushmen whom
we had known at Gautscha, and many Bushmen from Gam,
including the husband of Beautiful Ungka, had been taken
away by Europeans to work on the farms. Three times
European farmers had come, having followed in the tire
tracks we ourselves had left behind the last time. They came
all the way to Gam, where they had found the Bushmen,
no longer shy of Europeans, and had "offered to take them
for a ride on their trucks but had promised to bring them
back." The Bushmen had believed them, had gone for the
ride, and of course were never seen again. That is why Gam
seemed so peaceful, so empty, and the people so lonesome
and sad. The worst of it was that families had been separated, both between Gam and the farms and between different farms.

One group of farmers had taken some young Bushman

children who had been playing in the veld. When the mothers had called their children and had got no answer, then had looked in the veld and found their children gone, they had walked in the tracks the trucks had left to follow their children to the farms. The mothers and the children had never returned.

The farmer who had taken the Chuana couple's son had offered him food and clothes but no wages. When his mother had refused to let him go, the farmer had told her that she herself would have to leave Gam and move to Bechuanaland (there has always been a dispute about the border between the two countries, which affects the Chuana people who try to move across). The woman, assuming that the farmer was a government official, had been too frightened by this threat to prevent her son from leaving. She had been building a large new house, even planning to put a pane of glass in the little window, but she had been too discouraged to finish it, believing that she would have to leave it soon.

It was extremely sad to sit there talking about such things. The Chuana man held his head in his hands and his wife was almost crying, and it seemed very empty and lonely there on the hot gray ground with flies all around us in the air and birds flying above.

When we went back to our camp it was already dark and we found that Lazy Kwi, his wife, and all her family had moved in beside us to be near us. They seemed rather cheerful because they were all together, and they expressed their optimism by burning an entire log. This is prodigal for Bushmen, who usually burn just one small stick at a time, or at most the end of a small log, letting the fire work up the log by inches. The people sat with their legs stretched out, allowing the fire to warm them, and in the firelight their skins seemed bloodred, all except Lazy Kwi, whose skin was as dark as the night. Lazy Kwi was always changing color. When we first had met him we had thought he must be the darkest-skinned Bushman anywhere, but this was only so because he had rubbed himself all over with medicine paste and the accumulating dust had turned him black. When the rains came that year he had scrubbed himself with sand and water and had turned paler than the palest gold. No one had recognized him for a minute and then people had made fun of him, so he had let his coating accumulate again.

That night the old man, Lazy Kwi's father-in-law, decided that his band would move with us to Nama, a pan near Gautscha Pan, for he and Lazy Kwi believed that if we went there they would help us find more bands of Bushmen whom we had known. No one, he said, was living at Gautscha this season and the people who belonged there were scattered through the veld because the rains had been so good that there was food and water everywhere. We said that we would leave in the morning to begin the search, but the old man hesitated to agree and finally told us that in the morning he had planned to rob a bee tree, but after that he would be free to go. As he had hoped, the following morning we went with him on his trip for wild honey.

The bee tree was in a little forest about two miles from Gam, a forest filled with tiny yellow leaves and tiny seed pods blowing from the trees and scattered all through the grass, which in places had been plowed up by a wild pig rooting for bulbs. Because it was early in the morning and frosty, turtle doves were singing and the clear air was filled with their voices. Honey is always gathered at the coldest time of day, for then the bees are dull and stupid and it takes them a long time to collect their wits. The old man and Lazy Kwi cleared some grass and lit a tiny fire; then, squatting beside it, they warmed their hands, waiting for it to burn well, for they would use its smoke to numb the bees. Lazy Kwi's wife and her sister had come too; they did not join the men by the fire but walked off in the bush, gathering sour berries for their breakfast. The women in their meanderings found a hollow tree, and, looking inside it, found that it was filled with rain water. They told the rest of us, who went to get a drink. It was just a dead and blasted tree full of murky water, but, standing in front of it, Lazy Kwi began to fumble in his hunting bag for his drinking straw. He slipped the straw into a crack in the bark, drank, and held the straw for the next person. The straw was a reed with a hollow center and very hard to drink from, I found when my turn came to take a sip, for it was badly cracked. It was all one could do to suck hard enough to moisten one's tongue, the water was stagnant, and the reed tasted strongly of the inside of Lazy Kwi's hunting bag, but everyone drank, and when they had enough they returned to the fire. Something must have reminded Lazy Kwi of the European farmers on the way, for he announced naïvely: "They did not give me a shirt to put on my body."

When the fire was burning well the two men went to the bee tree. It too was dead, taller than the others in the forest and quite conspicuous. Lazy Kwi knocked on it with his ax and it gave forth a hollow sound. Then Lazy Kwi picked a straw and poked it into a tiny hole in the wood, and when he withdrew it there was honey on it and two bees. One bee detached itself and stung Lazy Kwi on the ribs and Lazy Kwi shook his skin like a dog. His father-in-law came forward with a smoking branch and held this near the hole. He blew smoke inside and the bees began to moan, low and ominously, the moan mounting in volume as Lazy Kwi chopped a piece from the tree above the hive. Four or five bees flew out of their hole; one flew at me and stung my face. The sting felt like a blow and in a moment the side of my face was numb and swollen. Lazy Kwi saw what had happened and he scratched the sting out with his fingernail. The old man by now had chopped away a large section of the tree and the bees poured down from the opening like water from a tap, but the smoke had confused them and they did not sting, although they flew everywhere looking for us. The old man turned his back, hunched his head between his shoulders, and hid from them as one would hide if one were being pelted with stones. When the swarm had dispersed a little he finished the opening. The Bushmen say that when bees are disturbed they are vicious only at first. After a while they become disorganized and confused and they fly about but do not sting you. When you smoke bees you must be careful not to burn them or smoke them too much because they are magic creatures with medicine to control fire, and if you harm them they will cause fire to burn you. A young boy whom we knew once burned some bees, and that night, when he was asleep by the fire, the fire sought him out and burned the skin of his belly, touching him only and no one else.

Lazy Kwi and the old man did the work perfectly. They were not stung badly, the tree was open, and no bees were seriously harmed. Inside the tree we could see the brown combs hanging and the bees as thick as fur around them. Lazy Kwi took out the combs and put them in a wooden bowl, licking his fingers afterward, and before we went back we ate some of the honey. There were two kinds, old honey and new honey, and the new honey was pale yellow and very sweet and mild, winter honey made from the small, dry flowers of the veld. The old honey was much sweeter and strong enough to burn your mouth. Before we left, the old man and Lazy Kwi carefully wiped their hands and arms with grass, for they were covered with honey and things were beginning to stick to them. Then we went back to camp and in the afternoon we packed to go on toward Gautscha Pan.

Lazy Kwi packed a skin bag full of tsi nuts and the seeds

of baobab fruit, alumlike powdery stones that ripen at the start of the dry season. The old man had a huge net bag filled with his possessions—bowls, fire sticks with which the Bushmen kindle fires, skins, and little bags of food.

Just before we left, the Chuana woman came to say good-bye and I gave her some tea and a bottle of perfume that was given to me when I left America. My mother gave her a silk scarf and some bars of scented soap, and the woman, overwhelmed, sat down on the ground with these things in her lap and with the aid of the interpreter she started to thank us, but then she said: "Too much thanks is like a curse. I sit here with my delights."

After that we climbed on the trucks and drove away, looking back to see the sky of evening and the dry hills around Gam, and the Chuana woman still sitting on the ground waving to us. In back of her, a group of serf Bushman women were thoughtfully carrying away the firewood we had left behind.

Many miles from Gam we camped for the night and all the sky in the west was hazy red with the flat-topped thorn trees blue below it, and suddenly through the haze a herd of giraffes ran from a thicket near us into the open plain. There were nine giraffes and eight were females, all strung out in a line with their strong legs slowly opening, then bunching as they ran and their heads on their long necks stretching out and back, out and back. Behind the females ran the bull, an enormous creature half again as tall as they were, half again as broad, mighty and ponderous as he reached his long legs forward to overtake his wives.

TOP: *Long reeds almost filled the waterhole at Gautscha.*
BOTTOM: *Even at the waterhole, water was treated with care.*

TOP: *I sometimes received presents of gum from trees, or soft, sweet caterpillars.*
BOTTOM: *Alone at his fire, Ukwane plays a mood song.*

TOP: *Toma the leader.*
BOTTOM: *Crooked Kwi and his wife.*

Tu made Norma clothes of ostrich-eggshell beads.

Beautiful Ungka.

*Beautiful Ungka's cousin, and the little girl who was content
to follow her and be her handmaiden.*

*The young musician—the lonely, brooding man
who played the guashi.*

TOP: *Dikai made a bow from a branch and an arrow from a reed,*
and gave them to her younger son.
BOTTOM: *Tsamko, Toma's son, became the owner of Short Kwi's*
crown of badger hair.

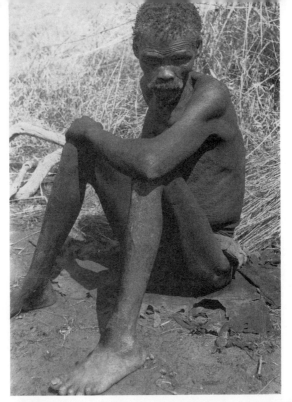

TOP: *The old man who had never shot an antelope, who had never married, now almost blind, very thin, and without people.*
BOTTOM: *The shining lake of Nama.*

In the middle of the circle the great tree rose,
pink-skinned and mighty, the claimer of two lives.

CHAPTER ELEVEN

TOMA
the Leader

IT WAS VERY cold and the wind blew all night long, sweeping the haze from the sky and leaving the brilliant hard white moon. In the bitter hour before morning we were all too cold to sleep, so we got up, finding that the Bushmen had risen before us and were crouched shivering on the ground between the small fires, partly sheltered by the grass.

When the sun rose the air got a little warmer and shortly after dawn we moved away from the camping place, on toward Nama. We went through little forests, over slanting plains bordered with trees, past an outcrop of rock where I once had seen a leopard lying on his side, sunning his white belly, past a graceful tree which was one of the trees where the people of Nyae Nyae got their poison. At noon we reached Nama Pan.

Nama was a grassy field in the center of a scrub forest, and in the field was a great rock slide, basin-shaped, which now was filled with crystal water, and around the water was a beach of sand six inches wide. Around this beach the green grass grew, very dark, almost rotten with the water, the rich earth, and the sunlight.

- - -

It used to be that no one lived at Nama Pan, although there was a deep waterhole brimming with water always, even when the lake was gone, and fruit in the bushes around the shore, and plenty of game. It had been an empty and unwholesome paradise abandoned in the veld at the time I once visited it with a band of hunters and women who went there in search of food. It was just before the heavy rains, when all the veld was blooming, and the hunters picked the sweet gum that oozed from the trees with the tips of their spears. The women gathered karu plants, little green fruits that look like cucumbers hanging on vines like grapevines, and that day one of the children saw a ratel, a honey badger, which the hunters speared. This was the badger that no one would eat but Lazy Kwi, the one that made him vomit. At that time the pan itself was empty of water and the dark, rank grass was growing where the water now stood. As we approached the pan a crowd of vultures moved in the grass, ran clumsily toward us, and launched themselves into the air. They heaved their great wings and rose higher and higher and soon a column of vultures hung above the pan, the highest ones almost invisible, the strong wings of the near ones beating the air just over our heads. A shower of feces came spattering down.

When the vultures saw that we were staying they flew gradually higher and higher until they were lost in the air and we walked over the dark grass trampled flat by them toward the waterhole which stood in the center of the pan. On the way we found a vulture egg among the droppings, small and pink and newly laid, for it was covered with a thin coat of slime, as though it had slipped out of a vulture accidentally when she was frightened and hurrying to fly.

A stench hung over the pan which got stronger as we neared the waterhole, a dark cavern in the grass. The stench was coming from it, and though the adult Bushmen knew what to expect and didn't waste time investigating, only pausing for a moment at the brink to glance inside, then going on, the children stopped to gaze and I stopped with them. The sides of the well overhung the water in a lip about four feet high. The water itself was the color of clay, and on its smooth surface a hairy back and a pair of pointed ears were floating, the back and ears of a drowned hyena floating on its belly with its nose pointing straight to the bottom. White maggots crept from one ear to the other and the rotting smell rose from the corpse. Obviously, the hyena had been thirsty and when trying to drink had fallen in and drowned. A little boy who was watching the hyena, fascinated, began to howl faintly, *"Mmm/ /ao, mmm/ /ao,"* the way a hyena howls, but putting a click in it the way Bushmen usually do, and then for my benefit acted the scene as it must have taken place. He rolled out his tongue and edged his hand toward the lip of the well, then jerked away, staring at the water with yearning eyes and saying: "No, I can't reach it. Yes, I must." He edged his hand toward the lip again, then shrieked "Ai! Ai!", waved his arms, pawed the air as the hyena had pawed the sides of the well, twisted his head from side to side, eyes starting, then closed his eyes and let his head roll back, his face calm and his lips parted, turning his hands limply, palms up. "Finished," he said.

"Yes," I said. "Too bad."

"Oh, hyenas are worthless animals," he said. He meant that they were not good to eat. Then he ran off and after a short time came back with a long stick, which he pushed into the water. "Help me stir," he said, so I did, and presently the carcasses of two wild dogs and a vulture bobbed to the surface, rolled over slowly, legs in the air, and sank again. "You see?" he said triumphantly. "Many things die here."

The water was darker now and roiled, and the stench was stronger. We went on after the Bushman women to find gum in the trees and then went home, and after that I had not been back to Nama.

- - -

Since then, the heavy rains had come three times, filling the waterhole and the lake and washing away the putrescence, leaving only the white bones sunk in the bottom of the well. Now the water of the lake seemed very pure indeed, with the ripples that the wind made shining like mica in the sun, and so clear that we could see every blade of grass and ice-cold stone on the bottom. Lazy Kwi and his family climbed down from the truck and squatted at the edge of the water to drink, scooping up water in their cupped hands. As they drank, Lazy Kwi found some Bushman footprints on the little shore which were many days old, just dents in the hard sand, but after glancing at them once or twice he said they were the footprints of strangers, a man barefoot, a woman in sandals, and a barefoot child, on their way to a place called Naru Ni, somewhere in the west. I don't know how he could tell all this, but I believe that he was right. Bushmen are always right when it comes to tracks, but also it is very unusual for Bushmen to travel through country that is not theirs, as these three must have been doing or Lazy Kwi would have known them. Naturally, we were very curious to know who they were and what they were doing, but their footprints told Lazy Kwi no more than that, and we never learned.

These were the only footprints that we found, but Lazy Kwi still believed that some of the people we had known at Gautscha in 1953 might be living there, especially Toma, the headman, for he had been there when Lazy Kwi had heard of him last.

Toma the headman, sometimes known as Male Toma, an honorary name, sometimes known as Toma the Short, so-called because of his stocky build, was a famous person, and once had been a serf. He was born of serf parents at Gam, and as a boy had worked for the Chuanas, drawing their water and herding their cattle and goats.

When Toma was a boy, his father was murdered by a child, the result of a terrible accident which took place one day when Toma's father was arguing with the father of a boy named Gao. Gao, who couldn't have been more than ten years old, became upset and angry when he heard his father quarreling and, taking his father's weapons, shot To-ma's father in the chest with a poisoned arrow. The old man was helped to the shade, the arrow was drawn out and the wound sucked, but as there is no antidote for arrow poison, the old man lived only for the rest of the day and by night he was dead.

Oddly enough, the crime was connected with the old man and not with Gao, the young murderer, for ever after that day the old man was referred to as Tsamko Bone Arrow, while Gao in later years became known as Gao Wild Pig, after a pig he had killed which was in some way re-markable.

Toma flourished as a young man and became an excel-lent hunter with tireless legs, tireless eyes, and a deadly aim, and it was said of him that he never returned from a hunt without having killed at least a wildebeest, if not something larger. Hence, the people connected with him ate a great deal of meat and his popularity grew. He once said of himself: "From the day I was born I was born for meat."

When Toma was in his late teens, some say, his powers in hunting attracted the attention of the headman of Gautscha Pan, who offered Toma the hand of his daughter, Tu, in marriage. Toma accepted, went to live with his wife's people, according to custom, and, when the old headman died, took over the leadership of the people in the area. He was not the true headman—his position would not be inherited by his son, for headmanship is passed only from father to son—but he was recognized as headman while he lived and it was a great honor to him that this was so.

Tu's brother was the rightful headman of Gautscha, but he had abdicated to live with his wife's people in the north. Her elder sister's husband, a man named Gao Big Feet, also had a right to the leadership in that his wife, Dikai, was older than Tu. But neither ever contested Toma's position as leader, for it was not a position which Toma held by force or pressure but simply by his wisdom and ability, and people prospered under him. No Bushman wants prominence, but Toma went further than most in avoiding prominence; he had almost no possessions and gave away everything that came into his hands. He was diplomatic, for in exchange for his self-imposed poverty he won the respect and following of all the people there. He enjoyed his position, and, being strangely free from the normal strains and jealousies of Bushmen, he saw justice clearly and hence he led his people well. At Gautscha his werf had been right beside the werf of his father's murderer, for Toma was friendly even with him.

Toma had a short, stocky body and a shock of tangled hair. He was strong, too, and very coordinated, so that every motion he made was quick and controlled, and not a gesture of his was wasted. As a result of this enormous and unconscious control, accidents almost never happened to him. His face was broad, lined with many deep wrinkles at the corners of his eyes and mouth as though from smiling, though it was not from smiling that he got them but from years of squinting at the sun. His expression was usually dark and wondering, his forehead drawn intently into a frown, but sometimes he would abandon his gravity and laugh a high, reaching laugh that one could hear from far away, a laugh that came from his very soul, or, as Bushmen say, from his stomach. He listened diplomatically and intently whenever he was spoken to, staring at the ground, and had a habit of echoing, in a loud falsetto voice, the important phrases of every sentence he was told.

"We went to Keitsa Pan," someone might say to him.

"To Keitsa," Toma would reply.

". . . and we slept there, but the blind flies were very bad . . ."

"Oh, bad, bad . . ."

". . . but in the morning we saw two porcupines . . ."

". . . yes, porcupines . . ."

". . . and we killed them there. We made them cry . . ."

". . . made them cry . . ."

". . . made them cry."

Toma was considered to be very fortunate in his marriage. Of course it was through his wife, Tu, that he gained the leadership of the Gautscha people, his life free in the veld rather than in serfdom, and his two young sons, but besides all this his wife was beautiful, having a smooth face and great, clear eyes like those of a cat. Also, she was five feet tall, considered to be a very desirable height, and although no Bushman has ever been too fat, Tu was not too thin and her arms and legs were round. She had soft blue scars curving on her forehead which made her eyes seem to lift at the corners, and blue scars on her thighs that showed when she walked. Her chief virtues, in the eyes of

Bushmen, were that she decorated herself with ornaments in her hair and she observed propriety, cared what people thought of her. She didn't leave her fire at night to go visiting, even to the scherm right next to hers. Rather, if she had something to say, she would shout it across the werf.

Her deference to appearances and public opinion seemed to make up for her faults, for she was considered to be almost a model personality in spite of her extremely jealous and vindictive moods which caused her to accuse others, often unreasonably, of selfishness, greed, and other such things. Her husband and sons were not excepted, but this was something that Toma had learned to ignore. He would simply shrug his shoulders if she railed at him, pretend he didn't hear if she railed at others.

When she didn't assault her family with her tongue she sometimes harmed them actively. Very often she would lie sullen with narrowed eyes in front of her scherm watching the other women walk out to the veld in the morning on their way to dig veld food, and on these days her husband and sons would eat nothing unless, driven by hunger, they went to the veld themselves, the three of them together, to dig up a few roots and eat them raw. Tu herself did not experience hunger as a result of these moods, for she would have saved herself a morsel from the day before. It was her right to do this: among Bushmen every root is owned by its digger and is shared only at its owner's wish.

Toma might ask but would never command Tu to feed her family, for as he had learned to ignore her biting tongue he had learned to accept her moods. This was his way, appeasing her, and because Toma wanted peace perhaps as much as he wanted Tu, he pampered her.

This was not always so. One day gossiping people told us that early in their marriage Toma shot a kudu and Tu said: "Don't cook all the meat because my mother will be coming to visit us."

Toma remarked that the meat was there for any use, but Tu misunderstood him and, thinking that he denied meat to her and to her mother, she flew into a rage, attacked Toma, and gave him a nasty bite on his arm. Toma lost his temper entirely and pinched her cheeks together until his fingers met in her mouth. His anger had come now, the people said, and he threw her into the fire, saying: "She is a woman. Why does she make me so angry? Shall I take a stick?"

A small crowd had gathered, and, as usual, the family quarrel became a public affair. Several people helped Tu out of the fire, found her barely scorched, but her cousin seized Toma and began to shake him. This enraged Toma so much that he caught the cousin around the waist and threw him into the onlooking crowd. The people said: "We must stop Toma because if he is so angry he may kill someone," and with that they led the cousin out of Toma's sight.

Toma shouted: "If you do that again, we will get our arrows and fight to the death. Stop here. I am very angry. Do not make me more angry."

One of the men who had helped Tu said to the cousin: "I took his wife from the fire. You almost got killed for the way you went at Toma. If you want to help people, don't get angry with them. Keep calm. Don't increase anger as you did with Toma." With these words the incident was over.

The people said: "After that everyone knew how angry Toma could be, so from that day on he never had another fight." Everyone honored and respected him, everyone except his wife.

When Tu was in a good mood she was charming. She would smile at everyone, speak in a light voice instead of the low, menacing voice that she used when she was angry, a cat growling, and would be affectionate to Toma and her sons. Very often, when she was happy, she would dance a light, short dance to a song that she sang herself.

Tu had borne four children, four sons, to Toma, but the first two sons had died. One of these had died at birth, "had died in the veld without a name," said Toma. The oldest living children, born after the others were dead, were a boy of about eight years old and a boy of five. While we were there in 1953, Tu bore her first daughter, a strawberry of a baby who was named for two people—named first for Toma's sister, but also Norna for my mother; her name is Lorna, but Bushmen have trouble with the *l*. In order to fit us into their society, the Bushmen had given us names and niches in the kinship of Toma's family. My father was named for Toma's father, my mother was named for Toma's mother, my brother was named Toma for Toma, and I was called Dikai for Tu's sister. Toma therefore named his daughter for the person who was named for his mother— not at all unusual, as it often happens that a child may bear the names of two of its relations.

Now, hoping to find Toma once again, we started the truck motors, fired a rifle, called and called, in case he might be living far from the water, but no sound came from the great veld to answer us and we began to search in the bush around the pan for signs that might show us where he was. We found two empty scherms built in the rainy season, their grass thatches gray with weather, their little piles of fire ashes sunk into the ground, and near these scherms we found the skull of a bird and the shoulder blade of an antelope, all white, bleached, and dry. Farther on we saw a tree where the woven grass nests of weaver birds were hanging empty, swinging with the wind, which made us think of the empty scherms, and still farther we found one more empty dwelling, the tiny grass nest of a mouse that hung on a bush, from a thorn.

We went around and around the pan in three huge circles, occasionally calling Toma's name, and when at last we were sure that no one was there we went back to the pan and sat in the shade of some bushes to think. Lazy Kwi sat with his chin in his hands, gazing into the sunlit veld. He was sure, he said, that no one lived at Gautscha Pan, so there was no use going there. Toma and his family had not lived at Nama for a whole season and since wind and rain had erased all traces of their passing we could not tell where they had gone. Lazy Kwi thought for a long time and at last he said that he had heard from the Bantu people at Gam that Toma had been indentured by Bantu people at another cattle post called Kai Kai, near Gam, and had been set to work minding a herd of goats. Lazy Kwi had not believed that this could have happened, but now he said that it was possible and in that case Toma would have to live not far from Kai Kai, somewhere in the veld but not too far from water. And there was such a place, said Lazy Kwi, but in the east and far from Nama Pan.

It was early afternoon, so hot that even the insects of the veld were silent. We decided to leave at once in order to reach the waterhole that Lazy Kwi had mentioned before night. We put a little meat, some water, and our blankets in the jeep, and my brother and I, Lazy Kwi and Ledimo, the interpreter, got ready to go, leaving the others to make a camp.

Before we left, Lazy Kwi took leave of his family, then got his bag of tsi beans and baobab seeds from his wife and put a handful or two into another bag which he would take with him, leaving the larger share with her. When his little son saw what he was doing and realized that his father was preparing to go, he began to cry, saying: "Father, Father," and when Lazy Kwi hesitated a moment, then said he was going anyway, the little boy picked up a handful of stones and threw one at him. This amused Kwi's wife, who smiled and tried halfheartedly to take the stones away, but it angered Lazy Kwi, who caught his son by the arm and boxed his ears. That made the little boy so furious that he had a tantrum; he screamed and cried and arched his back to draw away from his mother, who tried to pick him up, both mother and child doing exactly what they had done when the little boy was a baby and no doubt had been doing ever since. His mother often had a terrible time managing him, and he was still nursing although he was now five or six years old. Before his father left, his mother had managed to mollify him somewhat, and she sat on the ground, letting him sit on her leg to nurse. He drank from one breast and held the other in his hand as he glared over his mother's shoulder at his father, who was already in the jeep.

We drove all afternoon, going fast because the ground was hard and not too bumpy, and the plains of Nyae Nyae seemed even longer, even wider than the plains of Ai a ha'o, being more slanted. We saw the Aha Mountains, a series of large rock outcrops quite separate from each other, blunt-ended like drumlins, which the Bushmen call "The Knife's Back." They appeared on the horizon shortly after we left Nama, distant and blue over the yellow veld, so surprising to see in that flat country that we stopped to look at them. They seemed so misty and far, so infinitely alluring, that we longed to go there. When we drove on, they stayed as relatively fixed as the moon would, which showed how far away they were. Lazy Kwi said that once on a clear day he had seen them from the top of the Gautscha baobab.

We reached the waterhole at the end of the afternoon, a shallow well between two rocks and hidden in a thicket, but we saw no sign of goats or people, only the tracks of wild animals around the waterhole and down a lonely little path that led there, and we wondered what had happened to the goats and Toma. Perhaps he had become a renegade, hiding from the Bantus, on the run with his family; perhaps he now was wearing a goatskin and cracking the bones of his charges out in the veld somewhere.

On the eastern horizon we saw the smoke of a veld fire which Lazy Kwi said might have been lit by Toma and we drove toward it and reached it just before the sun went down. We found a way through the wall of flames and found what we thought was the source of the fire, but the burned area was very large and it was hard to be sure. It was almost dark then, very cold, and when we came to a clump of bushes we stopped the jeep and walked about, gathering dead wood that lay nearby. The camp was on a rise and we could see about for miles. In the north rose the brown backs of the Aha Mountains, and on the other side the land fell away, down and down, until all the trees were obscured, then beyond that until the horizon looked like the sea, just a blue line, darker and a little hazier than the sky.

It was very quiet and lonely there except for a few birds that flew high and far above us calling, and we called Toma's name again and again and our voices rang in the cold air, but we did not get an answer. Lazy Kwi, naked and barefoot in the frost, walked over the plain with his arms hugged against his chest for warmth and called more: "Toma . . . *Toma*," a little annoyed as he was tired, then waited, called again: "Toma—my brother . . ." and as his voice died away no answer came; but a koorhan, a dark bird the size of a chicken, flew out of a clump of bushes far away and rose cackling up to the sky, where we saw it, black and clumsy, before it dropped to the earth again. The last pale light faded on the horizon and for a minute the sky looked like the cold sky over tundra or over an icy sea before the empty veld turned dark.

To clear the grass from our camping site we lit a little grass fire, being too tired to pull up every blade of grass by hand, and the little flames seemed so cheerful and warm that we felt better right away. We made a cooking fire and cooked our meat, then unrolled our blankets to lie upon, and we found that because the wind had died our cooking fire shed so much heat that we were as warm as we would have been in a shelter.

We made coffee and talked all evening, and unnoticed, our fire burned very low and we got colder, the night seemed darker and in the dark the koorhan began to call again, and when we looked far over the veld for the light of another fire but saw none it came to us that Toma might have been taken by the farmers after all. We talked for a while about that, but then Lazy Kwi said he believed that Toma was somewhere not very far away but was too clever to show himself. After our last expedition had left Nyae Nyae the last time, Lazy Kwi told us, Toma had waited months, whole seasons, for us to come back and when he had heard the trucks of the farmers he had gone to them, thinking it was us. "Now he is angry. Now he is too clever to make that mistake again," said Lazy Kwi.

That did seem possible, so we stood up and shouted Toma's name again; but even at night, when sound carries best, we heard only our echo, distant and diffuse, and at last we built up our fire and got ready to sleep. The night was perfectly quiet. No sound came from the wind or animals, only the sparks snapping from our fire, which burned for a while but soon died to embers and the smoke rose white and ghostly into the dark.

As we lay in our blankets, before we went to sleep, Lazy Kwi told us a story, told us something that had happened to him and to Toma while we had been away.

- - -

After Toma had mistaken the trucks of the farmers for our trucks, the rains had come. After the rains, when the veld was lush and tropical, when Gautscha Pan was full of water and succulent reeds, several herds of animals that do not ordinarily live in the desert had migrated south from the swamps and marshes of the Okovango River to eat the sweet grass of the pans. A herd of elephants had come and gone by, but some small herds of buffalo had come and these had stayed in the veld of Nyae Nyae, living among the pans.

One day the buffalo had come to Gautscha, and Toma, crouching on a limb of the baobab tree, had seen them wallowing in the pan and had taken his bow and arrow and, running fast and silently, had circled behind them, then had crept toward them, and from the reeds at the edge of the pan had shot a big male. The herd had bolted and Toma, after having inspected the tracks so that he would know his wounded bull when he saw its track again, had gone home. He had waited a day and a half, longer than usual because of the danger, and when the time had passed, returned with Lazy Kwi to the spot where the buffalo had been wounded. There he and Lazy Kwi had taken up the trail. The buffalo had separated from its herd and the two men had followed it silently, carefully, aware of the danger, avoiding the trail when it led through bushes. When, that night, they had not found the buffalo but knew from the freshness and pattern of the tracks that it was near and restless, they had waited in the veld, eating nothing themselves so that the buffalo would not eat and gain strength, remaining awake, moving around so that they would not get stiff but remaining silent so that the buffalo, not hearing them, would relax, lie down, and itself get stiff and sore. In the morning the two men had found where the buffalo had slept, also a damp spot of its urine with black flecks in it (which I believe were flecks of blood) and Toma had pushed a poison arrow into the spot of urine so that the buffalo would be unable to urinate again, unable to rid itself of more poison.

The men had followed the buffalo's track for three days, knowing from its footprints that it was getting weaker, staggering, and in the morning of the fourth day they had come over a rise of ground and had seen it far ahead of them, lying on its side as if dead. The two men wisely had not gone up to it, but had squatted where they were to watch it, remaining this way for most of the day, and when the buffalo had not even flicked its tail or heaved its sides in breathing, Toma had considered it safe enough to approach. He had done this cautiously, very carefully, balancing his long spear in his hand, but just as Toma had stood near the buffalo, spear poised for the stab that would kill it surely, the buffalo had lurched to its feet, had chased Toma, and had tossed him on its horns.

The great boss, the heavy mass of horn on the buffalo's forehead, had cracked Toma's ribs and one curved horn had hooked in Toma's side, passing through his body and out his back. Toma had lain unconscious and Lazy Kwi had carried him home; later, other hunters of Toma's band had found the buffalo truly dead, partly eaten by vultures, and had taken the meat; but nothing, no medicines or cures that the Bushmen had used, had helped Toma, and the people had expected him to die.

Gautscha was the country of Toma's wife, and when Toma had realized how sick he was he had wanted to return to his own people, the people of Gam. Lazy Kwi and another man had carried him there and it was there that the second group of farmers had found him, unable to escape or to resist, and they had taken him away. His wife was still waiting at Gautscha and Lazy Kwi had returned there to tell her that her husband had gone.

At the farm, though, Toma's luck had begun to turn.

The farmer had gradually managed to heal his wounds with medicine and treatment, and by the start of the dry season Toma had felt quite well. One night, when the veld was quiet and dark, Toma had thanked the farmer in his heart, had gathered all the Bushmen on the farm together, and had led the people over the veld, all the way back to Nyae Nyae. It had been a long walk, a long way, but Toma had managed. Now, said Lazy Kwi, Toma's wound ached on cold days and sometimes his vision was blurry, but he was pleased with himself and pleased to be back in his own country.

Lazy Kwi was pleased with him too, and he smiled when he finished the story.

- - -

When the first light of morning came, the air was so cold that our breath made clouds. We got up, fed the fire, and cooked the remainder of last night's meat, then drove off in the jeep again, for in that early light we had seen the smoke of three veld fires on the horizon, one in the south, two in the west, perhaps kindled by Bushmen during the night, perhaps revived by the wind from old embers, and we planned to make a circle to investigate them all.

On the way we found a bee tree that had been raided for its honey and we believed that Toma had done it, although the break was old and the bees were gone away; but after looking at it a moment Lazy Kwi rememberd that he had done it himself during the last rains. He remembered too that there had been very little honey and that he had got stung, and since that was all he remembered we went on again to the source of the first of the three fires.

It was there that we found Toma. He had been there all the time, only a few miles from where we had camped, and when he heard our jeep coming he watched us over the top of a bush to see first who we were before showing himself.

We saw him when he ran toward us. He was quite far off and we saw first his dark figure detach itself from the bush and run with long, swinging strides toward our jeep. He waved his arms and we knew at once that this, at last, was Toma. Before he reached us a second figure appeared from behind another bush and ran beside him, and we knew from the disjointed stride that this second man was Gao Big Feet, Toma's brother-in-law. We turned our jeep toward them and soon we met and the two men embraced us and laughed and said that they had known we would come back someday, and then they climbed in the jeep and took us to their werf, stopping first to get their spears and quivers, which they had left in the bushes, for no Bushman, no matter how excited, ever greets people with his weapons on his back because this might be taken as a sign that he was quarrelsome, looking for a fight.

Their werf was in a tiny thicket of thorn trees at the edge of the plain, screened in front by bushes, carefully concealed, but on a rise of ground where a man standing could easily scan the surrounding plain without being seen himself. There Toma and Gao Feet could observe the movements of the antelope that crossed the plains below them, waiting patiently in the dappled shade of their trees' broad leaves as lions do. The two families stood in front of their bushes to meet us and they, too, embraced us and they all climbed in the jeep to do this, then climbed out again and stood back to see how we were.

We got out and sat with them in their werf to talk before deciding what we would do next. Looking around, we saw that only the two families lived here, for there were only two sleeping places, set, for the sake of a little privacy, on opposite sides of one of the scrawny trees. The women had not built huts, but had scooped little hollows for themselves and their husbands which they had lined with soft grass bedding, and had put up two arching sticks at each of these

hollows to mark the place where the door would be if a
scherm had been there, for the Kung as well as the Gikwe
need a sense of place. In fact, the Kung need it even more,
for without their grass and marking-sticks the Kung feel
homeless. Their sleeping hollows were like the soft grass
nests of pheasants, hidden in the leaves.

The Bushmen all lit pipes and passed them—each pipe
reached everybody, everybody shared and smoked, and the
pipes circled slowly for an hour or more until the tobacco
was gone. There was a brass pipe made of an old cartridge,
a bone one, a horn one, and last of all a copper one that
tasted very bad. The Bushmen cracked roasted tsi nuts and
passed the fat little kernels around to each other, offering
them on the palms of their hands. My brother told Toma
that he had missed tsi because there was none in America.

"What?" said Toma. "No tsi? Why didn't you plant
some?"

"The soil is a little strong for it," said John.

"So."

"But tsi is good."

"No good," said Toma sadly. "I used to be fat. Now I
am thin." He stuck out his leg and slapped it. "Where is
my fat?" he said.

He did not seem to be thinner than he used to be,
though; he had only a scar on his belly and a scar on his
back where the buffalo's horn had wounded him. Otherwise, he looked very well. All the people seemed well,
especially the children. Toma's oldest son wore a crown of
badger skin with the long hair standing up on it, and two
safety pins that we had given him, which he wore as earrings
in his pierced ears. With all this he looked bold as a pirate.
His brother was nearly as big as he was, and his sister,
Norna, now three, was a slender, graceful child who regarded the world with dark, wondering eyes.

Norna's sixteen-year-old uncle, Tu's brother, was there

too. He was a lame boy; he had been crippled in one leg since childhood and could hobble only with the help of a long stick. People had despaired of him, believing that he would never be able to hunt and therefore never marry or inherit the headmanship of Gautscha Pan, but when we saw him now and looked at him closely we noticed a fine row of scars between his eyes and on his arms and chest and we knew that he had hunted and killed an antelope and had been scarified in his initiation. We had planned on this trip to give him presents of all kinds, to make him rich, so that he could marry whether he could hunt or not, but we saw now that this would not be necessary. When he knew that we had noticed his scars he told us in great detail the story of the hunt. He told us how he had gone out with a group of hunters, how he had first seen the two horns of a kudu above a clump of bushes, how he had silently hobbled near it, propped himself on his crutch, and shot it with a poisoned arrow. The arrow had penetrated deeply and the lame boy had returned to tell the others. They had followed it with him for a day and in the evening had found it dead. It was the lame boy's kudu, though; he shot it, and to Bushmen that is the important thing. He was scarified with a paste made of the kudu's meat, and ever after that he was a man.

Toma's son, Tsamko, said that he, too, had shot a buck during the last rainy season, but while the hunters were following it a rainstorm had come up and had washed the tracks away, forcing them to abandon the hunt, although for days they had searched the sky for the column of vultures that would show where the buck had fallen. Lions must have got it, said Toma, and eaten it in one night, and this was a great shame, for boys younger than his son had already proven themselves. Tsamko shrugged his shoulders at these words. He had been the first person we had met

when we first had come to Gautscha Pan, and we had seen
him in the veld, a naked child hardly more than an infant,
standing in grass that came over his head with a toy bow
and a wooden arrow in his hand. He was far from home,
all by himself, but he had stood up to talk with us so boldly
that our interpreter, vastly amused, had asked him what he
would do if he met a lion, and with great self-possession
Tsamko had said: "If he let me alone, I would let him go,
but if he came for me, then we would fight."

Young Bushman boys do not always seem anxious to
become adults. Like Tsamko, in Toma's opinion, they prefer to play at hunting because as soon as they know how
to hunt they have to, and hunting, say adult Bushmen, is
very hard work. We felt, though, that it wouldn't be long
before Tsamko did succeed in killing an animal. Besides
playing at hunting as a child he used to hunt beetles, moths,
and large caterpillars by shooting them with thorns; but he
was twelve now and seemed to have left his childhood behind, for while we talked, his younger brother and sister
played in the sand but he sat quietly with the men and
listened.

Gao Big Feet and his wife, Dikai, Tu's sister, had had
a second baby, a little boy named Dabe ma, Little Dabe.
Their first child, Little Gashe, now four, was blind in one
eye, possibly as the result of a very prevalent eye disease.
He had been blind when we knew him as a baby; now his
infected eye had shrunk away, leaving a socket. As I
watched him, I noticed that his good eye had become infected too and bothered him; he had developed a habit of
turning his head from side to side, squinting with his good
eye, trying to see depth or judge distance, and also a habit
of rubbing both eyes with his knuckles. When Dikai saw
me watching him she pointed to her own eyes, then to
Dabe's, to show that she and Dabe, too, had the infection,

and when I said that I would give her medicine when we got back to Nama she nodded. "I was waiting for you to come," she said.

Hearing me speak of medicine, Little Gashe glared at me balefully. I had treated his eyes before and perhaps he remembered that the medicine was painful, or perhaps he was afraid that I would harm his eyes. He scrambled into his mother's lap to nurse and, facing toward her for safety, glared at me over her shoulder. Little Dabe, seeing this, climbed into Dikai's lap too, and she had to nurse them both, one on each knee, at each breast. Her lap became a battlefield. They kicked and pushed and got in each other's way.

Dikai and her two boys were only half of Gao Feet's family, for he had another wife, his first wife, who had a daughter and a grandchild. We were not surprised that these people were not with Gao Feet; his two wives did not get along well. Since Dikai was young and pretty, Gao Feet spent his time with her. We asked Gao Feet where his first wife was, and he told us that she was living with her daughter's family and with Dikai's mother in a dry forest not far away where tsi was growing. We asked for other people, the other members of Toma's large band, and Toma told us that they were well, living far away in a mangetti forest. Naturally, Toma's family had not seen this group for some time because of the distance, but Toma said now that he would take us to see them someday soon because he believed that we would be able to help them; one man in their band, a man called Short Kwi, or sometimes Kwi the Hunter, had been bitten in the leg by a puff adder and was very badly hurt. We got the impression that he had been bitten recently and, hoping that we might draw the poison from the wound, we said that we would leave at once. But Toma said that it had happened during the last rainy season, so there was no use hurrying; other Bushmen had cut the wound and had sucked the poison, saving Short Kwi's life, but his leg was so badly hurt that he couldn't use it. It had turned black, said Toma, and black liquid ran out of the wound. We thought then that there would be nothing we could do to help; but perhaps rumor had exaggerated the misfortune, and so we told Toma that we would certainly go to do what we could.

Short Kwi came from a famous family; he was the younger brother of the man who murdered Toma's father, but Short Kwi was famous in his own right, famous as a hunter. He often killed more game in a year than many other men kill in their lives, a great hunter among a hunting people. The other Bushmen told stories about him—about the time he had killed four wildebeests in a herd of many, about the time he had killed an eland, a wildebeest, and a wild pig all in one day. It was his technique of hunting to be relentless in his pursuit; therefore, if he shot an animal and suspected others to be in the vicinity he would let the wounded animal run where it would while he hunted on and shot another, and another, and when all were as good as dead he would rest, then return to pick up the trail of the one that he felt would die the soonest. He almost never lost an animal, for his eyes were sharp and he could follow a cold trail over hard ground and even over stones; he could tell from fallen leaves whether the wind or passing feet had disarranged them; and the meat that resulted from his prolific hunting was never wasted, for he would bring other hunters to help him dry it, then carry it off to a werf somewhere to share with others.

He knew the habits of animals from the ways of the largest antelope all the way down to the smallest species of mice; in fact, he must have known animals very well, for he could always find them. He knew when he was in danger and when he was safe, and he was as brave as he was careful. Once, Short Kwi, John, and two other hunters were tracking a bull wildebeest that one of the hunters had shot. They came upon it lying down, surrounded by a very large pride of lions. There were twenty or thirty lions in all, having got there first and claiming the wildebeest as their own, for the bushes were full of lions walking back and forth, watching several other lions brave the fallen wildebeest, still able to protect itself with its horns. The braver lions were standing near the wildebeest, obviously steeling themselves for the attack, when the hunters arrived. The bushmen had followed the wildebeest's trail through thorns and over the parching desert and were not to be deprived, and, speaking softly to the lions, they said: "We know you are strong, Big Lions, we know you are brave, but this meat is ours and you must give it back to us."

Even after these words the lions did not give ground. Their round eyes watched the hunters and they began to growl, and the four men, quite unarmed except for their arrows and a spear (to use a spear would have been folly), said respectfully: "Great Lions, Old Lions, this meat belongs to us," and then advanced on the lions, throwing little stones and clods of dirt. The lions in the bushes began to back away, while the braver lions stood their ground until a clod struck one of them, causing him to huff and run back a little. At this, the courage of the other lions broke and they all turned and scrambled for the safety of their companions, by now quite far away.

The hunters, victorious in this battle of nerves, had the bull wildebeest all to themselves, but now found that they could not approach it either. Having fended off the lions (it thought), it now tried to lunge to its feet to fend off the men. Short Kwi borrowed the spear from its owner and hurled it into the wildebeest's neck, where it stuck fast. Now they had no weapon at all. Their arrows would be useless. The sticks and stones they threw at the spear did not dislodge it and all their efforts to retrieve it by creeping up on the wildebeest from behind did not succeed, for as soon as one of them would edge near enough to touch the spear the wildebeest would toss its horns so quickly that the man would have to jump back, grazed. At last, while one of the men distracted the wildebeest from the front, Short Kwi backed off and rushed at it, and, as he passed over its back, jerked the spear free. The bull lunged and the curved horns hooked upward, but too late. Short Kwi was gone. Wanting a picture, John asked Short Kwi to do it again, but Short Kwi shook his head. "This time he will remember," Short Kwi said, and dispatched the bull by hurling the spear into its throat.

Sometimes, as on these occasions, Short Kwi hunted with others, but mostly he hunted alone. He knew every bush and stone in the area of thousands of square miles that he ranged over, and he lived for hunting. Caring more for this, his passion, than for society, he often hunted as he did when we had first heard of him, alone in the veld with only his wife—a young woman who was intelligent and gay and almost pretty, to whom Short Kwi was devoted—his baby daughter, and his mother-in-law.

We had met him for the first time at Gautscha. He had come in from the veld one night to visit his brother, and we had met him in the morning. Short Kwi was a young, small man, shorter than his wife and so slender that he looked almost like a child. With long, light feet that took him everywhere, with heavy thighs but light calves like the thin shanks of a greyhound, and with a narrow, deep chest and lungs that never winded, he was obviously built for hunting. In the rainy season when the veld was soft and muddy he often hunted with only a spear and ran the great antelopes down, for though their hooves sunk and split in the mud, causing them eventually to tire, Short Kwi never tired and his strong legs bore him after them relentlessly, sweeping him down the long plains like a wind of death.

His life in the veld seemed lonely, but I doubt that it was; he had his wife, who adored him, for company in the evenings, and although she may have missed companionship more than he did, they were both shy, both quiet, and it may be that they both enjoyed their life apart. Short Kwi hunted most of the time. He would hunt on and on and when word would reach the large band of his wife's family that he had killed, the band would go out to where the animal was, dry the meat, and eat it. When there was enough meat Short Kwi would rest, would relax in the sun, would talk with his wife or make himself a new skin bag or garment, and when word would reach him that all the meat was gone he would move again. The men of his wife's family hunted too, of course, but never as successfully as he, yet his great ability set him so far apart from ordinary mortals that for once the Bushmen forgot their jealousy and agreed that he was the best hunter the Kalahari had ever known.

It is a custom among Bushman hunters to cut strips of skin from the foreheads of the antelope they kill and fashion them into bracelets which their wives wear on their arms. Short Kwi's wife and daughter wore dozens of these; their arms were covered and heavy with them. Short Kwi himself wore no ornament of any kind, nothing except a crown of badger hair which he owned for a while but later gave to Toma, the very crown that Tsamko wore.

One day, said Toma, Short Kwi had been walking in the veld and had failed to watch where he was going. He had stepped on the tail of a puff adder, which had risen up and bitten his leg, just below the knee. It was a rare and terrible accident; in all the time we had been in the Kalahari we had known of only two people besides Short Kwi who had been harmed by snakes—a young boy bitten by a mamba who had died the day he was bitten, and a young woman who had been pulled into a waterhole by a water python and had drowned. Usually, snakes move away when you come near them, of if they don't, you can usually see them; but you can't walk with your eyes on the ground all the time, especially if you are hunting, as Short Kwi had been. His misfortune was regarded as a horrible accident and it was felt that the spirits of the dead were to blame. They had led Short Kwi down the very path the puff adder had chosen, and perhaps had even placed the snake where his foot was sure to fall. Toma and Gao Feet were very depressed to think of it. Although the talk turned to other things, Gao Feet mentioned the accident again and again; everything seemed to remind him of it. At last Toma said to us: "Perhaps you can help him hunt again. Since he was bitten his people have had no meat."

Toma told us that he had been with Short Kwi near Nama Pan when the third group of white farmers had arrived. The farmers had looked at Short Kwi and had offered to cut his leg off for him then and there. This had frightened the Bushmen so badly that they had fled in all directions into the veld and the white farmers had not recruited any labor. We wondered how Short Kwi had managed his escape and Toma told us that his brothers-in-law had helped him. They had carried him on their backs to a far place, taking turns.

CHAPTER TWELVE

The Grove

LATE IN THE afternoon of the day we met Toma, we decided to find the rest of his band—his wife's mother and the other part of Gao Feet's family. There were now nine adults and five children all intending to ride in the jeep and we were very crowded, but to relieve this condition as much as possible Toma left some of his possessions behind. He left a large, dry hide, scraped but not yet cured, rolled up and thrust in the branches of a tree, and a skin bag stuffed full of bedding grass under a bush. Someday he would return for them, perhaps when a season or two had passed, when he would be roaming near that spot again. Bushmen commonly leave their things anywhere they wish, for the things are never touched by others; theft is so unknown that Bushmen do not even forbid it, having no need for taboos or laws against that which never happens.

When Tu was in the jeep, wedged in tightly between others with her youngest children in her lap, she gave the werf that she was leaving one last glance and noticed the bag of grass that Toma had left behind. It was her bed too, after all, and when she saw it she pushed aside her children, pushed aside the people who crowded her in, and, clambering out of the jeep, ran back to retrieve it. It was an enormous bundle, but she dragged it to the jeep and tried to stuff it in, paying no attention at all to the others who insisted loudly that there was no room. She finally got in, climbed in after it, and sat on it to squash it down. She completely ignored a lofty glance from her husband, a reproach for her impoliteness, and searched through her clothing for her pipe and her flint, with which she struck a light and smoked. In a sense, she and Toma were mismated, for the idea that she would have fewer things, less conveniences than someone else seemed to taunt Tu, while Toma seemed possessed with the fear that he would have more. When Tu took, Toma gave away.

We drove down the plain, leaving the nests in the forest behind ourselves forever, toward the eastern horizon, which was blue and shimmering in the heat of the late afternoon. We were too crowded and too jostled to talk much, everyone preferring to crouch quietly and ignore discomfort, exept Tu, higher than the others on her bag of grass, who seemed very cheerful indeed and talked on and on. We stopped several times along the way—in fact, we had hardly started before Tu plucked at John's shoulder and asked him to wait. She had seen a gemsbok cucumber growing on a vine in the grass and wanted to pick it, so John stopped the jeep. Tu climbed out and found several, which she tossed in, letting them roll about freely on the floor. We were about to start again when Dikai also saw some cucumbers and we had to wait while she gathered those, and no sooner had we driven on again, the little cucumbers rolling against our ankles and prickling us with their spines, than Little Dabe vomited and we had to wait a third time while Dikai cleaned him up with a tuft of grass.

Toma sighed. Men plan to spend several days traveling with their families on trips that would take them only hours if they were traveling alone. We stopped a fourth time in the middle of the vast plain, for John had seen a shattered ostrich egg on the ground and wanted to let the Bushmen gather it to make beads. Toma motioned him to drive on. The egg, he thought, belonged to a man named Crooked Kwi, who had left it there one season and would return for it someday soon. Toma had heard of this event from Crooked Kwi himself when they had seen each other last, and, observing that the shell fragments were gathered into a pile, he supposed that this must be the very egg that Crooked Kwi had mentioned. It was just where Crooked Kwi had said it would be, too.

We left the eggshells behind in the immense plain and went on our way toward the eastern rim. When we got there we found the rest of Gao Feet's family—his older and uglier first wife, his old mother-in-law, his first wife's daughter, and his daughter's husband, none other than Crooked Kwi himself. These people were living in a most beautiful glade of thorn bushes that were growing thickly together among tall trees, their branches arching just over people's heads. A fire had cleared out all the grass and leaves, leaving just the brown earth and the gray lace of branches; the people were brown and their things were brown and white and the ashes of their fires were gray in the little hollows on the ground, for these people, too, had built no scherms. Tu got right out of the jeep and went straight to a fire, where she began to crack some of her tsi nuts between a stick and a stone.

The rest of us exchanged greetings and the old woman, Dikai's mother, embraced me. "You are my daughter. I bore you," she said. When I had first come to Gautscha Pan I had been named Dikai for her daughter, and among the Kung one is strongly identified with the person one is named for; as the namesake of Dikai, I had acquired her set of relationships and was expected to follow the rules that applied to her. I could act in a familiar way with those people whom she treated familiarly and was expected to avoid those whom she avoided. I called Dikai "Big Name," the term usually applied in such a relationship, she called me "Little Name," her nephews called me "Aunt," her mother called me "Daughter," and often her husband, Gao Feet, with roars of laughter, would say he would marry me someday.

We sat down in the werf in the delicate shade of the arching branches and Dikai's mother produced a bag full of tsi nuts, which the people began to roast and eat. The bag was made of the entire skin of a duiker—a little nocturnal antelope no bigger than a small dog—turned inside out with the legs tied together as handles, the neck tied off as the bottom of the bag and the rump open as the top. When it was full of tsi it was solid and formed and looked eerily like a little, headless duiker.

When the day was over and the sky was getting dark I made a camp for myself a few feet from the werf. The Bushman children helped me pull the grass. We built a fire in our clearing and I cooked some beans and tsi nuts that Dikai's mother had given me for myself and the children, and as Bushmen from the werf began to come over, I cooked more and more. There wasn't much—the Bushmen had only half a day's supply and we hadn't expected to be away from camp so long. Everyone had a little, though, and afterward we filled ourselves up with water and we smoked. It was very cold. Before the night was over, the water we had in our water pail had turned to ice. On nights such as this the Bushmen prefer to sit up and talk, to keep their minds off the fact that the air is cold and they are naked and hungry, rather than to try to sleep; they wait to sleep the following day, warm in the sun. That night it was so cold that no one wanted to leave the fire and when finally everyone was at my camp, settled close to each other, side by side, with their bellies warmed by the heat and their shoulders covered by their capes, their backs turned against the enormous veld where the cold wind blew and where the dark was coming, they began to entertain themselves with conversation, their favorite pastime.

The adults held their elbows on their raised knees and cupped their hands under their chins to cast little shadows into their eyes, for in this way they could see clearly over the bright fire. Close to the fire even the children were not cold. The older children sat up like the adults, although they were naked and the adults had capes, and the younger children slept in their parents' arms, warm between the fire and their parents' skin.

Before the darkness had come totally I left the fire to look through the little forest for wood, and as soon as I was off among the trees a way I was quite alone; I could not see the firelight and the voices did not reach me, and as I walked around in the frost and the gloom I could hear my footsteps crackling the grass. When I stopped walking to pick up an icy stick I could still hear the grass crackling, and when I looked around I saw, not too far away, a pair of mongooses, a male and a female, with five little ones. They were eating seeds from the pods of a plant and when they saw me they ran, all in an orderly line, and when they

were gone the forest seemed very empty, for I could see
through the trees to the desolate plains beyond, and up
through the branches to the sky, where stars were showing,
far away. A partridge rose in front of me—I had chased it
from its bed. I could hear it calling as it flew, lost out in
the veld now, and when I had a bundle of sticks I found
my way home.

Dikai had been out for sticks in the opposite direction
and when we looked at the pile we had, we judged that we
had enough for the night, but we burned only one at a time
to save them.

For a while, sitting at the fire, everyone was quite gay.
The adults began to talk about food they had gathered and
eaten and Toma's children asked me to tell them a story.
"A true story," they said. Casting about in my mind for a
story that would amuse them, I remembered a night when
we were camped on our way to the Gikwe Bushmen in
Bechuanaland and six lions had come into our camp. Someone in our party had shot at them and had wounded two
of them, and then we had followed the wounded ones on
foot through the darkness, a dangerous business, had finally
found one and killed it, and had found the other one dead
in the morning. I tried to say all this in Kung, but though
I could understand quite a bit of it and could speak on some
subjects, this time I found that my vocabulary was lacking;
all I could say was "We killed two lions," a terse statement,
and though the children were looking at me wide-eyed, I
couldn't go on and had to get John to finish the story. "Ah,"
said the children when the story was told, not nearly as
impressed as I had thought they would be, but then I myself
had seen their father walk through a valley where several
lions were roaring, at night, alone, armed only with a spear,
depending on his wits for safety and on the fact that lions
have a musky odor. He had been in our camp on one side

of the valley when he had heard the lions roaring, and had slipped across among them in order to be with his wife and children, asleep on the other side.

Crooked Kwi, his wife, and his daughter had all turned away from the fire to warm their backs. They sat in a row, Kwi first, then the baby, then his wife. They were relaxed and they had let their heads tilt back to look at the sky. Crooked Kwi and his wife were very young, and, being one of the few men between their adolescence and their thirties in the entire area and not an excellent hunter, Crooked Kwi was sometimes a figure of ridicule. He was nicknamed Crooked because of the way he walked, the Bushmen said, although I could never see why, and now, tonight, the men began to taunt him. For a while Crooked Kwi just looked idly over his shoulder at the men and smiled.

"Why did your wife run away from you?" Lazy Kwi asked finally. This went too far; his wife really had run away from him once with another man, and Crooked Kwi had been grieved and humiliated. His wife had been persuaded to return to him, but the incident had not helped Crooked Kwi's position as a figure of fun. Now, when he was reminded of it, he turned his head away. Bushmen can be quite cruel with their joking.

Perhaps to turn the conversation to other things Toma reminded me of a time I had driven him and some other Bushmen in a truck and had bounced them quite badly. He told me that the Bushmen had agreed that women should leave trucks alone. "Your husband would drive if you were married. Why aren't you married?" he said.

I said it was because I was too young (I was twenty-three), intending this as a joke because Bushmen, even old grandfathers, always say they are too young when they are at a loss for an answer. "Oh no," said Toma. "You are old enough now. Even the last time you were here you said you were going to be married. How is it that you are still alone?"

"Well," I said, "I *will* someday."

"Yes, that is what you told me last time and here you are again." I couldn't think of a thing to say, and Toma added: "Well, never mind. Your father will help you, just as I will help Norna here when she is a little older."

At these words Norna lifted her head from her mother's lap and looked drowsily at her father. "Ehe," said Toma, pointing at her, pleased that she still remembered her European name.

The talk returned to food and hunting and Toma remembered an eland the people had eaten which Short Kwi had killed, and this reminded everyone of the puff-adder bite, and Gao Feet, who had seen Short Kwi, began to describe the wound. He stammered and repeated whole passages again and again, but finally he finished and those who had not seen Short Kwi drew in their breath and seemed very depressed. Short Kwi had been sick a year and had not died, but the flesh had gone from the calf of his leg, said Gao, the skin had gone from his foot, his foot was curled and the bones were showing. The wound stank, too, said Gao, and at this Tu said she didn't think she could bear to see him. Her children were asleep around her and she looked very sad, but by now all the faces lit by the fire were depressed and sad, and soon after that people began to go home, carrying their sleeping children. The night was almost over, the Southern Cross lay on its side and the Firewood Star was high over our heads. Last to leave was the old woman, Dikai's mother, who got stiffly to her feet and waved good-night to us.

"Good night, Old Grandmother," I said.

She turned her head to face me. "You should call me Mother. I embraced you when you came," she said.

Quite far away a fire at the werf flared up, the center point between two tall trees whose branches formed a delicate, pointed arch lit from below, showing the fire's brown owner sitting with his back to us, his elbows on his knees, perhaps gazing into the flames. It was Crooked Kwi, and he seemed very small beneath the high trees but very bright in the firelight and, somehow, very important. In a moment his wife walked into the firelight and sat beside him and they sat together without speaking and then his wife lay down and he lay down and their fire began to die. Soon all the werf was dark.

- - -

In the morning, in the salmon dawn, the first light, we woke up to find doves singing and a fresh, warm wind blowing. It was easy to sleep now, and the people slept for hours, rolling away from their piles of ashes as the day warmed, until they lay curled or sprawled in all parts of the werf with Toma's son, by chance, asleep in the center, flat on his belly with his head in the curve of his arm, relaxed and strong and breathing deeply.

At noon the adults began to get up. The women went into the forest behind their werf for sticks to burn and a few roots to eat, and when they had built up their fires they roasted the roots and shared them with their families. Toma said that we would go back to Nama Pan right away, but his wife and the other women wanted to gather tsi; it was very abundant right beside the forest and they hated to leave all that food just lying there. "Perhaps other people will come here and eat it," said Tu, so Toma changed his mind and everyone took bags, nets, skins, anything that could be used as a container, and they spent the afternoon gathering tsi. They got mountains of it. There was plenty in the patch that they had chosen and with all of them picking the nuts from among the round leaves of the tsi plants they filled every bag, skin, and net that they had. They gathered almost three hundred pounds. The women felt so happy that they were singing a gay, light song in three or four parts. When the people had picked all they could find, when every possible bag was full, they said they were ready to go to Nama, but when we brought the jeep and began to load it they were already busy with their endless preoccupation, that of giving and receiving, and had already begun to give each other presents of tsi. Bushmen feel a great need to give and receive food, perhaps to cement relationships with each other, perhaps to prove and strengthen their dependence upon each other; because the opportunity to do this does not occur unless huge quantities of food are at hand, Bushmen always exchange presents of the foods that come in huge quantities, these being the meat of game antelope, tsi nuts, and the nuts of the mangetti trees, which at certain seasons are scattered abundantly all through the mangetti forests.

As we waited by the jeep Dikai gave a huge sack of tsi to her mother. Her mother gave another sack to Gao Feet's first wife, and Gao Feet gave a sack to Dikai. Later, during the days that followed, the tsi was distributed again, this time in smaller quantities, small piles or small bagfuls, after that in handfuls, and, last, in very small quantities of cooked tsi which people would share as they were eating. All this was very hard to trace, especially for us while we waited and loaded the jeep, for the large sacks were not handed around but rather were tossed into the jeep one on top of the other while the transactions went on vocally.

There is a further complicating factor in food distribution. The owner of the bag which is full of tsi or mangettis is the owner of all the nuts inside, no matter who gathered the nuts, just as the owner of an arrow, whether man or woman, is the owner of the largest share of the buck killed by the arrow, no matter who shot the buck. This is a practical arrangement, since all three of these important foods, oftener than not, are very far from the waterholes where the bands would be living. Usually, Bushmen have to travel for several days over waterless, scorching veld to reach tsi fields or mangetti forests, then have to carry their heavy loads back again to water. These journeys are too hard for young children, old people, cripples, women who are pregnant, or people who are ill. In fact, the long journeys for the two kinds of nuts are undertaken only by strong adults, who therefore must gather for all those who stay behind. The system of Bushmen in these matters ensures that everybody gets enough. As it turned out, that afternoon we found that both Tu and Lazy Kwi had filled bags belonging to Lazy Kwi's wife, the bag that Lazy Kwi filled being the only one he had with him, and in this way his wife, who wasn't there and who so far knew nothing of her windfall, owned two bags of food which she would probably share with Lazy Kwi, who actually, that day, owned none.

At last, when many bags had changed hands, when everything movable including Tu's bag of grass—which she had emptied, tying the grass into a bundle with a strip of bark in order to free the bag for tsi—had been loaded into the jeep, the people began to climb in and the jeep sank down on its springs, groaning dangerously as each person got on it and found a place to sit. When finally everyone was on and the springs still had not broken we drove away with extreme caution, barely moving when we came to bumps, with Toma and Gao Feet sitting on the hood and pointing the way to Nama.

As we crept along Toma told a lion story concerning some Bantu people at Kai Kai who tried to rid themselves of three lions that were attacking their cattle. As his story was extremely funny, his voice was often drowned out by the laughter of the others. He spoke so fast we could not understand him, but his wife laughed until she cried. Toma told the funniest parts of the story two or three times.

- - -

Just before we got to Nama, when the shadows of the bushes reached far over the veld and the western sky was bloodred, thick with smoke, we reached a tiny waterhole with empty veld around it, veld without veld food, without tracks of game, and we stopped to drink. The waterhole's name was Nam Ta Kwara (Here Is Nothing). Crooked Kwi was the only one who was thirsty, so he climbed alone out of the jeep, the hunting bow on his shoulder arching over his head, and walked to the water's edge, where he crouched on the white sand all pocked by the tiny feet of birds to dip up water in one long hand and drink it out of his palm. With his body bent easily, his back arched, he was so grace- ful and lithe that he looked like a serpent or an otter and I wondered again why his name was Crooked Kwi. A white moth touched the surface of the water to drink beside him, and afterward a wasp.

Behind Kwi's head the smoke in the north and west was so thick it seemed that all the Belgian Congo and Angola were in flames, and the sun was swallowed by the smoke, and a gray, soft darkness fell long before the sun had really set.

When we got near Nama Pan it was dark and we saw our camp by its fires, but greatly expanded now as there were perhaps twenty fires where before there had been three. It looked like the camp of an army, for there were fires all over the rise above the pan, arranged in little groups, cluster by cluster, each fire casting light on the branches of a little tree or bush. These were the fires of Bushmen who had come in our absence and at the sight of them the Bush- men in the jeep put up their heads to see who the newcomers were.

At camp many people had got to their feet and were

standing silhouetted by their fires as they peered into the dark; they had undoubtedly been listening to the sound of our jeep for hours, and when we stopped there was a crowd already waiting. The people who had been riding, relieved to have arrived at last, climbed out stretching to greet them. The children were taken out, yawning sleepily, the youngest ones whining by now, cranky from the long ride; the bundles of tsi were unloaded, the bundles of belongings, and Tu's grass bed. Lazy Kwi went off to find his wife and family, but the others, all Toma's people, looked around for a place to live and finally chose a tall tree, where they dropped their bundles and began to clear grass. In a very short time the werf was ready, fires were lit, tsi was roasting, and several of the Bushmen who had watched us come had gathered there to see if they should have a share of the tsi. Of course everybody got some and then sat down to eat it, burying the nuts in the hot ashes and scooping them out again with a stick when they were done. Dikai gave some tsi to me and said that I could use her fire, a courtesy, so I buried the nuts in the ashes and when I thought they were done I poked for them with a stick but I couldn't find them. Pretty soon they began to explode with loud reports and puffs of gray ashes which showed where they were, but of course then it was too late. You might as well throw them away if you forget where they are, the Bushmen say.

Some of the newcomers were eating giraffe hide, roasting great pieces of it, dried and thick and curling; they passed chunks of it around and it looked like the soles of shoes, all that remained of a giraffe hunted long ago. When it was roasted the people put it in a wooden mortar and pounded it into powder, and then licked the powder off their palms. Again, Dikai gave some to me and I found that it was salty and not unpleasant, tasting like bacon.

Gao Feet plucked my elbow and when I turned to him he pointed at Dikai, sitting on the other side of the fire. He had pointed his lips at her, pushing his lips forward and gesturing with his chin because Bushmen think it is rude to point with the finger. "She wants to tell you what is in her heart," he said. I looked at Dikai and she passed her hand over her two sons' eyes, first Little Gashe, then Little Dabe, as they slept beside her, and I remembered the eye medicine I had promised to her, so I nodded and went to get it, but when I returned with it I found that she had mistakenly awakened her sons and they now crouched behind her, peering out at me, their small faces distorted with distrust and apprehension. I held out my hand to Little Gashe, but he retired completely behind his mother, pushing Little Dabe out the other side, so I held out my hand to Little Dabe, causing him to shrink back, pushing Little Gashe. Finally Dikai stood up and left them both exposed, and then Gao Feet held Little Gashe, Dikai held Little Dabe, and I put the medicine in as quickly as possible, but both children had tantrums of rage and arched their backs, and as soon as they were released, they would have nothing further to do with their parents, but went to sleep at their grandmother's fire instead, on the opposite side of the werf. The light was very dim, only the stars were showing and the fires had died, and these two forlorn children made two red little shapes as they lay down at their grandmother's fire; their skins reflected the red glow of coals, for they lay right in the ashes for warmth; they had forsaken their parents' karosses and there was no room for them under their grandmother's—another child was sleeping there.

Gao Feet gave up trying to urge them to come home and at last he, too, lay down to sleep, snug between his two wives, who were resting, not sleeping, for whenever someone at one of the other fires said something of interest, one or the other of them would put up her head and remark upon it. Tu slept alone with her children, for Toma had gone visiting, and one by one the people at Tu's fire moved away toward their own werfs, calling to each other in the dark. At last only a few voices were heard at one of the werfs; they seemed very gay and very lighthearted, all talking at once, and now and then Toma's voice was heard above them all. Hearing him, Tu lifted her head and her face showed in the firelight; her eyes shone quite yellow and she looked dangerous, like a leopard, as she glared in the direction of his voice.

On my way home I passed Lazy Kwi's house, which his wife had started in his absence, and as she had planned a large scherm and had already built the framework, many large branches stuck upright in the ground, but had not yet covered it with grass, I could see Lazy Kwi inside. He was between me and his fire, and in silhouette against the red light he looked like a creature in a cage, for he was peering through the lattice of branches to see who was passing by. I stopped to show who I was, and noticed a bird roasting by his fire, a little duck which must have been snared by Lazy Kwi's old father-in-law. It was plucked and trussed and tied to a stick which was pushed into the ground so that the duck hung over the coals. It looked about done to me, so I asked Lazy Kwi, who was obviously alone with it, awake only to tend it, if it wasn't ready, and Lazy Kwi looked first at me, then at the duck, then up at the sky, and shook his head. He was timing it by a star, he explained, and the star had risen but wasn't high enough yet, so I said good-night and went home and left him in his lattice; and just before I went to sleep I heard great shouts of laughter, for Toma had found someone who hadn't heard the lion story and was telling it again.

- -

CHAPTER THIRTEEN

SHORT KWI
the Hunter

THERE WERE ABOUT forty people who had moved in beside us at our camp by Nama Pan, having settled overnight into seven werfs, each concealed from the others in the privacy of the grass and forming a community that was superimposed on ours, for the werfs, each a little clearing containing several grass nests or several scherms symbolized by sticks thrust in the ground, surrounded us on all sides and life went on as if we weren't there. People walked back and forth through our camp on their way to patches of veld food or to the water pan, and soon little paths appeared which we had not made.

Mostly, the people were Bushmen from Gam who had

left there right after we did and had walked along after us, taking their time, sleeping one night on the way. They had brought all their children and old people, all their belongings, and evidently planned to stay. Even the Chuana woman had come, riding her donkey, followed on foot by two of her Bushman servants, and she had made herself a camp quite far away from us to prevent the donkey from annoying us with its brays.

The other werfs were much nearer us, as the people wanted to keep an eye on each other, to see that we gave food or presents to all when we gave to one, but also because they enjoyed being together and wanted to be able to visit each other quickly at any time at all. Next to our camp on one side was Lazy Kwi's werf, and on the other side lived Toma with his wife and Gao Feet with his wives. At the far end of their werf lived Crooked Kwi with his wife and the old grandmother. They were between our camp and the pan, and beside their werf ran a pathway, the way used by the people on the other side of us to reach the water.

On the other side of the path, in the shade of a tree, lived one more small band, the band of a young man of perhaps thirty, who lived with his twelve-year-old son and his eight-year-old wife, whom he was nourishing while waiting for her to grow. These young people had chosen their spot because the little girl was Gao Feet's daughter by his first wife and was still so young that she wanted to live near her mother. She was a sad little girl with a grave face and troubled, wondering eyes; in fact, all these young people were very grave and sad—the young man's first wife had died and he now had no one to care for him because the little girl, his new wife, spent a great deal of time with her mother and he was left alone. The son was lonely too, having no mother and no one to care for him except his sad young father. His father was too troubled, too preoccupied, to be a companion to him, his little stepmother was too young, and he spent most of his time sitting on a rise of ground overlooking the werf where he lived, watching other people going by.

The little girl took after her mother, Gao Feet's ugly wife, but her two men, her husband and her stepson, were a family of great beauty. Both had wide, grave eyes and golden skins, and both were musicians, but the young father himself was an Orpheus. He owned a *guashi*, a stringed instrument which he had made, and he carried his guashi wherever he went. As he plucked the strings, playing chords with his long fingers, he would hum the notes of a song that were not the same notes that his fingers were playing; he wove two themes and made a web of music, the guashi playing an intricate accompaniment while he sang a melody.

The guashi was made of a hollowed log about a foot long with a wooden lid fixed over it, forming a sounding chamber. At one end of the log, five wands were fixed which held five sinew strings that reached from the tips of the wands to the opposite end of the log. Anyone but a Bushman finds it hard to play a guashi, for the strings are always slipping out of tune and the position one plays it in is awkward. The guashi is set on the ground and the player squats before it, holding it steady with his feet or the edges of his hands; but the sound is beautiful, sometimes full, sometimes thin, and makes very deep and various music, for Bushmen, their music being by far their greatest art, are not given to whistles or clear, shrill sounds—all their instruments make blurred and vibrant music with a richness in every note. Their compositions, too, are never simple, not even the music of their musical games, but always mixed, always subtle, partly gay but partly sad.

The songs and rhythms of the Kung are in no way as precise as those of the Gikwe, but the effect of Kung songs is deeper and, as the songs are freer, more impassioned. Like the songs of the Gikwe, the Kung songs are mood pieces. Because the guashi is made of mangetti wood, the songs are called "mangetti songs." The young man who owned the guashi knew many of these, but there were four that he sang very often, all wistful and quite sad, sometimes touched with irony. One of them was called "The Stump," a song about a man lost in the veld and wandering until at last he saw another Bushman, and because he was so happy to see someone and imagined the two of them passing the night together talking by a fire, he waved and called and ran up to the other Bushman. But when he got there he found that he had been mistaken—what he had thought was a man had been only a stump.

A second song was about two jealous co-wives, and the song, more ironic than sad, was composed by the husband to ridicule them. The names of these two women were Nunkwe and Aite, which sound for all the world like Gikwe names, as perhaps they were, and we wondered how far this song had traveled, by how many ears and mouths, before it found itself at Nama Pan.

The third song was called "*Chiviba*," a song composed by a young man who had brought veld food to his people in a chiviba, a basket made of branches. His people laughed at him and said that he was lazy not to have a bag to carry the veld food in, but nevertheless they were not too proud to eat what he had brought. The fourth song was called "*Ka Te Te*," the song of the redwing partridge. The redwing partridge is most strongly tabooed as food, may never be eaten, and *ka te te* is an imitation of its cry. The song was composed by a man who heard a redwing partridge making a sound in the evening and knew that the sound foretold a misfortune or a death.

Because the young man who owned the guashi was lonely and brooding, it was natural that he should play. The other people loved to hear him and often when he played several people, usually men, would gather to lie in the shade near him or sit beside him with their chins on their raised knees and listen, sometimes singing softly as he sang, very harmoniously, but paying no attention, just singing in their own way within a set harmony, dreaming and soft, and although the young man played for his own ears, not theirs, he could infect them with his moods and when he stopped playing and they went away, they, too, were brooding.

- - -

Many young people had come to Nama, and together they made Nama very gay. The boys played a game with wands, throwing the wands at a hummock of ground and watching them bounce off and sail into the grass on the other side, the nearest that Bushmen come to a competitive game, for the young boys like to see whose wand goes the farthest.

The girls played a singing game with a melon. They would stand in a row that formed a half-circle, dancing in place while the girl at one end would spring into the middle of the circle and toss a melon to the girl next to her in line. The game is accompanied by a rapid, intricate song of several parts sung in falsetto voices, as pretty to hear as the game is pretty to see, for the girls dance with their arms and heads as well as with their feet, like the dancers of Bali.

At that time there were only two adolescent unmarried girls at Nama. One of these was Beautiful Ungka, the other was her cousin, and they both lived with the cousin's parents at one of the werfs of the people from Gam. They were both extremely beautiful and they were lilies of the field. Since they were their parents' only children, they had no younger brothers or sisters to mind, and did nothing at all from one day to the next but adorn and amuse themselves, and this they did together, for they were the best of friends. They were straight and slender, with pale-gold skin not yet darkened and weathered by the sun of the veld, and they had flat bellies and high, small breasts. Beautiful Ungka had nipples like knobs, rounded like balls. Both girls wore ornamented aprons, soft leather capes—the best that there is. Many bead ornaments hung from their hair and swung when they walked, and almost hid their handsome faces.

A sound and fragrance accompanied them wherever they went; the sound was the sound of their ornaments clanking like crockery, dry and dull, and the fragrance was heavy and sweet, the perfume of the leaves of *sa* and the wood of *tchambuti*, which Bushman women grind to powder and rub on their bodies. We would always hear these two girls coming, for they talked loudly, and a moment later we would see them appear around a bend in the path, one in front of the other, heads high and eyes cast downward, as light and long as two Egyptian sacred cats. Usually they were followed by a homely little girl years younger than they were, a forlorn little creature who would run errands for them and was content to trot after them and be their handmaiden, and usually they were on their way to visit a friend of theirs, a young married girl who was visiting at Toma's werf. When the two beauties would arrive to visit her, their married friend would stop whatever she was doing and the three of them would sit together in some shady spot to string beads or weave blossoms into crowns which they would wear, the blossoms fetched by the handmaiden, who searched the veld for aloes, the only flowers blooming in that season.

While they were stringing beads or weaving blossoms, a group of young boys would gather to play the wand game, and now and then, of course, a wand would land among the girls and the boys would jostle each other to retrieve it. The girl of Toma's werf treated these happenings with gaiety, for she was responsive and kind, but the other two wouldn't even turn their heads to see. Beautiful Ungka had been married, after all, and kidnapped, and widowed and divorced; grown men had fought over her and it was natural that the jostling of young boys would seem trivial. She would laugh behind her hand at them, though, then pull a long face when they would turn around to see.

Those were two willfull girls, too beautiful, too proud, too much admired, but the young boys couldn't do enough for them. It was one of their admirers who cleared the grass for the werf that the cousin's parents were building, and though the two girls teased and ridiculed the boy all the while, snickering contemptuously at him from behind their swinging beads, he worked on happily until not a blade of grass remained.

But Beautiful Ungka and her cousin were not as sophisticated as they thought they were, really, for when they would hear the music of the melon game they would abandon their poise and decorum and run for the sound, arms waving, ornaments and clothing streaming out behind, and when they found the game they had been hearing they would jump into the middle of it and play with abandon, singing loudly and dancing fast for fun. Also, Beautiful Ungka could spit through her teeth like a man. She could draw back her head and spit ten feet and she did this often, smiling scornfully, an astonishing accomplishment for such a handsome girl. Her cousin used to try it too; she could spit a little way but not nearly as far as Beautiful Ungka.

After all, they were only sixteen. There is a Bushman mood song with these words:

> *I am tired and old and without people,*
> *I wish I could marry a young girl.*

- - -

There were so many great fires around Nama that the sky was dark with their smoke, and when the sun rose in the morning, one day shortly after we had got there, we could not even see it until it was far above the horizon and then it appeared red and enormous, murky. In the west two new fires had sprung up, perhaps lit by Bushmen to show where they were or perhaps kindled by the wind from old embers, and their new smoke rose white against the sulphurous sky. The dawn was warm, the north wind blew and, though the smoke it carried stung our eyes, it carried too the sound of insect voices and frog voices from the pan. These songs and cries of creatures made the air seem alive, the veld large, quite different from the deathly quiet dawns of frost.

We were getting ready to look for Short Kwi and his people, and that morning we packed a truck. Everyone felt apprehensive, and at Toma's werf Gao Feet, a medicine man, was throwing oracle discs to see what would happen. He crouched in front of his kaross, which he had spread to throw the discs on, and beside him sat Toma and several other men, their lips pressed against their hands, absorbed, watching. We watched over his shoulder; at a distance, for oracle discs are men's business, the women were standing up to see.

Gao Feet had five discs made of antelope hide, which he would shake in his hands and then drop upon the kaross. When they fell in certain positions, they would tell him certain things. Before he would throw them, though, he would assign identity to them; if he was wondering where people were he would call them men and women, or name them after people he wanted to see, and if he was trying to predict the outcome of a hunt he would call them kudu or gemsbok or wildebeest, male and female, then would see in which direction game could be found, and how far away. Sometimes, too, he would call one disc a hyena and then, if this disc fell upon the disc that was the wounded antelope, he would know that hunting that day would be useless; the hunters would never find their prey.

Sometimes he threw them with a particular question in mind and sometimes, as this morning, he named them and then threw them just to see what would turn up. Perhaps he felt uneasy with no specific worry in mind. He did ask them one specific question, though; he wanted to know where an outbreak of diarrhea that everyone had got came from, and when Tu's brother, the lame boy, who was watching, heard what was asked, he said that our cameras had sent the diarrhea, and the people almost choked themselves laughing at that. Toma laughed until he cried. "We do not really believe this," he said through his tears, looking over his shoulder at us lest we should be uneasy, "we are only joking."

Toma, Gao Feet, and Lazy Kwi took turns throwing the discs, and presently the discs told them that the diarrhea "came from the fires, from people to the east." I don't know how to interpret this, but perhaps the Bushmen meant that the disease blew down the wind. The discs also foretold that someone in the west would kill a buck, that visitors were coming, and that some Europeans and some Bushmen would sit at a fire to talk. Later all these things came true. Because the oracle discs predict conservatively, their predictions often come true.

Toma lost interest in them and told everybody how he had been walking home the evening before and had heard a voice which had sounded to him like the voice of a European speaking English, but when he had investigated he had found a Bushman man sitting alone in a clump of bushes practicing the sounds of English, possibly hoping to speak it, and Toma's audience all thought that was very funny and they talked on and on about it. Incidents like this are talked about forever by Bushmen, who drag them out infinitely, remembering every detail, savoring them to the fullest. This is because very little happens outside of routine. (We once asked some Bushmen if they ever made up stories to tell and they, a little righteously, said no, they did not, because Bushmen do not care to hear about things that are not true.) Then the young boys began to speak sounds that were for all the world like the sounds of English, with flat, nasal tones, perfect in cadence and inflection, and the people laughed again.

Because it was getting close to noon and the sun, now only veiled by the smoke, was burning over our heads, we decided to start our search for Short Kwi. After Toma, Toma's son, Gao Feet, and Lazy Kwi decided to go with us and the others decided to stay at home, we got on the truck and drove away, lurching over the stones at the edge of camp and out to the wild veld, to the west, where the soft wind was blowing and the horizon seemed dim because of the smoke. Ledimo, the interpreter, came too, and my brother and myself, and that night we slept in the veld, not even bothering to build a fire, but eating a few handfuls of cold food and sleeping in our blankets around the truck. The following afternoon we reached the werf of Short Kwi and his people. This werf, too, was hidden in the bushes and if the men of the band hadn't come out into the plain to meet us we might have gone by it, for Toma himself hadn't known exactly where it was. They came out because they knew it would be us they were meeting, for, they explained later, the European farmers couldn't possibly have found them there.

Six men and several young boys suddenly stepped from the bushes and appeared in front of our truck, all of them brown and naked and waving wildly to us, and the truck stopped so fast that those of us on top were nearly thrown off, and we all climbed down to greet them.

Three of the men were brothers, the brothers-in-law of Short Kwi, for their old mother had a strong hold on her family and kept them all beside her. Her sons and her daughters all lived with her; the sons at least might have been expected to live with the families of their wives, but they had never left her and they were here with her now. They stood together in front of the truck and when we climbed down they embraced us.

We went on toward the werf with these men and boys clinging to the sides of the truck and laughing loudly at those among them who were raked by thorn branches that the truck drove through, and at the edge of the werf we saw the women standing all together, waving and calling to us, and we stopped again and they too embraced us and kissed me, and the little children gravely shook my hand.

Short Kwi's mother-in-law was there with a wide and toothless smile, her face all wrinkled like a little shriveled pear, and many other people, among them the old man who had never shot a buck and whose sister had died in the forest; he now was nobody's close relative and we noticed he had lost an eye and seemed even more malevolent and sad. He greeted us distantly, but the others were enthusiastic. The little children tried to climb on me and finally someone put a baby in my arms. The baby bit me, but he meant me no harm for when he bit I felt the sharp edge of a new tooth coming, which probably itched.

We passed through the bushes and came into the werf, where the people had obviously been living for a long time, judging by the size of the ash heaps at the fires and the depth of the nests that people had dug for themselves. Looking around, it came to us that many people whom we had expected to see were not there, Short Kwi for one, and his wife. When we asked for them, Short Kwi's brother-in-law said that he would take us to see him presently. When we asked for the others who were missing—among them the man with two wives named Kushe and two daughters named Xama—we were told that these people had all been taken by the farmers and had never been seen again. We were very sad to hear it, for many of them were too old to have to do the heavy work required on the farms, and also because certain members of the families were still here and now these families were broken forever.

On our way to see Short Kwi, the brother-in-law led us to the far end of the werf, behind a clump of bushes, to the scherm where Short Kwi lived. We saw him there, sitting with his wife and little daughter by the ashes of their fire, side by side, and we caught our breath at the sight of him. He looked tiny, no bigger than a child, and his flesh had wasted away so that his pale skin stretched tightly over all his bones. His leg was hidden by a blanket, his hands were as thin and fragile as a girl's, and his eyes were huge. He looked up at us when we came and smiled wanly, wryly, and his wife also smiled wanly, but his daughter did not smile at all. The first thing Short Kwi did was to rearrange the blanket over his foot to hide his toes, but not before we had seen them, dry and black, dead entirely like the toes of a mummy. His leg was the first thing in his mind, but this was natural; we reminded him of better days.

We sat down at his fire to talk, all of us who had come from Nama and most of the people from his werf, and his wife gave those of us from Nama a palmful of sa, the finely powdered yellow-green leaves that smell halfway between roses and sage. We crossed our faces with it, sprinkling a stripe up the bridge of our noses to our foreheads and another stripe across our cheeks. It smelled very nice, a sweet present to give to someone who has arrived from a long journey. Hours later it was still fragrant and we could smell it, faintly, for days.

We asked Short Kwi to show us his leg and as he started to unwind the blanket the Bushmen from Nama leaned forward, fascinated, but the other Bushmen did not look because they had seen it before. Short Kwi drew back the blanket and revealed a tiny, skinny stick that was his leg wrapped in some kind of rag, bound by a thong that tied the calf to the healthy thigh above, with the black foot showing below, and then he slowly and carefully unwound the thong and then the rag and opened it.

The leg was even worse than people had described, all dead and black at the ankle, and above that, rotted away down to the bone, which was gray now, but while the foot was rotting and dry, the leg was rotting and wet and oozing a little black slime or juice. It was gangrene. A faint stench rose. Those of us who had not seen it had to look away, and Short Kwi, perceiving this, looked calmly down at the ground, at his ruined black leg, and he wrapped the rag around it again, tied his calf to his thigh with the thong, and covered it all with the blanket.

Short Kwi's wife had watched the whole thing with calmness and composure, her hands in her lap, and when the leg was covered she opened one of her hands, revealing a palmful of little white beads, which she began to drop, one by one, into a tiny bag she wore around her neck. With her head bent to see the mouth of the bag she looked very girlish and young; someone said something unusual, an unfamiliar word, and Short Kwi glanced at his wife to see if she had heard it but saw instead what she was doing, and he looked at her with such a deep look of adoration and affection that I wondered how it was she didn't feel it and look up. The word was the word for European doctor, *docteri*, which is not part of the usual vocabulary. Short Kwi's wife had not understood it and when she had finished dropping the beads into the bag she whispered to ask her husband what it meant. He answered her softly, in a masculine, affectionate way, and the other people chimed in, so for a moment everyone was speaking except Short Kwi's wife, who looked around at them all gravely, listening, and when they had finished she nodded her head. "A medicine man of Europeans," they said.

"So," said she.

We talked about the foot for a while, for although he had covered it we could still see the toes. The people of the werf described how Short Kwi was bitten and everyone claimed credit for his part in saving Short Kwi's life. One man had killed the snake, another had cut the fang punctures, and others had given advice at the time and later. The leg had swelled enormously and the medicine men had cut the swollen skin to let blood; the scars of this still showed on the healthy thigh above the blanket. All the people seemed very depressed when talking about it, though; for one reason, they ate meat less often, but also they truly admired him and did not seem to enjoy watching the disaster. Toma asked Short Kwi how he felt and Short Kwi said he thought that his leg had seemed to be getting a little better during the last few days.

It was almost evening, and we heard voices singing in the veld. Two women and a young girl were coming home from a trip for veld food. These three were also very happy to see us and the little girl kissed me but not the men, then asked for her mother, who lived at Nama and whom she had not seen for seasons, and we told her that her mother was well. The girl had been newly married and she was as pretty as she could be, with lots of beads, and with long ornaments of tsi nuts hanging beside her face. She wore a fine kaross which she had rubbed with red powder, often a sign to men that a girl is menstruating, as perhaps she was, that men may be careful not to touch her and endanger their powers to hunt. Marriage seemed to have agreed with her. She looked very happy. She was only ten, but already she had lost her childish belly, although her breasts had not yet begun to grow.

Now everyone was in the werf and people had begun to go back to their fires, leaving Short Kwi alone. When most people were gone, Short Kwi's brother-in-law squatted beside him and, taking his injured leg, began laboriously to help him move toward the veld, toward a little pathway that we had not noticed before. Short Kwi's wife had cleared the path; it led to a place in the veld where Short Kwi could urinate, and slowly, painfully, Short Kwi and his brother-in-law moved down it, the brother-in-law duckwalking, carrying the bad leg while Short Kwi—he who once could run great elands down—edged himself forward on his buttocks, using his hands to brace himself and his good leg to pull himself along.

We were not at his fire when he got back, but we could see him through the trees, inching, and then, when Short Kwi was alone with his wife and daughter, we could watch him sitting by his fire, looking idly around. He was like a wild goose with pinioned wings, squatting there before his fire, watching the sky, the veld, and other people come and go.

Those of us from Nama made a camp apart from the werf, through long grass as high as our chests, inside a little glade of thorn trees. We cleared some of the grass and built a fire, and even then the Bushmen could not stop talking about Short Kwi, although they tried to change the subject; they spoke of him creeping along on his buttocks, even this impossible without someone to help, and all because he had failed to notice an adder that was waiting in his path. Of course, the Bushmen said, he was lucky to be alive. I felt that he was luckier than they supposed, because of his wife, that quiet, gracious, gentle, pretty woman, and his grave little daughter, the image of her mother. The people felt, said Toma, that Short Kwi's wife would leave him now for a better man, but she had not and was not going to. He was, after all, the same husband, only sadder.

Later in the night we went back to talk with Short Kwi once more, to tell him that we thought he could be helped to walk again, but not that we thought his leg would have to come off, for we did not want to frighten him. Our plan was to drive him to Windhoek, the capital of South-West Africa, where he could go to a hospital and perhaps be fitted with an artificial leg. We planned eventually to tell him this, but gradually. The long grass was wet with dew when we pushed through it this time, and we were drenched. Short Kwi was still sitting where we had seen him, still beside his wife, not speaking. When we asked him if he would come with us because we believed he could be helped, he smiled such a heartbreaking smile of pure happiness that we felt sickened because we knew what he thought. His wife looked at him and smiled and then they both looked up at us and their smiles faded and their faces fell and I think that when they saw us they knew we couldn't restore his leg to him.

- - -

Early in the morning when the sky became light, misty yellow—for the sun was still swallowed by smoke—we broke camp and made a comfortable bed for Short Kwi on top of the truck, then went to the werf to get him. He and his brother-in-law were just creeping back on the path from the veld, but Short Kwi's belongings were ready, tied up in bundles by his wife. We waited a long time while Short Kwi made his way toward us, sweat standing out on his forehead although the air was cool, but, oddly, even his slow and painful creeping seemed graceful. It did not have the heaving awkwardness of movement that one associates with injured human beings, but rather the liquidity and coordination of a three-legged dog. This morning, though, he did not look at anyone and seemed more silent even than he had been before.

The men made a carriage of their arms and lifted Short Kwi to the top of the truck, and in the process one of them lost his footing so that Short Kwi was jounced, which must have hurt him although he did not show it, Bushmen being very good at concealing pain or despair. His wife climbed on to help make him comfortable and to receive their bundles, which were being handed up, and at the sight of this his baby began to cry without a sound, slow tears rolling down her cheeks and dropping to the ground. I lifted the baby and tried to play with her, jumping a little and smiling to make her smile, although of course I could not cheer her, and when Short Kwi's wife looked over the truck's side the baby twisted away from me and held up her arms.

When Short Kwi was ready we asked who would come with us, and most of his relatives decided to wait and join us later because one of the young boys, a child of twelve or so, had shot his first buck two days before and as the buck had still not been found, the people did not want to leave it. Toma's son himself wanted to remain because, it turned out, the buck had been shot with an arrow which he had given to another boy, who in turn had given it to the young hunter, and Toma's son, as original owner of the arrow, wanted his rightful share of the meat. When Toma said that his son could wait if he wanted but that we couldn't wait for him, his son turned to some other little boys who stood near him and began discussing the possibility of his joining the search for the animal. It was very interesting to see this conversation, these adult dealings beginning among the ten- and twelve-year-olds, these new, young hunters, these small figures of hope and strength, and we waited a long time while Toma's son rubbed his head with his tough little fingers to make up his mind. Finally he left his friends and climbed on the truck. Home was too far to walk to, he said, and he was going to forfeit. As we drove away, his friends ran after us, shouting that they would bring him his share if they were able to.

- - -

We reached Nama Pan late in the afternoon. Toma and Gao Feet cleared a werf for Short Kwi, and when he was settled comfortably with his back against a tree and with soft grass and blankets arranged all around him he said softly, just to himself and anyone else who might be listening, that during the night his leg had fallen off. After he said this he began to cry, and Gao Feet slowly crouched beside him, unwound the blanket slowly, and untied the bark, then gently lifted the knee away from the calf, which remained on the ground, just like the leg of a mummy. When the calf had fallen off, Short Kwi was crying and biting his hand and his wife was crying, and Toma and Gao Feet stood beside him for a minute looking, the expression on their faces as dark as night. Then they picked up the leg and carried it away to the veld, where they buried it in a hole, exactly as if it were a person, they were so sad.

Later, when we had dressed the stump, Toma and Gao Feet came back to sit with Short Kwi and talk with him. Gao Feet told about a Bantu man he had seen far in the north who had been injured in a mine accident and had been fitted with a false foot. Short Kwi could have one too, Gao said; but Toma said, almost too depressed to speak: "What does it matter? He is a cripple now."

Then the men went away and left Short Kwi to rest, and during the evening the children and young people were talking happily, but all the adults in all the werfs were too depressed and sad. Finally, one by one, the men went back again to Short Kwi, who by now had rallied and was sitting up, surely having been through the worst of it the night before, and talked to him about the antelopes he had killed and about the time he killed a wildebeest, an eland, and a wild pig all in one day.

It has been said that Bushmen abandon cripples or people who are old or sick and cannot travel. This is not true.

Far into the night, people who could not sleep sat up and talked at each other's fires. We heard the guashi being played, its long strings sounding in repetitious little songs of four or five notes which themselves were played over and over, for the guashi was being passed from hand to hand, played idly by people who just wanted something to do.

It was a warm night. The frogs in the pan were croaking and the north wind blew the cooking fires around. Later, when the moon rose and made a bloodred fire all its own, the people began to go home, Toma and Gao Feet and their sons stopping to visit us on their way; they walked silently up to our fire from the darkness and dropped to their haunches one after the other, and sat quietly, their grave faces tilted back, hands shading their eyes. Toma's son wore the crown of badger hair, which moved in the wind a little. Presently the men and their sons stood up again one at a time and walked on, as silently on their bare feet as they had come. We heard the low voices of other people who were passing, then saw fires flare up at the werfs, and much later, when the wind had died and even the frogs were silent, we knew that some of the people were dreaming, for they groaned in their sleep.

CHAPTER FOURTEEN

The Sun Dance

EARLY IN THE morning, when the sun was rising red into the smoke and the sky was bright, we heard a woman quarreling at Short Kwi's werf. Her voice was strident, harsh, and loud—and carried well above the ordinary sounds of morning—children talking, firewood breaking as limbs were snapped for the breakfast fires—and, solicitous of Short Kwi, for today was the day he was going to Windhoek, we went over to see.

We saw a startling sight. Many people had got there before us, hearing the quarrel and being moved to go there out of curiosity, and it seemed as if everyone had already taken sides, for the people had arranged themselves in two groups facing each other and were fighting. The speaker, the woman whose voice had awakened us, was an old woman who lived at one of the farthest werfs, and her opponent, the person whom she was berating, was Gao Feet. These two sat on their haunches on opposite sides of Short Kwi's fire, leaning toward each other, glaring sourly. Arranged behind them were all the others. The larger group by far, including Toma, Tu, Dikai, and Lazy Kwi, crouched behind Gao Feet. Short Kwi himself, on Gao Feet's side, was sitting propped on the blankets we had given him to keep him warm in case of shock, feeling better and obviously taking an interest, for the matter was clearly close to everybody's heart. In fact, everyone was so interested in the quarrel that no one looked up when we came, for the people all sat with their ears pricked, waiting for a chance to speak. They, too, were glaring, deadly earnest, as though the argument were for their lives. Now and then someone would contribute a word or two, but for the most part the old woman did the talking. She looked bitter as gall; her eyes were burning and she hissed like a goose; she was accusing Gao Feet of having failed to give her a present of tsi nuts when he had come to Nama. Gao Feet was rubbing his face and it began to look as if he were losing. He said, obviously having said it before, that he had brought only a few. The woman said, also not for the first time, that she had expected him to give her a present and now he was refusing to do so. It was her right, she said, her due. Toma edged himself forward until he was beside Gao Feet, his friend and brother-in-law, and together they tried to pacify her, telling her that really Gao Feet had none to give, but her eyes burned so fiercely and the people behind her glared so that Toma and Gao Feet lost conviction and before long they fell silent again, defeated by themselves, for what they had tried to say was true. Finally the argument centered itself at its probable source, a gift given to

Gao Feet's father by the woman's father which had not completed itself in an exchange. The woman's father, now long dead, could not receive it, Gao Feet's father, living far away at another pan at the farthest end of Nyae Nyae, could not give it unless he moved to Nama, so it was up to Gao Feet to assume responsibility.

Throughout the two crowds, children were sitting wide-eyed and open-eared. Things like this are remembered and talked about always; Bushman children listen for hours to discussions of this kind and thereby know the history of every object, every exchange between their families, before they are ten or twelve years old. A debt unpaid is a sword against the debtor, to be used against him any time, for any reason. Jealousy and spite had surely preyed on the old woman's mind when she had started this discussion, for she had got up to seek out Gao Feet very early, just at dawn.

In the end, the argument was concluded and the crowd scattered by us when we told Short Kwi that we were ready to take him to the hospital in Windhoek if he would go. He said he would, and the people, glaring bitterly at him, at each other, and at us, stood up and went to their scherms, saying to the other members of their families what they would have said to their opponents if they had had a chance.

Soon Short Kwi's werf was nearly empty. The only people who remained were Short Kwi, his family, ourselves, Toma, and Gao Feet. Toma and Gao Feet talked together, vindicating themselves, and then, before long and before we had a chance to discuss our plans to move Short Kwi, some of the people who had been on Gao Feet's side in the argument came back and crouched beside us stolidly, waiting to hear what might now be said. Jealousy had been aroused.

Because of the long journey and Short Kwi's condition, we thought that it would be best for him to leave at once, but his wife spoke out against this, saying that the rest of her family, probably at this moment on their way here, would be heartbroken to find them gone. She would like to wait for them, she said, to say good-bye. Gao Feet agreed with her. He added that if her mother were to come and find her gone the old woman would cry and cry for days, but Toma shook his head. "Perhaps Short Kwi can be helped," he said. "Perhaps he had better go anyway. The old woman will just have to cry."

Short Kwi's wife began to put her things in a skin bag. She seemed to be resigned. Short Kwi did not say a word, but he smiled, and he seemed to be in good spirits, ready for whatever might happen to him.

Short Kwi's wife called her daughter and when her daughter came she took one of the child's arms; another woman took the other, and together they stripped off every ornament the daughter wore, every bead string in her hair, every band of antelope skin on arms, the great wealth of them that once had shown how Short Kwi had hunted, and they did it quickly, cutting some and pulling others, although it hurt the little girl and she cried sadly. The two women piled the ornaments in a mound which grew higher and higher, to be left with Tu for safekeeping. Perhaps Short Kwi was resigned to leaving, but we thought then that his wife was not.

When the little girl's arms were stripped completely Short Kwi's wife let her go free to rub the pale stripes that the bands had left and to wipe away her own tears. Short Kwi's wife then stood up to ask us to feed her mother when she came. We said we would.

Everything had happened so quickly that we hadn't had a chance to think or plan, and when we looked at Short Kwi and his wife now and pictured them in the streets of Windhoek, we knew we had to do something, so my mother and I and our interpreter, Ledimo, took Short Kwi's wife aside so that no one would be embarrassed and told her everything we could imagine she would have to know in order to take care of herself and Short Kwi in the city; we racked our brains and started with the simplest things. We taught her how to open a safety pin; we told her how to find a toilet and drew a picture for her of what a toilet would look like; we told her where she could get water and how to turn a tap, how to handle menstruation when she was alone in the city in the clothes of a European, without the absorbent leather strip that Bushman women use. We told her, in order that she might not seem strange and perhaps be the object of ridicule, to wash very often and to let her hair grow, for she had recently shaved the top of her head like a monk, very decorative among Bushman women. We told her that the traffic in the city streets could kill her, that she must be extremely careful, and we did not even venture into the subject of money, for she had never heard of such a thing and, although we could have taught her the denomination of coins, we could not think how to explain the system to her, how to tell her that Europeans keep tiny discs which possess a value beyond themselves, for Bushmen have no tokens of exchange.

We told her what clothes people wore, both men and women, from the inside out, that she must clothe herself and cover her breasts always or be stared at, which is abhorrent to Bushmen, and then at last we tried to tell her what a city was, what it would look like, what buildings were made of and what they were.

At the end we told her to remember everything we said, for very few Europeans or Bantus can speak the Kung language. This was her last chance to learn. She would hereafter be unable to ask.

After that we took her to our tents and dressed her, stripping her as she had stripped her daughter and giving her a set of clothing put together from what we had. I gave her a dress which I had brought with me to wear if ever, in our travels, I should need one. It was cotton and required very little ironing; she could wash it at night and wear it dry and quite smooth in the morning. It fitted her and became her—it was pink and made her skin look gold. My mother gave her underclothes and a bright bathrobe which my mother found hastily in our bundle of cloth that we intended to give away as gifts, the bathrobe intended to be cut into pieces as scarves for children, for we ourselves had no need of bathrobes in the desert. Short Kwi's wife could wear it while the pink dress dried. We sent a set of clothing out to Short Kwi, robbing my father and brother, and last of all we quickly made a little red dress for the daughter from more of our gift cloth, fitting it on her as she stood there, for we heard the truck motor starting and knew that we had very little time. All this we did in less than two hours.

When we came out of the tent we found ourselves in the middle of a crowd of women crouched together in a mass. Tu and Dikai were at the front, nearest to us, for they had been looking under the tent flap to see what we were giving Short Kwi's wife and wondering, no doubt, if they would get the same. They glared at us when we came out, and Tu was yellow-eyed.

The truck was ready, Short Kwi was braced with grass and blankets comfortably on top. His wife tried uneasily to join him, her new skirt binding her legs badly, for the apron worn by Bushman women is supple and free, and falls between the legs when the woman is in motion. People boosted her; she finally got up, and reached out her arms to her daughter, who stood, a lonely baby, by the truck's great wheel, waiting to be seen, to be taken. Toma lifted the little girl and her mother caught her.

The motor had been running, and almost before we knew what had happened the truck had gone, had disappeared among the trees. The two, Short Kwi and his wife, had taken one last, desperate look at the veld, the werfs, and all the people, and their little girl had seemed frightened even though she was with her father and mother, though perhaps not nearly as frightened as she would be later when she was far away from Nama Pan in the streets of the city.

- - -

It was a very sad and heavy day the day that Short Kwi left. It depresses Bushmen terribly to see one of their number crippled, which, of course, in almost every case means the end of that person's productive life as a supporter of the people—one becomes a poor person and depends upon the enforced charity of one's near relatives while suffering avoidance by one's remoter kin; but it depresses Bushmen even more to see one of their number taken away. It is the end of a link in their unity, and when it happens part of the chain of their relationships, part of their pattern is destroyed. That day many people who surely expected never to see Short Kwi again stayed alone by their fires or played the guashi idly, but spoke not a word. The rest of the people, all but Toma, Gao Feet, and Lazy Kwi, were beset with jealousy and quarreled on and on all day, with us, with each other. They were jealous because we had given Short Kwi and his wife clothing and within the hour after Short Kwi's departure a crowd of people was squatting in the dust around our camp. The crowd was so thick that we could hardly get through. No one budged an inch to let us by, and when they would catch our eyes, the women, particularly those who had waited outside our tent when we had given Short Kwi's wife the clothes, pointed to holes and frayed spots in their karosses which clearly showed that they, too, needed clothing, and when we did nothing (we had presents of blankets, cloth, beads, shirts, pants, pipes, and knives to give to everyone when we left, but could not give dresses to all the women and could not give the presents now) they glared at us with stony faces and hard eyes.

In the afternoon the people were still there, quite dusty now but motionless; in the evening they began to get up, one by one, to go to the veld for food and firewood. Dikai had relented entirely. Before she went off to her evening's work she put her arm around me and told me that she and I were cemented together by our names. But Tu, who suffered from jealousy more than Dikai, was angry still and chose that moment to make a scene, to force someone to do something for her as well as for Short Kwi. She arose from the vigilant, crouching people and, followed at a distance by her baby daughter, went up to our cook, Philip, and demanded that he give her firewood. He refused because there were three dead trees right outside of camp that Tu could easily have got, in plain sight, not twenty feet away, but she did not look at these. Instead, she began to scream at Philip in a most bitter harangue, and though she became aware at last that everyone had fallen silent and was listening to her, she couldn't stop her tongue but went on and on until her entire audience was embarrassed and didn't know where to look. Worse, Philip lost his patience and told her to go away. She bit her lip, glaring, and suddenly there was perfect silence; her words had left her and she just had to stand there, too proud to leave, alone in the center of the crowd of crouching people watching, and she looked very silly and forlorn, robbed of her dignity by her tongue and with her hair ornaments askew on the back of her head. No one would speak to her; this time she had gone too far.

It was Norna, her daughter, who provided her with the chance to escape. Norna, frightened and bewildered and embarrassed too, had crept up beside Tu and had taken the string of her kaross. Tu must have felt a tug, for she looked down suddenly and, seeing this, turned on Norna, slapping the string out of Norna's hand. There was another agonizing pause and silence while Norna slowly took the string again, and again Tu slapped it away. This time Norna began to cry, lonely and forlorn in front of all the people, turned on by her mother, and she looked very small and defenseless and bereft; she cried sadly, not angrily, big tears running down her face, her fist in her mouth, looking up at her mother with enormous eyes. This was Tu's chance. She snatched up Norna and carried her back to the werf.

It was a terrible incident for everyone. That evening Tu still felt her shame and when I went to the werf to visit for a moment she took the occasion to fix me with her eyes all the way across the werf and tell me loudly that in the morning I would have to help her clear grass for another werf, for she was not going to "live among these people anymore." Tu's mother, a shameless old woman, came up to me to tell me a joke and Tu smoldered.

Not only the adults felt a sense of tension. That evening Dikai, looking rather worn and tired, was sitting by her fire rubbing her shoulders, which usually ached, she said, when her two sons, also tired, threw themselves down each on one side of her and began to nurse, each leaning heavily against her, each at a breast. Perhaps because she was tired or perhaps because she had been about to put some tsi nuts in her fire but now could not because her sons were in the way, she looked down at them and mildly suggested to Little Gashe that perhaps he could bring himself to stop nursing altogether, being old enough now. Little Gashe did not take this kindly at all. He looked up at her, then took his mouth from her nipple and cursed her with a formal, deadly curse. "May the spirit of Nisa, who is dead," he said, "take you by the throat and choke you." He then took the nipple back in his mouth and sucked on, thoughtfully.

I could hardly believe my ears. Children are expected not to curse their parents, but, worst of all, Little Gashe had invoked those supposedly unmentioned beings, the spirits of the dead. Dikai was not offended, though; she gazed down at him calmly. "You, you little thing," she said, "no curse that you could say would hurt me."

- - -

Much later in the evening when John and Dan and I were sitting at our own fire just before going to bed, Dikai and her nephew, Toma's son, came to visit us, Dikai with Little Dabe asleep on her back. It was a quiet evening, people were sitting at their own werfs and though they were screened from us by grass we could hear their voices talking and see the light of their fires. When Dikai came, Lazy Kwi, whose werf was on the other side of our camp, heard her speak and stood up to see what was happening, looming suddenly from where he had been sitting only a few feet away. He came through the grass to visit also, and we sat by the fire listening to Dikai as she told us about various relatives in the north and what kinship terms we should use for them, I being named for her and John for Toma. Lazy Kwi told Dan that Dan had been named for him, but named Kwi Cheeks instead of Lazy Kwi, and when Dan asked why his nickname was Cheeks all Lazy Kwi could say was: "Because of your cheeks." We thought, but we could not think of a reason, as there was nothing about Dan's cheeks that might attract attention, except that he had recently shaved his beard so that his cheeks were visible.

Dan said that now he had no beard, no hair, no name, which Lazy Kwi thought was terribly funny and said: "Throw away your beard hairs, throw away your name, but take Kwi instead and be my namesake." Shortly after that we went to bed. Relations seemed less strained.

- - -

One morning about a week after Short Kwi had gone, when the people were resting and the werf was quiet, we heard a rumble, a faint roaring in the veld, the sound blown to us on the wind. Toma must have heard it first, for he stood up from his nap and squinted his eyes at the veld. "A truck," he said. "Your truck. Not the farmers."

He was right; it was our truck. Soon we saw its top among the bushes; when it burst through the bushes at the edge of the pan the Bushman men ran to meet it and, as it did not stop, ran along beside it, craning their necks to look in the front and the back. Soon they dropped behind and walked slowly in its dust cloud. Short Kwi had not come.

The news of Short Kwi was good. At the hospital, his gangrenous flesh had been removed and enough of his calf was left so that a peg leg could be attached to it. A peg leg had been chosen instead of an artificial leg because, in the veld, an artificial leg would be impossible to repair or replace, but a peg leg could be replaced with the carved branch of any tree. It would be months before Short Kwi and his family could return to Nama because Short Kwi would have to learn to walk again, using the peg. When he was able to come, a truck from the government of South-West Africa would bring him.

We told all this to the Bushmen, but they were not really pleased. The miracle which they had perhaps expected had not taken place, for Short Kwi was still a cripple, and he always would be. They did not think of Tu's brother, the lame boy who would someday be a headman, who managed his lame leg and his crutch so well that he had hunted successfully and was initiated into manhood; they turned their sad faces away from the truck and went back to their scherms in silence.

- - -

The following morning, adding somewhat to the tension and unease, the rest of Short Kwi's band arrived. They looked very sleek and prosperous, for they were staggering under loads of food, their bags and nets bulging with tsi and their carrying-poles strung with the meat of the gemsbok. They put down their loads and the women began immediately to make a large and busy werf on the far side of Toma's. In a very short time the werf was built and strewn with food and objects, and the people sitting among their possessions looked so comfortable and settled that one would never have thought that they had just arrived.

The old woman, Short Kwi's mother-in-law, did cry when she found her daughter gone. She squatted sadly on the ground and wiped her tears from her wrinkled, dusty cheeks with her fingers. All her relatives clustered around her, trying to comfort her, telling her that, after all, her daughter would return, that she herself would be looked after and not allowed to starve, and presently the old woman stopped crying, wiped her eyes, and got up to build herself a tiny hut, a shade of grass and branches.

That night, when darkness fell, when the moon rose bloodred among the trees and the frogs in the pan began their singing, we were again sitting by our fire, again hosts to a good many visitors, when we heard high voices singing a medicine song. We stood up to look over the grass and saw a fire where no werf was, with five young girls around it singing, clapping a rhythm, their faces lit red by the fire and their backs lit palely by the moon. They were all alone there, far from their homes.

We asked our visitors if there was going to be a dance, which did not seem likely, everyone being in such low spirits, and those who wanted to dance said yes while those who didn't said no. Soon some little children joined the dance, though, among them Little Gashe and Little Dabe. Little Dabe was evidently being minded by his brother, for he arrived riding on Little Gashe's back, a heavy load, and Little Gashe carrying Little Dabe danced in a circle behind the young girls, then, perhaps getting tired, stopped dancing and shook Little Dabe off. When Little Dabe was standing Little Gashe climbed on Little Dabe's back to let Little Dabe do the dancing for a while. Soon these children were joined by some older boys and they all bobbed along happily, one behind the other, quite small and lit dimly in the big dance circle they were making for themselves.

The girls sang well. Their songs and the sharp rhythm of their clapping floated over the dark veld to us, mixed with the voices of the frogs. The frogs croaked so loudly by the pan, their croaking floated so clearly over the water, that for a while the girls just clapped their hands and let the frogs sing for them. The girls and the frogs kept time, and as the frog voices gradually faded the girls began to sing again themselves and presently, two or three at a time, our visitors went away from our fire to their scherms and later, a few at a time, appeared again at the dance fire with wood to burn or dance rattles to wear, some joining the singers and dancers, some others building small fires of their own in the veld a little apart from the dance fire. Before long, every werf was represented.

In the veld, where we were standing, the moonlight shone, making black shadows and pale, cool light. The air was still and warm and fragrant with the grasses of the veld and the voices came to us softly. At the fire the dancers wheeled slowly in their course around the circle, and the firelight shone in flickering beams through their stamping, naked legs, red on their naked backs. We could not see them plainly because they were far away, but we moved toward them and the singing got louder, we heard the low sound of stamping feet and the low singing of the men's voices, no longer obscured by the pure, high singing of the women, and when we were there we were inside the cloud of red, luminous dust, and the sounds of rattles and clapping rang in our ears.

More and more women joined the singing girls, each throwing some sticks on the dance fire as she came, then finding a place to squat in the circle, the others shuffling apart to make room, and soon the fire burned up brightly, lighting the dust stirred up by the dancers' feet and showing the huddled circle of women, who by now looked like a flock of birds crouched on the ground, they were so tightly crowded, their karosses like hunched, folded wings and their heads up alertly; the bright dance fire showed too the oval faces of the visitors, the smallest ones near the ground, the larger ones a little higher, and as more and more men appeared from the darkness to join the dance the dust cloud rose higher and thicker until it seemed to shine of itself, like a veil or an illusion, and you couldn't be sure if what you saw was there before you or reflected.

Within an hour everyone was there. It behooves one to go to a medicine dance because the spirits of the dead, waiting in the shadows around the dance fire and on their paths above the veld, might carry off a person if he stayed at home alone.

In the circle, one man was dancing with his child on his shoulder, and the child, naked and golden-skinned on the naked brown shoulder, looked gravely down. Other children were dancing. Little Dabe and Little Gashe among them, Little Gashe carrying Little Dabe again, going slower and slower because he was tired. At last Beautiful Ungka picked up both Little Gashe and his passenger, put them in her kaross, and carried them to their mother; in this way, one by one the dancing babies were eliminated and the circle was left to the men.

- - -

The dance went on all night, reaching a climax after midnight when the moon was high and sailing overhead. The medicine men were seized with trances that shook their bodies and rattled their teeth and sent them rushing head-long into the black shadows to curse at the spirits of the dead. Dust mounted, the sound of the high singing and the rattles was deafening, and even in the pauses between dances the medicine men screamed.

When hours had passed, when the moon was low and only its thick red glow showed on the horizon, the dance reached a lull and many people went home. Soon only a core of dancers and singers remained, perhaps twenty people in all. These were the strong young men, wiry enough to have withstood ten hours of dancing, and the old widows and middle-aged women, those who had no small children to worry them, women who were tougher than the young girls and did not mind that they felt tired. It is a strong thing to dance all night; it brings powerful, enduring medicine, and these few people, willing to withstand fatigue and cold, wore away the night to dance for the medicine of the rising sun.

When the moon was down and the dance fire had burned to embers, was almost out, I went to the veld to gather firewood. Just then the first stars began to dim in the soft, cold air, the eastern sky turned pale; faintly, the first birds began to cry, and from where I stood in the veld I heard the song change to the sun dance. The song lasted only for a moment, as the singers acknowledged the paleness, and a little later, as the light in the east became brighter and the colors of the veld began to show, the women sang the sun dance fully, a song quite different from the others, very even, very simple, steady, dignified, and grave.

The dawn wind lifted and blew away the smoke and dust and made the people shiver. The light showed the dancers moving stiffly, the singers hunched together for support and warmth, and revealed dusty, dirty faces and dirty teeth. Dust had made mud in the corners of our mouths and eyes.

Only about ten women were singing in the circle now and they sat all together at one spot, leaving a lot of space around the fire; only four men danced and they moved slowly in their track, burdened by their rattles. They, too, stayed close together so that most of their huge track was bare.

When the sun was over the horizon the dance stopped. The women ended their song abruptly, stood up, shook the dust and straw from their clothing, and walked away. They did not speak to one another because they were tired. The men talked for a moment as they sat down, stretched, untied their rattles, before walking off two by two toward their werfs. Soon all that remained was the dance track, a deep circular rut in the ground, the big heap of dead white ashes, and the dusty bushes and trees.

- - -

The people who had been dancing during the night slept all through the heat of the day and as the afternoon came, lying in the shade of trees and bushes. Flies buzzed over them, the afternoon shadows lengthened and the day cooled, and still they slept on.

When the light was red and the sun was almost setting, the women began to stir, getting to their feet slowly, and then alone or in twos and threes, followed by their children, walked down the path to the water, the last ones to leave hurrying because one of the little boys had found a millipede and was trotting behind them carrying it. Bushman women do not like millipedes; millipedes make them very nervous. Someone persuaded the child to drop it, which he did reluctantly. It was a giant, shiny black and a foot long, and it ran away with the front of its body in the air, its head bent like a curbed horse. The little boy watched it go.

The women walked through the acacia trees and reached the pan, the shining lake, red now with sunset, and even though the air was getting cool the children ran in the shallow water, splashing, the women crouched on the rocks to bathe. They took off their karosses and bathed their arms and legs and faces, washing all the dust away, then brushed their teeth with their fingers. Beautiful Ungka called for Little Dabe and hung her ornaments on him while she bathed. He ran through the water playing, splashing with the other children, quite unconscious of his gorgeous array. Beautiful Ungka was so supple that as she sat bathing she could lay her body down on the rocks between her raised knees, which she did to reach the water, saving herself the trouble of moving forward.

After they had bathed, the young girls made aloe circlets for their heads, red in the red light of the sky, and they seemed very innocent and beautiful, fresh and clean; they dressed themselves slowly as the sun went down, then walked into the water, where they danced, slowly, idly, kicking to make a rhythmic splash.

Little Dabe, on the shore now, found the rocks hard on his feet and began to wail, and all alone on top of the rocks, picking his feet up one after the other, he was like a peacock in his ornaments, with his complaining, raucous cry. Beautiful Ungka carried him then, although she too was barefoot, bouncing him up and down while the other women rinsed and filled their ostrich eggshells. The air was soft and fragrant with acacia and now the tiny, bright birds of the desert came out of the bushes where they had spent the day to fly over the pan and dip up water, and when it was almost dark the girls and women wandered home.

CHAPTER FIFTEEN

The
Medicine Bees

THE DAY AFTER the dance was the day before we left Nama to return to the United States. In all the time that we had stayed at Nama we had not been to Gautscha Pan, and now Toma said he wanted to go there to gather honey from the Gautscha baobab tree. Before we left, he sat in his werf telling me stories of people who thought that they could climb baobab trees but whose self-confidence had been excessive, because they had fallen, each and every one.

Steinbok Gumtsa was one of these, said Toma, and he was an excellent climber. Baobabs that others could not climb he managed, and ate honey from the upper branches every time. One day, while watching bees fly about the top of the very high baobab at Gautscha Pan, Steinbok Gumtsa thought to bring himself luck and said: "I am going to climb, but I will slip and fall and be killed." The others told him not to try it, but he did. "He thought he was too good," said Toma, "and that is why he did fall. The others found him dead at the bottom."

One-eyed Nishi was another good climber. He also tried to reach the honey at the top of the Gautscha baobab, but he slipped and fell and the other Bushmen found him dead at the bottom too, "with his head driven down between his shoulders," said Toma laconically, hunching his own neck to show how it was.

A third man whom Toma did not name climbed for honey in the Gura baobab, a tree somewhat north of Gautscha Pan, and he also fell; but, happily, he survived his experience. His sister and her husband were below him, watching, and when they saw him fall they held out their arms to catch him. He fell through their arms, of course, but his fall was broken and though he was unconscious for a long time he finally did recover.

The moral of these stories, Toma said, was to show that young people should listen to older people and not act rashly. I believe that he thought I was going to try to climb the Gautscha baobab (which I had already done, though only to the lowest branch, fifteen feet from the ground), for he went on to say: "When Bushmen tell young people not to climb baobab trees they should listen. It is seldom that a person lives who falls from a baobab tree, they are so high. Even those good climbers I told you about, they all fell." I assured him that I did not even want to climb it and he said: "Good. When we who are experienced get the honey you can watch from below. Then you can see just as well."

The Gautscha baobab was somewhat east of the pan, and we could see it rising from the plain when we were almost a mile away from it. It loomed up at the horizon, towering, its mass of upper branches hazy because we were so far. As we moved toward it, it seemed to move away from us like a distant mountain, but gradually, after a long time, it began slowly to get larger, looming higher, its top branches reaching up to the sky, where the clouds of spring were already forming as the desert got ready for the rains, three months away.

It was noon when we reached the tree; we broke through the bushes that surrounded it and came into its clearing, a circle thirty yards across of stony, barren ground from which the long roots had sucked the nourishment, and in the middle of the circle the great tree rose, pink-skinned and mighty, the claimer of two lives, twenty feet in diameter and almost two hundred feet high. Its lower branches were heavy and enormous, but the branches got smaller toward the top, the upper ones very thin, crisscrossing each other like lace. On the eastern face of the tree there were no branches; the pink trunk towered up and up, smooth and bare. On this side was an ascending row of pegs driven in by Bushmen long ago who had been after honey, used in later years by Bushmen hunters trying to rob the hives again or to scan the countryside for game. The pegs led from the ground around the trunk to the lowest branch, then up the trunk again to the next branch, ending finally at the top of the great tree, almost out of sight.

I knew this old tree very well, for during the year that we had lived at Gautscha we had camped beside it. It had been the home of many creatures then; and now the eastern face of the tree, the great bare slab rising like pink stone, was pocked with little holes. Some of them were empty, surely, but some had tufts of dry grass showing in the openings, little creatures' nests, and here and there, between the roots or in the forks of branches, were the caves of larger animals.

Bees had lived in a hole among the branches halfway up, though Toma said the bees had now moved higher; a mongoose had lived in a little cave between the roots on the south side, though now the mongoose was dead, snared and killed by Toma's son; a python that had lived in a hole on the north side was also dead, killed and eaten by an old Bushman woman we had known; but a colony of green-furred squirrels that had lived on the lowest branches, we saw, were still there. Bushmen do not eat squirrels because squirrels have no meat on their bones. Birds of all kinds lived in the great tree too, and there was a hawk's nest in the upper branches; I once had seen the two gray hawks that built it, but now they too were gone.

It was the bees that interested the Bushmen, though, and those of us who had come from Nama—Toma, Gao Feet, Crooked Kwi, Lazy Kwi, my brother, and I—sat among the rocks at the foot of the tree, the men planning what they would do. I was so tired from having been awake all night to watch the dance that I lay down on the stones and fell asleep, and when I awoke, in an hour or so, the men had built a fire but were still arguing about who would brave getting stung to find the honey. No one really wanted to do it; but I saw that Crooked Kwi was almost persuaded, being very amenable and the youngest person there. Sure enough, taking a smoldering brand in his teeth, he at last began to climb the pegs, clinging to them with his fingers and toes. Toma followed at a distance, cautiously, urging Crooked Kwi on, and the two climbed higher slowly, Crooked Kwi looking down from time to time to be encouraged. When he did, Gao Feet and Lazy Kwi would shout for him to continue. At last Crooked Kwi reached the branch beside the hive and squatted there, blowing on his brand to make it smoke while Toma climbed past him, around to another branch, where he, too, squatted with his feet apart and his hands on his knees exactly as though his feet were on the ground, the branch was so wide.

Crooked Kwi found the hole, a small opening, though even from the ground we could see a few bees humming idly outside, and blew the smoke from his brand into it, then, encouraged by Toma, reached his slender arm inside to find a honeycomb. He was stung, of course, and snapped his arm out instantly, though even then the bees were not angry, none came out of the hole. From the ground below, Gao Feet called up to ask why Toma himself didn't try to reach the honey and Toma said: "No! I might get stung!" then went on talking loudly to encourage Crooked Kwi. But when Crooked Kwi tried to smoke the bees again he must have blown in too much smoke or perhaps a spark which set the hive on fire, for clouds of smoke and many bees poured out of the hole and dead bees began to drop to the ground like rain. It made me sad to see them lying there, furry yellow, covering the ground.

It is dangerous and bad to kill bees, and we paid for it. Crooked Kwi, slapping at the bees that stung him, climbed down as fast as he was able. He jumped the last few feet and, pushing through the people watching, ran out among the bushes, trying to elude the bees that followed him in a swarm shaped just like a cornucopia, the small end at the nape of Crooked Kwi's neck. No bees stung the rest of us, not even Toma, who was still clambering down. When Toma reached the ground he said that Crooked Kwi was no good because he had failed.

Thus Crooked Kwi paid for his crime, though the rest of us paid for it later. A few miles farther to the north, at Gura Pan, another baobab was growing. We could see the top of it from Gautscha and Toma said that we would try now to get honey there. When Crooked Kwi came back, rather embarrassed, we went on toward Gura, and even when we were far away from Gautscha we could still hear the bees that Crooked Kwi had angered moaning, a loud but sleepy sound. One of them must have followed us, for it stung my knee.

The Gura baobab was very tall, though not as wide as the baobab at Gautscha. The southern face of it had been charred by a veld fire and was also bristling with pegs, old ones, new ones, in trails or little pathways up its side, as Bushmen had been robbing its hives of honey for years. Gao Feet said that its hives were raided every few months or so and wondered if there would be any honey left for us. While pondering this question we stopped at the base of the tree and looked up, high above us, at a crack in its trunk where bees were flying, and in a moment, to my great surprise, the whole hive of them had poured down over our heads and were stinging us badly. We dropped everything that we carried and ran as fast as we could into the bushes, slapping wildly at ourselves, scattering in every direction, and each of us, as we reached thick bushes, hid in the branches, only to be routed out again by someone else pursued by bees, and in this way we were scattered further. Far from the hive though we were, the air around us was full of bees; they kept us hiding and cowering like jackals, peering out from under bushes, away from our water jars and ostrich eggs, which we had dropped in our hurry, and they held us in this way for hours. We were tired and wanted to go home, but we could not leave our water. I, at least, was astonished that such a thing should have happened, but to the Bushmen it was no surprise. The bees, those magic, medicine creatures, were having their revenge. As a group, we were responsible for having killed the bees of another hive. The Bushmen were only surprised at themselves for not having foreseen the disaster.

In the middle of the afternoon my brother borrowed everybody's clothing and, swathing himself in it while the lenders crouched naked in the bushes, braved the swarm and retrieved our water. Then we went back toward Gautscha, pausing on the way to dig a water root which Lazy Kwi had known was there. The root was quite large, very wet, and though it was as puckery as alum it did quench thirst.

Late afternoon had come now, and I was so tired that I sat down to lean against a bush, where I almost fell asleep. Toma pointed to me and said: "Look at Dikai. She wants to go home. Let's go home." And so we did, and as evening came we went by Gautscha Pan.

We had not seen it before; we had been in the bushes on its eastern side when we had looked for honey, but now, as we emerged from the bushes, we found ourselves on its farther, eastern rim.

Great Gautscha Pan was full of water, shining gray water. Smoke overcast the evening sky all around the horizon and high into the air, and all we could see was the great stretch of gray water with yellow grass like islands in it and flocks of small black ducks breaking its surface, and yellow grass all around. The line of bush on the horizon was gray-green near us where we stood on the rock slide at the eastern rim, touched with yellow spots, acacia trees with their soft, pale-yellow fuzzy flowers round as balls, looking like clouds, like dreams, pretty and fresh with a sweet fragrance, and as the bush went around the pan the haze dimmed it, giving it the subtlest colors and a wild, still look like trees before a storm. Among the bushes to the north of us rose the two visible baobab tops, eerie and far away, and in the water the yellow grass was reflected upside down.

There it was, Toma's great country, magnificent and solitary, for no one lived there now, no person, no animal, except the black wild ducks that swam on the water, some near, some far away, in lines of three or four, in pairs, moving gradually in their even, deliberate processions as though they were being drawn slowly over the water by hidden streams.

The sun was sinking; high above the horizon it was deep red, a perfect circle, almost hidden by the haze and reflected by a red path in the water, and as it sank into haze that grew thicker and thicker the sun got paler and more obscured until it vanished long before it set.

That was beautiful, the sun, and there was no sound as it went down except the sound of doves calling among the trees on the far bank, whirring, cooing, a call that was pulsing and thick, urgent, throbbing, rising in intensity as the sun got dimmer, reaching a peak as the sun disappeared. It was as though they had brought it down, and when it was gone there was no sound at all; the silence was complete.

Gautscha Pan was more than a mile square and we, Europeans and Bushmen alike, held our breath with the majesty of it, its great solitude, the great drama of sunset going on reflected in its water for no eyes to look at; and when the sun was down and the colors of the veld were dull and dark we started home, but that was an impressive last look at a place and the last I ever saw of Gautscha Pan.

- - -

In the morning our trucks were packed and ready. We were not happy to leave and the Bushmen were not happy to have us go. We gave them presents of all kinds, presents of pipes, of knives, of beads, of clothing, of cornmeal and tobacco, and all this pleased them, but Dikai cried when we said good-bye and asked me if I would ever come back. I said that I hoped so and she kissed me and I felt wet tears on her face.

The people who had come from Gam wanted to ride a little way back with us to a mangetti forest, and we were glad to have them, but the others, Toma and his band, Gao Feet and his family, wanted to return to the tsi fields where we had found them, the veld food at Nama being almost gone, and before we left they had their bundles packed and were ready to go; as our trucks moved away they waved good-bye and before we were out of sight we looked back and saw their small groups going in every direction, scattering to the four winds. When we reached the mangetti forest the others climbed down, helping the children; Lazy Kwi and his wife were with them and they stood by the truck until we left and even then, when we had driven on, they were still looking at us and Lazy Kwi watched us out of sight. I saw him standing among the thorn trees, smaller and smaller in the distance, and just before he disappeared he waved.

- - -

That evening we camped beside an omaramba where the air was warm and pale, lit by the three-quarter moon; the wind made the dry leaves of a mangetti tree over our heads tap together and before we went to sleep we heard a leopard coughing far away, then growling nearer, a rattle, a rumble of a growl. In the morning we got up long before dawn because of a veld fire that someone had seen coming toward us; it made a huge red light in the black sky, like the open doors of an inferno, but as the dawn winds lifted, it blew back on itself and went out. The sky slowly got gray, then pale rose, and then, hundreds of miles away, the great sun lifted from the veld's horizon and with the light we found the leopard's footprints which he had left as he had walked around us, in two great circles, as though he had cast a spell.

EPILOGUE:

The Bushmen in 1989

THIRTY YEARS AFTER the publication of this book and forty years after our family began to record what we could about the ways of two groups of Kalahari hunter-gatherers, I offer an epilogue as a brief description of the profound changes that have come and of the people's struggles to survive. The epilogue is dedicated to the memories of Ukwane, who died in 1955, and of Toma, who died in 1988. It is also dedicated to John Marshall, Tsamko, Claire Ritchie, and Megan Biesele, all of the Ju/wa Development Foundation.

- - -

Before proceeding, I should say a few things about the book itself, about spelling and terms in particular. On the occasion of its republication I was offered a chance to make changes. I might have added clicks, for instance, to make the spelling look more official. But I don't believe the click symbols would really help the general reader, for whom this book is intended. In any event, even today there is no standardized spelling of Bushman words, and in any publication about Bushmen, the spelling is never more than vaguely phonetic at the very best, so except for use of the spelling *Ju/wa* in the epilogue replacing the original *Zhu twa*, the original spelling used in this book has been kept. *Zhu* (meaning "person") follows the International Phonetic Alphabet; *Ju* follows the spelling used in the numerous publications of my mother, Lorna Marshall.

I have identified two mistakes since I wrote the book (although there may be others): the birds I call "doves," which in the evening crowd at water's edge, are really sand grouse, and my beloved "huge pink hunting-spiders" are really solifuges, sun-spiders or wind-spiders, not true spiders at all but a subclass of arachnids like the scorpions.

Still with us is the problem of what to call people who neither perceive nor name themselves collectively. Such people are the Bushmen, who perceive their many groups as different and distinct. Not so the outside world, which by and large ignores the differences. Hence the English "Bushmen," the Afrikaans "Bojesman," the Bantu "Masawara," the Arabic "Wakwak," and the Nama "San" are all collective terms. Unfortunately, all are more or less pejorative. "San" is what the Nama, who own livestock, call poor people who own no animals but instead live like animals, eating wild food rather than agricultural produce or food bought in a store. Whites can be "san," if they fall so low. (Mathias Guenther, in Biesele, 1987)

Ironically, nowadays not only the Nama but also a number of academics call the Bushmen "San." "San" is thought in certain academic circles to be more dignified than the English "Bushmen." In the 1970s some well-meaning anthropologists known as "the Harvard group" adopted the term to avoid the pejorative which they felt in "Bushmen." Why they chose to replace one pejorative with another is unclear. They seem to have followed the lead of the British anthropologist I. Schapera, who used "Khoi" for the Nama (once called pejoratively "Hottentot") and "San" for the Bushmen when he invented the name "Khoisan" to describe collectively the Nama and the many groups of Bushmen. "Khoikhoi" is the Nama people's name for themselves, although to the outside world they call themselves by the name of the main dialect of their language, Nama. Obviously, Schapera took both "Khoi" and "San" from Nama vocabulary.

On top of the San/Bushman dilemma is the fact that the latter excludes women. To remedy this, attempts are sometimes made to introduce the term "Bushpeople." But "Bushpeople" probably will not take hold, or not for a while. Unless the term "bush" is frozen into idiom (Bushman, bushmaster), it has in English-speaking Africa a derogatory quality all its own.

Although in the United States "San" is finding its way into use, "Bushpeople" is not. In rural South Africa, in South-West Africa/Namibia and in Botswana, both terms are unknown or unacceptable. The Bushmen I know don't call themselves San and, unless they change their minds, neither will I, because in Namibia and Botswana the Nama speakers surely outnumber the English speakers. Meanwhile, the pejorative of "Bushman" and even its more often heard Afrikaans form "Bojesman" is, I believe, going or gone. According to the anthropologist Mathias Guenther, in the Gambia district of Botswana the appellation "Bushman" is "the distinct and stated preference" of the Bushman people, and in Namibia, when I last visited in 1987, I felt that people used the name with pride.

Interestingly enough, I noticed this because of cattle. By 1986, the Gautscha people owned a herd. Surrounded as they were by ranchers—Herero, Kavango, and Afrikaner—the Gaustcha people strongly felt the stigma of eating wild food, of owning no livestock (of being San, so to speak), and were pleased to have become ranchers themselves, running about sixty head including a magnificent, slow-moving bull, the biggest thing in the landscape except the baobab tree, a bull with half-shut eyes whose testicles hung to his hocks, a bull who had fought off a lion but who still bore the claw marks on his shoulders. This bull's owner had named him Bushman.

- - -

The fate of the group of Gikwe Bushmen in Botswana (then the Bechuanaland Protectorate) shows what has already happened to many southern African Bushmen and what, for others, may be still to come. When we met Ukwane in 1955, he and his people were staying in the southeastern part of the area that had been traditionally theirs to use. The area, as described herein, was dangerously dry. Each year in September and October Ukwane's group would travel northwest to the Ghanzi area of Botswana to their traditional permanent waterhole. By the time we visited in 1955, the land around this waterhole had become part of a white person's farm. Perhaps because in those days the white farmer did not intrude much upon their lives, Ukwane's people did not mention his existence, and we didn't know to ask. But in fact, although neither they nor us perceived it, they were already locked into the situation that quickly brought about their destruction.

Before World War II, the white farmers who had settled at Ghanzi allowed the Bushmen of the area to continue their old way of life. The farmers, frontiersmen all, rather enjoyed the Bushmen and liked hunting with them. Some men married a Bushman woman. Some men married two Bushman women.

After World War II, many white South African farmers came to the Ghanzi area from the Republic, bringing strong attitudes about commercial ranching and apartheid. They replaced the natural waterholes with covered boreholes and denied Bushmen the use of the pumps. Their commercial attitude was almost identical to the attitude most people of all nations display toward animals. Displacing an animal hardly merits anyone's slightest consideration; the idea that the food and water of an animal are features of specific places where there are springs or streams, where edible plants grow, is extremely far from the thinking of most people. Just so with the South African farmers, who thought Bushmen could and would simply move off to another part of the bush. The farmers who evicted the Bushmen didn't know or didn't care that some parts of the bush grow only grass and thornbush (although they knew well that most parts are waterless).

Denied their former sources of dry-season water, many Bushmen used a central source of water in the middle of the Ghanzi farm area—the Ghanzi Commons—but the area lacked food, so while there they more or less starved. What food they got came from begging, from dancing for tourists in front of the Kalahari Arms Hotel, from selling small artifacts.

As far as my brother, John Marshall, could learn when he visited in 1972, Ukwane's people at first were an exception. The farmer who owned their old dry-season area had allowed them to stay, living as always. In 1955 Ukwane's people postponed traveling to that farm. This in itself was dangerous, since the year was a dry one and water on the journey became a problem. On the way they found almost none. Ukwane died of thirst.

When the rest of the people reached the farm, as far as John could determine, they found a new farmer in residence. The new farmer wouldn't let them stay, so they, too, were forced to the Ghanzi Commons. There, Kutera and Dasina died of starvation. Gai, the young man, got a job on another farm where his wife, Tsechwe, was raped by a Tswana man with syphilis—Tsechwe got syphilis and Gai got it too. The farmer didn't take them to the doctor in Ghanzi for antibiotic treatment (of which Gai and his wife knew nothing). In time, Tsechwe died. Their little boy, Nhwakwe, died too. Gai became more and more ill until he was too ill to work but clung to life because the other workers fed him the scrapings of their three-legged iron pots. In 1972 that was how John found him.

John was in Botswana making a film envisioned, in part, as a sequel to his earlier film of Ukwane's people shot in 1955, a film called *Bitter Melons*. John had brought a copy of *Bitter Melons* with him, and also a screen and a projector, as he had planned to show the film to the people who were in it. One evening on the farm, John set up his screen in the veld to show the film to Gai, who sat on his heels in the grass beside the stand of the projector. The farmer brought out a table and chair and a bottle of beer and sat down to watch the film too. Gai had never seen a film. John told him more or less what to expect and sat on his heels beside him.

The film started. It shows how all the people of Ukwane's group lived in the far reaches of the Kalahari, and shows Ukwane playing the guashi and singing the mood song which is the film's title. There was Tsechwe again, young and beautiful, and little Nhwakwe, and all the other people living together in the old times. There was Gai himself, with his fine, healthy body. There was Ukwane singing the old songs. Taken off guard, Gai was overcome. He caught John's hand and began crying. John and Gai held each other's hands and both wept while the film ran.

John later brought Gai to Maun for medical treatment and arranged for his prolonged care until he was well. Later still, after a search, John found Giamakwe, Ukwane's son. Giamakwe, then in his twenties, was trying to get work from another farmer, and appealed for John's help in persuading the farmer to hire him. John succeeded in getting the farmer to at least give Giamakwe a little training in driving a tractor. In the process, John asked Giamakwe if he remembered his father's music. Giamakwe seemed puzzled. "What music?" he asked.

- - -

Unfortunately, popular fantasies and notions sometimes hold that the Bushmen still live in a precontact, pristine manner. In the mid-1980s the fantasies were inflamed by a fanciful film called *The Gods Must Be Crazy*, and by statements of the producer, Jamie Uys, who claimed to the press that the Bushmen he filmed actually live in the precontact manner the film presents and that some had never seen whites. But, in fact, his film was made at or near Tsumkwe, once a baobab tree about twenty-seven kilometers northwest of Gautscha, but, by the time Uys reached it, an army post and the government center of Bushmanland in Namibia/ South-West Africa. The male lead in the Uys film was played by a young man whom we knew quite well, and the female lead was none other than the daughter of Dikai, a woman named Nai whom we have known since her childhood, very well.

John by then was also at this Namibian outpost making a film about Nai's life for PBS. In his film, *!Nai, the Story of a !Kung Woman*, he shows the South African camera crew shooting a scene for the Uys film. It's a strange little scene—

in it a man walks down a path to a hut. Like any suburbanite, the man is coming "home" to his "house" in the evening. There's only one "house" present, and the man's family, awaiting him, is grouped in front. His lone child runs up the path to meet him. This scene the Uys crew shoots over and over. Patiently, the Bushmen redo it.

There is a strange truth to the scene, a truth the film crew never intended. The nuclear family is not a hunter-gatherer institution, the little home, suburban-style, at the end of a walkway is not a hunter-gatherer residence, and the acts of leaving home in the morning and returning to the waiting family in the late afternoon are not part of a hunter-gatherer's day. Yet the suburban vision of Western culture which the film crew unwittingly laminates over Bushman life is poignant, because in truth, no Bushmen today are out of reach of it. As the film unwittingly twists their image, the world beyond theirs blindly twists their lives. The concept of Bushmen in a faraway wilderness, pleasant as we may find it, is simply and perniciously untrue. No Bushmen lack contact with the West and none is undamaged by it. And their own way of life, the old way, a way of life which preceded the human species, no longer exists but is gone from the face of the earth at enormous cost to the individuals who once lived it.

- - -

Although most of the people we knew in Botswana are dead or scattered, our family has been able to keep in touch with the people we knew in Namibia. My parents, Lorna and Laurence Marshall, visited the Nyae Nyae area of the Kalahari throughout the 1960s. My brother John (who speaks Kung fluently) visited Nyae Nyae during the late 1970s and 1980s with his colleague Claire Ritchie in part to make films and in part to study and to try to reverse an alarming decline in Namibia's Bushman population. From them, from John Payne and Ann Edwards, from Megan

Biesele (so fluent in Kung as to be nearly bilingual), from Robert Gordon, and from my own visits to Bushmanland in 1986 and 1987, I have gathered the data for this portion of the epilogue.

- - -

In 1959, foreseeing that the farming and ranching areas on all sides of the Kalahari would encroach on the center and deprive the Bushmen of their land, and foreseeing that certain white farmers (known as "blackbirders") would persist in capturing Bushmen as slaves, Mr. Claude McIntyre, an officer in South-West Africa's Administration of Native Affairs, established a government presence in the central Kalahari. He chose Tsumkwe. Mr. McIntyre believed that, faced with the loss of land, the best preparation Bushmen could have for the future was some education and a knowledge of subsistence farming. Subsistence farming, if practiced under the right conditions and in the right way, allows a more intensive use of land than does hunting and gathering. When subsistence farming succeeds, more people can live in less space.

McIntyre's idea met opposition from both sides of the political spectrum. On one side were people like myself, mostly foreigners, who felt that all Bushmen who so chose should be left alone to continue their ancient life-style unmolested. On the other side were South-West African farmers and ranchers, both white and black, who by coincidence agreed—despite their own racial hatreds and differences—that hunting and gathering made poor use of land and labor, both of which should be made available for commercial exploitation. The farmers and ranchers were more numerous than the foreigners and, of course, the white farmers voted. It was they whom McIntyre was trying to circumvent.

McIntyre went into the Kalahari to broach his idea to the Bushmen. "When McIntyre first came," Toma recalled, "he found us at Gura in the winter. He said he was going to make a settlement at Tsumkwe and we should come and help him. He said he was going to teach us new things like gardening and raising goats, so we could live in one place. He said our children would go to school and someday he would bring us cattle.

"At first we didn't want to go. But we talked about it and decided it was a better life for us and we would learn to live like other people. So we came to Tsumkwe in the hot season, before the rains." (Marshall and Ritchie, 1984)

McIntyre then left his home and his friends in Windhoek and took his family out to Tsumkwe to live for the next ten years. Thus Tsumkwe was established by McIntyre and his family together with Toma and his people—it so happened—on Christmas Day, 1959.

McIntyre's plan was long-range, to say the least. He introduced wage-work with nine people employed at the unskilled level to build a road and dig postholes. McIntyre taught two of the nine people how to drive a tractor. The rest of the participants of the Tsumkwe experiment were taught how to plant gardens and herd goats (purchased through McIntyre in exchange for cutting fencepoles—so many poles for a goat). People continued to hunt and gather in order to supplement the rather meager produce from their farming. To accommodate their groups to the new way of life, the groups would divide, some remaining at Tsumkwe to mind the planting and the goats, and some venturing far into the Kalahari for the old food staples of mangetti nuts, marula nuts, and the ground-nut, tsi.

People found that not all their old customs blended well with the new economy. Many families with gardens and goats became discouraged because their kinsmen came to Tsumkwe from afar, expecting the Tsumkwe people to share even though the newcomers hadn't contributed anything toward the gardens or goats. To some at Tsumkwe, it seemed that all a person got for his hard work was a group of hostile, jealous relatives to take everything away. Some gave up the experiment and went back to hunting and gathering. Others, perhaps more diplomatic or with fewer relatives, persisted in spite of jealous visitors.

Toma and the people with him managed to persevere. Their perseverance was possible partly because their entire group came to Tsumkwe together. If Toma had established himself with a garden and goats while his brother-in-law Gao Feet had stayed in the veld, Toma might not have been able to refuse to kill his goats for Gao Feet later. As it was, the families of these two men took part in the experiment together.

In 1970, just as McIntyre had foreseen, the 45,000 square kilometers of Nyae Nyae in South-West Africa/Namibia was carved into three parts. In each part was one of Nyae Nyae's three permanent waterholes, Gam in the south, Gautscha in the middle, and Tsho/ana in the north. Around these waterholes, the Bushman population of about 1,200 had been distributed.

The southern waterhole at Gam was given to Hereroland. The northern waterhole at Tsho/ana was given to Kavangoland. The middle waterhole at Gautscha remained to the Bushmen and became designated as Bushmanland, to whose potential population then were added the 27,000 people from all over the country whom the government had meanwhile classified as Bushmen. In reality, only 6,000 square kilometers in the eastern portion of the Gautscha area, the new Bushmanland, had ever been habitable. Only here were there food plants and water. With the new plan, the proposed population density increased from one person on 37.5 square kilometers to five people on one square kilometer, or, in other words, if all people classed as Bushmen had gone to live there, the density would have been two hundred times greater than before. In any case, the addition of the northern and southern populations to the central population was so great as to finish hunting and gathering. The environmental conditions necessary to support the old economy were gone.

McIntyre's seriously failing health eventually forced him to leave Tsumkwe. His successor abolished the policy of helping the Bushmen to help themselves and instead put as many of them as possible into his labor force, to build houses for the administrators of Tsumkwe and to work on the roads.

The number of people employed in menial wage-work jumped from McIntyre's original nine in 1967 to eighty-five by 1972, accounting for most of Tsumkwe's able-bodied men. These men had to stay at their jobs and couldn't spend the long periods of time necessary to obtain food in quantity. This created difficulty, since the wage structure was based on Western economic standards, with each unskilled wage-worker on the starting-level pay deemed suitable for black workers, barely enough money for a man to feed himself, not enough to nourish his dependents. As the division of Nyae Nyae had taken away the land for hunting and gathering, large-scale wage-work took away the personnel.

The government didn't employ women. In the old economy the women had contributed a much greater share to the daily diet than the men. But without McIntyre's transitional policy of encouraging groups to divide, some traveling to obtain faraway staple foods while others stayed working for wages, the women—who never take long trips without men—soon picked clean the veld around Tsumkwe. Without food to gather or jobs to earn pay, the women as well as the children, the old, and the disabled became dependent on the pitiful wages of the men.

As the money economy displaced the old hunter-gatherer economy, it displaced the social usefulness of nearly everybody. By hunting, the men had once provided much-needed, highly valued protein food as well as the other animal products used for implements and clothing. By wage-work, the men provided a few coins which bought nothing in adequate amounts. By gathering, the women had often provided all the food for everybody, and at least had provided for themselves and their children. In the new economy, they provided nothing. The old people once had minded the children and made the clothing. In the new economy these services weren't needed. The old people also were the repository of information that might sometime serve the young. This stored information is hard for literate people to imagine, and its use is seldom witnessed. Nevertheless, it is there and can be lifesaving. For example, if serious weather conditions occur every fifty years or so, only the old people will remember the last occurrence and the tricks which were used to survive it. In fact, while I was there I saw a man in his forties make an error in tracking which his father, alive but not present, would have readily corrected. But in the new economy not even the old memories were useful, since they did not apply to the new way of life. The old people became burdensome. The number of old people in the population has dwindled as seriously as the number of small children.

Even non-Bushmen began to notice that the old and the young were dying. After putting up a small clinic, the administration tended to attribute the death rate to an unwillingness of the Bushmen to seek treatment. Because Bushmen who came for medication were shouted at and otherwise treated rudely, the administrative reason was partly true. But also the clinic made little effort at outreach—over time a woman who lived within sight of the clinic lost both feet to leprosy.

In fact, the administration didn't much care why so many died. And the Bushmen didn't know why. But after a few years of living in the government's housing project of tin-roofed, one-room, concrete huts, damp, crowded, and without sanitation, they were getting the diseases of over-crowding and poverty—tuberculosis, typhoid, meningitis, measles, venereal diseases, and many others—with tuber-culosis and the various kinds of diarrhea being the most pernicious and destructive, especially to small children.

And the diet was poor. The old diet of wild foods had been nutritious enough to sustain our ancestors for three million years. Not so the diet of posho or mealie-meal, the cornmeal porridge which eventually became part of or pur-chased by the workers' pay. This, the food ration generally provided for Africans by white employers, the staple for millions of poor people throughout southern Africa, pro-vides bulk but if used alone is nutritionally defective and can ultimately produce the disease called kwashiorkor. More immediately, in small children it can be an irritant which causes diarrhea, the primary cause of infant mortality. For many old people, it can be indigestible, creating bloody, cornmeal stools.

Shortly after McIntyre left, a store was established in Tsumkwe. It sold, along with cheap clothing and cornmeal (by then necessities to Bushmen), canned meat, canned fruit, canned vegetables, jam, coffee, tea, sugar, candy, soft drinks, flashlights, batteries, notions, ballpoint pens, tape recordings, tape players, plastic shoes, plastic jewelry, and gasoline. Of necessity, the storekeeper bought these items in fairly small quantities and had them trucked in from far away (about six hundred miles). This made them very costly.

But by now, people would pay his prices. For one thing, they had only store-bought food to eat. They had never really put their trust in their own beginners' efforts at gar-dening, so thornbush had taken over their old garden plots. Jealous relatives had long since eaten the goats. There was no veld food, not even a veld, just a vast expanse of thorns and dust as far as one could see. For another thing, many Bushmen were now ashamed to eat veld food (if any could be found). The stigmata of eating food taken off the ground, of picking food up out of the dirt, of having to go searching for food in wild places like an animal, of having no supply of food, no firm idea where a meal would come from, were by now deeply felt by the Bushmen, and were why many people (themselves included) didn't use the term "San." They were why Bushman people willingly bought expensive store food as well as transistor radios, ghetto blasters, ballpoint pens. To own such items, as the rest of us demonstrate so abundantly, was to rise in Western civilization—from the lowest, meanest edge where the Bushmen by then clung.

The picture of Tsumkwe would not be complete without a fundamentalist Christian church to decry the depravity—the drinking and fighting—and sure enough, Christianity came with its optimistic message that the Higher Powers of the white people care about the goings-on. If only because the sermons were in Afrikaans, Bushmen didn't rush to conversion.

Instead, some relief came for some people in 1978 when the army of the Republic of South Africa established a presence at Tsumkwe to combat SWAPO guerrillas based in Angola. Sometimes seen as part of the political left in the RSA (as opposed to the police of the political right), the army is racially integrated (to the rank of lieutenant colonel at the time of this writing). All white South African men are drafted for two years of national service, usually as soldiers in the army. Most of the soldiers, however, are professional black volunteers. Pay is determined by rank, not race. The pay of the lowest-ranking soldier was extremely high by Tsumkwe standards, in 1982 about $300 per month plus housing, food, clothing, comprehensive medical care, and education for the soldier and his dependents, many times greater than the approximately $100 per month without benefits which the administration paid. When the army came to Tsumkwe, some Bushman men enlisted.

So the army brought prosperity to some. These people owned ghetto blasters and good clothes. They bought candy, coffee, and even old junk cars which some used-car dealers in Namibia, sensing the potentially rich market, trucked to Tsumkwe to sell for high prices to those who couldn't drive them. Meanwhile, people who had no jobs begged to keep from starving.

That the tremendous need for sharing was often unmet gave people more cause than ever for jealousy and anger. Such stresses weakened their means of dealing with social tensions, for maintaining smooth human relationships.

Perhaps not surprisingly, yet dealing a final blow to the loss of control over social tensions, people stopped the *n/um chai*, or medicine dancing. The great dances discussed in this book, the dances through which people were able to rid themselves of "star sickness," which I believe is the stress that arises from bad feeling, anger, jealousy, and anxiety, are danced no more. Why not? Nobody seemed to know. Perhaps, like veld food, the old way of dancing was stigmatized. "The women won't sing the songs" was the only explanation anyone would offer.

A few years after opening the store, the storekeeper obtained a liquor license and, with the aid of a government loan to small businesses, he added hard liquor to his stock. It was an instant success—the store became a gold mine. Claire Ritchie, in a study of the store's profitability, found that after an army payday 102 Bushman customers spent R 715 in four and a half hours (in those days about $900).

Although they bought it and drank it, the Bushmen had had no previous experience with this addictive substance which chemically produces anger and anxiety. Like most of the rest of us, they took little notice but instead consumed alcohol readily, especially after they found that it temporarily relieves tension and dulls hunger as well as physical and emotional pain.

Interestingly enough, not everyone wanted alcohol. Some of the older people, people such as Toma and Tu, didn't like the sense of losing control. They might have indulged in a shot every once in a while, but they never became heavy drinkers. But the young adults drank heavily almost to the last man and woman. That people who could hardly afford food would spend so much money on alcohol was not surprising—they soon became addicted.

Claire showed me a photograph which to me characterizes Tsumkwe. It shows strewn trash, a skeletal dog, some nearby dirty concrete huts, and some distant white stucco administrative buildings in green gardens. In the middle of a vast expanse of dust, the main street, a beautiful, drunken, pregnant woman sits on her heels. Wearing a yellow dress, with a two-year-old child at her breast, she is looking at the camera with unseeing eyes and raising to her young lips her half-gone liter of cognac.

Adding liquor to the social situation at Tsumkwe was like throwing a match in gasoline. The old, low-voiced discussions with narrowed eyes and stiff, jealous smiles instantly gave way to weeping, screaming arguments, which erupted into blows and beatings which brought out the knives and poison arrows, which resulted in homicides. The death rate soared.

No one had been ready for anything like this. The people, so unused to fighting, were profoundly and horribly upset. John and Claire were present while some people had a terrible fight, showing knives to each other, accusing each other of whoring, selfishness, and stealing. At last a weeping woman ripped open the buttons of her dress to bare her breasts, hysterically calling on her adversaries to stab her.

Later, when Claire asked why, the woman said the quarreling had upset her so much she wanted someone to kill her. "Death was dancing with me," said Nai. Others would agree. Tsumkwe is the "Face of Death," "Face of Sickness," "Face of Fighting." At Tsumkwe "fighting follows you."

Sometimes I found myself comparing the Bushmen of Nyae Nyae and their plague of violence to a pastoral people, the Dodoth, whom I once visited in northern Uganda. Among the Dodoth, violence was so much a part of life that they hardly noticed it, neither admiring nor deploring outbreaks of it, shrugging off bloody beatings, stabbings, and killings. Not only did the Dodoth tolerate violence, but they divided it into categories with different kinds of rules and weapons for each kind they anticipated. They used clubs and wicker shields for fighting their own tribesmen whom they intended to hurt but not to kill. They used spears and rifles against members of other tribes, their enemies, whom they did intend to kill. Unlike people in the United States, the Dodoth weren't much excited by violence. Making our television violence seem like the work of overstimulated schoolchildren, the Dodoth didn't invent amusing nicknames for killing and death and they didn't make games or dramas or songs about violence as we do. To the Dodoth, violence was a fact of life, a simple necessity.

But not to the Bushmen. The feverish, uncontrolled fighting that resulted from the loss of their formerly well-established social controls upset people profoundly. Yet so it will be, since the elements of fighting are now fixed in Tsumkwe.

- - -

Here, as of 1988, are the fates of some of the people we knew after the new life found them. Gao Feet died of tuberculosis at Tsumkwe. His widow, Dikai, is living with her youngest son, who in the 1950s was the much-loved, self-assertive infant known as Little Dabe. Today he is a soldier and a drinker. Once when very drunk he smashed Toma's head with a rock, causing an injury that troubled Toma for the rest of his life.

Another girl we knew sustained head injuries that affected her sanity. Her husband, like many other people, had become a hard drinker and one day when very drunk he bit off one of her ears, then kicked her head severely and repeatedly. Nowadays, possibly because of her head injuries, she doesn't talk sense, says John. Even so, he says, she remembers me, and a red bandanna I used to wear. After almost thirty years, I in my bandanna stay in her damaged brain as a dream of security, immune in my safe life from the terrible troubles that have beset her. She once asked John if I remembered her. When he said I did, she told him she liked to imagine being me because the fearful things that kept happening to her weren't happening to me.

Lazy Kwi is living, still married to Kushe. Their only son, Gao, died of tuberculosis during his early twenties. So did Kushe's sister and so did their father, Old Gao. Lazy Kwi and Kushe stay at Tsumkwe but have no resources, no young people to help support them, no jobs. Kushe is ill and doesn't go out much, but Lazy Kwi is sometimes seen at the roadside by the store, where he begs for small items—a tea bag, a cigarette.

Short Kwi, who lost his leg from a snakebite, triumphed completely over his disability. He made himself a peg leg from a hardwood tree and walked wherever he liked, hundreds of miles at a time if he wanted to. He, too, brought his family to Tsumkwe, where his daughter (the baby for whom Mother and I made a little red dress to wear to Windhoek) grew up and in time married a highly paid, hard-drinking soldier who one night while drunk stabbed and killed Short Kwi. The soldier had no quarrel with Short Kwi and no reason for stabbing him. In fact, the next day, he was bewildered to learn that Short Kwi was dead, since he hardly remembered what he had done. So all of Short Kwi's courage, endurance, intelligence, ability, and ingenuity amounted to nothing. He lies in a shallow, trash-strewn grave on the outskirts of Tsumkwe. His widow moved to Gautscha, her traditional home. Later, in remorse, the son-in-law tried to kill himself by the method many people favor nowadays—he stabbed himself in the arm with a poison arrow. People rushed him to the infirmary, where a doctor saved his life by cutting off his arm. Now he, like his father-in-law, is an amputee.

Beautiful Ungka died at Tsumkwe. Another woman we knew, not named in this book, died in a coma after being kicked and beaten by her son, who came home one day blind-drunk to find that his wife, passed out from drinking, had accidentally rolled on and suffocated their baby. In drunken confusion, the husband blamed his mother for the child's death, saying that as the oldest person present she should have been looking after the others. He beat this frail and elderly woman so badly she never regained consciousness but died in coma six months later in an infirmary in Grootfontein. Two years later, again in a drunken rage, the same man killed his wife.

Claire points out that the police at Tsumkwe are not particularly worried by this man's murderous alcoholic rages—he doesn't drink at work (or if he's drinking he doesn't show up for work) and the murders he committed didn't cost him his good job as assistant to the Nature Conservation officer. Years passed before he was so much as arraigned. He is expected to serve a year in jail if and when the court gets around to sentencing him. I was told, to my horror, that Toma's widowed daughter Norna has meanwhile married him.

In time, the storekeeper's liquor license was revoked, to the great dissatisfaction of many Bushmen, who felt that it was no one else's business how much they drank. But, after all, the end of liquor sales didn't make much difference in alcohol consumption, since by then people wanted alcohol and would buy sugar to brew their own.

- - -

Thus ended the old ways. The Bushmen had learned that they were the scum of the earth, the poorest of the poor, that they lived in the meanest of houses, that the dogs owned by the whites at Tsumkwe were far more valued and much better fed. The Bushmen had found out that they were unskilled, despised, deemed lazy, ridiculous, and dirty. They had learned how the outside world saw them.

And they agreed. Their honor was lost—their culture, too. Whole families who once were able to feed and clothe themselves, once able to depend upon one another, became completely dependent on one family member—perhaps a young member, a teenage soldier, say, who had learned his values and priorities in the barracks. Everyone knew that others held back money, hid clothing, ate in secret, were not sharing—everyone felt harmed by others, ignored, not wanted, left out. Husbands and wives were burdensome to each other; most of their children had died; their parents, too; their reasonable ways were lost if not forgotten; they were drunks. Thanks to alcohol, they all had said things that could never be forgiven. All held grudges while fearing the grudges which were held against them.

The people were ashamed. They realized that in their old life they had been eating dirty food, living in the wilderness, owning nothing worth owning, knowing nothing worth knowing. They were ashamed of getting drunk and fighting, but they somehow couldn't help it. So they shamed each other during brawling drunken scenes.

Many people under thirty hardly remembered the old way of life. Others remembered but had forgotten the skills necessary to lead it. Even people in their forties who knew some of the skills lacked the fine knowledge that everyone once had. Only the old people remembered everything, and it was they who best realized what had been lost. Nowadays, perhaps not surprisingly, they seldom discuss the past.

- - -

"Among contemporary !Kung San," writes Edward O. Wilson, "violence in adults is almost unknown; Elizabeth Marshall Thomas has correctly named them the 'harmless people.' But as recently as fifty years ago, when these 'Bushman' populations were denser and less rigidly controlled by the central government, their homicide rate per capita equalled that of Detroit and Houston." (*On Human Nature*, Cambridge, 1978, p. 100)

As Jamie Uys in his film, *The Gods Must Be Crazy*, misrepresents the Bushmen, E. O. Wilson reverses their history. To my knowledge Wilson has never visited the Ju/wasi. His book never mentions how important it was to them to keep their social balance, how carefully they treated this balance, and how successful they were. That he discusses them at all is perhaps due to the fact that in the 1970s they were selected by academics as a sort of living laboratory in which studies could be made on attributes of human nature, the most intriguing of which at the time seemed to be aggression. As it is discouraging that Uys, in a film viewed by millions, exploits the myth of precontact Bushmen when the truth is so horribly different, it is discouraging that an academic as eminent as Wilson thinks that "control by the central government" gave Ju/wasi their social equilibrium.

When our family first went to the Kalahari, we realized that we were visiting a unique people who, living as hunter-gatherers, perhaps were living as our preagricultural ancestors may once have lived. We tried hard to find anthropologists or ethnographers to go with us, to help make a record of what might be there to find. But hunter-gatherers weren't of much interest to anthropologists in those days, and we couldn't find anyone of those disciplines to join us.

In the ten to twenty years after we started our work, many academics developed an enormous interest in the Bushmen. Many of them went to Botswana to visit groups of Kung Bushmen, and for a time in Botswana, the anthropologist/Bushman ratio seemed almost one to one. Yet although the investigators were numerous, the range of some of their investigations seemed narrowed to an emphasis on questions of violence and aggression.

In Namibia in the 1950s, we found people anxious to suppress their aggression. This seemed to be in contrast with the findings of the anthropologists in Botswana, where people seemed willing to express aggression. That differences were found between the two groups of Bushmen did not surprise us, for the Botswana studies were begun many years after ours, in another country, among different people living under very different conditions. How different can be seen from Marjorie Shostak's fine book, *Nisa: the Life and Words of a !Kung Woman* (Cambridge, 1981), which resulted from her work there.

What did surprise us was that the Botswana anthropologists sometimes suggest that the differences are due to personal predilections of the investigators, as if Bushman groups everywhere uniformly display, so to speak, a finite amount of aggression which our investigations overlooked but which the anthropologists in Botswana discovered. I wish I knew who first explained that anthropology now suffers from physics envy.

In consequence, from time to time the suggestion arises that we didn't really see what we say we saw. Shostak herself, and her husband, Melvin Konner, write as follows: "Briefly stated, the !Kung have also been called upon to remind us of Shangri-La [*sic*]. While they were spared the attribution of free love that came rather easily to the minds of observers in the South Seas, they have received considerable attention for other alleged characteristics that also drew attention to Samoa. These included a relative absence of violence, including both interpersonal and intergroup violence; a corresponding absence of physical punishment for children; a low level of competition in all realms of life; and a relative material abundance. In addition to these features that the !Kung and Samoan utopias seemed to have in common, the !Kung were described as having exceptional political and economic equality, particularly in relations between men and women.

"We are here consciously trying to avoid the mention of anthropologists' names. Partly we are doing this because the Samoan controversy has suffered so much from the emphasis on personalities rather than on facts, and we would like to avoid a repetition of that error. We forbear, however, also because there are no key personalities in the !Kung case. Most of us have participated to one degree or another in the dissemination of utopian ideas about the culture. Members of the Marshall expeditions of the 1950's tended to emphasize the absence of violence and competition while being more realistic about the questions of abundance and equality. Members of the Lee-DeVore expedition of the 1960's and 1970's tended to be more insistent about abundance and equality while being more forthcoming about the presence of violence. We ourselves, for at least the first year of our field work, were quite convinced that !Kung culture was superior in all these ways to many others." (Konner and Shostak in Biesele, 1986, p. 71)

Despite Konner and Shostak's omission of names, they mean my mother, Lorna Marshall, and me when they speak of "members of the Marshall expeditions," since we were the only members who wrote accounts. In them we both emphasized the absence of violence and competition. Indeed, we were struck by it.

That the Bushmen we knew had aggressive inclinations, there was no doubt. In the 1980s, I saw many manifestations. Perhaps the one I found most painful involved a young woman who was Short Kwi's relative, his niece or his daughter. In 1987 when she visited her mother at Gautscha, I glimpsed the distress in this young woman's life. In one hand she carried a leather strap with which she threatened her children, age eighteen months and three years. She undoubtedly used the strap on them, for she had only to hold it up to make them go unnaturally quiet and stay quiet, uneasy, shamed, and cringing. The young woman looked alcoholic and unwell. She kept her head lowered but couldn't hide the blue-green bruises on her face and body where someone had beaten her. One day I heard a sound one often hears these days in Bushman villages—a dog screaming (the *yi yi yi* of a dog hit by a car). When I went to look I saw her older child with the strap, whipping with all his might a puppy too young to walk. The puppy was screaming. Its skeletal mother looked on anxiously and unhappily, but helplessly, from afar.

In the 1950s such episodes just didn't happen. The relatively few outbreaks of violence seemed isolated and were discussed over and over, since they caused such distress. Through these discussions I remember hearing of the killing of Toma's father by a child, of a mass killing in which one man shot his wife with a poison arrow and ran into the veld only to return after dark and shoot several other people, and of two executions. The first execution was of the mass murderer by his in-laws and his relatives, who hunted him down. The second execution was of a man named Dabe who, like the mass murderer, also seems to have been unbalanced, since he lived alone in the veld, hiding in a warthog's burrow. It isn't clear what people thought of him, or exactly why they feared him, but he was thought to be dangerous even though (as reported) he did no more than startle people by shouting from inside the burrow. "You frightened us, so we killed you," one of the executioners said to Dabe's dead body.

I didn't emphasize the above killings because the little I could learn didn't strike me as extraordinary. On the contrary, the first killing was all but an accident, the act of a child (and what struck me about it was that the event became associated with the victim, not the perpetrator). The next group of killings were apparently the acts of one unbalanced person. The last, the executions, apparently were the controlled, premeditated acts of reasonable people who saw no alternative and who acted with the encouragement and consent of their groups. To my way of thinking, the two executions could not even properly be called acts of aggression—not by any of the usual definitions—since the killings seemed to have been reactive and for the groups' protection.

Unlike later investigators, my mother and I were not drawing conclusions about human nature. What we wanted to stress was the efficacy of the social controls which people held ready to exercise over their aggressive or competitive inclinations, controls which, as far as we could determine, in those days only rarely broke down.

And so it sometimes dismays me to find that we are called "romantic" and "utopian" because we didn't emphasize something which twenty years later other investigators chose to emphasize, and that our findings are sometimes held lightly because they don't synchronize with later findings about different people, distant in time and space.

- - -

For many years my brother John was prevented for reasons of apartheid from visiting Namibia. In time apartheid was abolished there. Then many people who had been excluded were given visas, my brother among them. When he went to Tsumkwe to make his film for PBS the conditions he found there shocked him. He went to Gautscha looking for people he knew and during his visit carved his Ju/wa name, /Toma / /Osi, on the baobab tree. By the name he carved "1950–1978," as if the person called /Toma / /Osi had died there.

When I visited Gautscha in 1986, when I stood once again under the magnificent baobab tree by the edge of the salt pan, I saw this carving. It gave me a turn to see my brother's name with "birth" and "death" dates by it, yet I had come to Gautscha via Tsumkwe, and could understand why he had done it. And John had not been idle in the intervening years. In a way, he had picked up where McIntyre had left off, although under far worse conditions than McIntyre could have imagined. Using his own money, using a gift from our father, Laurence Marshall, and with the cooperation of many of the Bushmen, including Toma and his grown sons, Tsamko and Gashe (who had taken the name of Gashe Martin), John started the Ju/wa Development Foundation to help any Bushman group willing to leave Tsumkwe and try subsistence farming in the group's traditional place.

The farm animals were to be cattle. Unlike goats, cattle don't necessarily destroy the environment by chewing the grass too short or uprooting it, and they are so very large physically that envious visitors can't ask their owner to kill one. The neighboring non-Bushman ranchers certainly didn't casually kill cows for the table, so a precedent existed. The Bushman rancher who would seem unreasonable and selfish to refuse to kill a goat for visiting relatives would seem prudent and upstanding to refuse to kill a cow.

And so, for people willing to return to their old places, to dig a garden and to build a large, safe, lionproof pen with a gate and a mangle, the foundation would provide gardening tools, seeds, fencing, a watering trough, know-how, physical assistance, and a starter herd of cattle.

At first, the response to the foundation's proposal was minimal. People didn't think they could live as farmers. But several families including Toma's, now more or less under the leadership of Toma's eldest son, Tsamko, were willing to try farming at Gautscha, so the second transitional experiment began.

The experiment met direct, obstructive opposition from the Namibian administration, which early on had decided that Nyae Nyae should be a game park cleared of people, like Etosha. Unlike Etosha, however, the game park would be a hunting preserve. Rich foreigners—Germans and Texans, mainly—would pay handsomely for big game licenses, safari getups, and the like, obtaining for a stiff price what local white hunters and administration officials had long been taking freely, the Kalahari's wildlife for trophies and meat to make jerky or biltong.

To attract the game, the Department of Nature Conservation had been increasing the amount of water available by drilling wells and equipping them with windmills. Many of these wells simply deepened the traditional water supplies of various Bushman bands. When the administration learned that groups of Bushmen were living at their old waterholes, giving their cattle water which had been drawn by Nature Conservation's pumps, local officials were sent to tear down the cattle pens and remove the water pumps. To counter this, the Bushmen made thornbush fences and the foundation bought hand pumps. The Bushman farmers also made bucket brigades with pails and tin cans to bring water from the very deep wells.

At Gautscha, Tsamko and others had dug down eighteen feet for water. Such determination unsettled the administrator, who could not quite bring himself to refuse publicly to let the Bushmen drink their own water. Instead, he drove to Gautscha, where he found Tsamko and others digging at the bottom of the well, all covered with mud and sand. If Tsamko would bring his people back to Tsumkwe, promised the administrator, the government would ensure food for the people and water for the cattle. Although this happened during the height of a serious drought, Tsamko didn't even have to consider the offer. He had lived for years at Tsumkwe. He refused.

Later, the administration learned that John and Tsamko were helping other villagers install a hand pump at a bore-hole drilled into the villagers' traditional water suppy by the government. This time the administration sent a policeman and a chaplain to make them stop. When Tsamko kept working, the policeman started to arrest John. But Tsamko stepped between them. "The water here is not John's water," said Tsamko. "The pump is not John's pump. It is our water, and our pump. We are asking John's help to put it in. So if you're going to arrest someone, arrest me. This is my work. Let go of John."

The policeman had not expected such words from a Bushman, and in near perfect Afrikaans, too. He obeyed, and did not arrest anyone or pull out the pump. That moment was in a way a hiatus, if not a turning point, in foundation-government relations. The matter has remained at a standstill, with moves now and then by the government to arrest, sue, harass, or evict people but nothing so serious it has not been overcome.

The foundation began to get grants from charitable organizations—first from the congregation of Our Lady of the Wayside in Shirley Parish, England, later from Oxfam, from Misereor, from Brot fur die Welt, from ICCO, and from the Ford Foundation. The foundation has now helped about five hundred people leave Tsumkwe and establish fourteen communities at their traditional sites. The cattle supplied by the foundation have increased to about four hundred head. And the foundation has hired its own drilling contractor, who to date has dug four new wells for villagers, plus many dry holes.

As envisioned, within these communities some people herd cattle, which provide milk, occasionally meat, and when sold, money. Other family members continue to work for wages at Tsumkwe. Other people gather wild foods, and some (fewer since the drought) make rain-dependent, nonirrigated gardens, growing melons, millet, or corn. A few children go to school, living during the week with relatives at Tsumkwe and if possible coming home on the weekends. Unfortunately, they learn only in Afrikaans, which is not widely spoken and in which few books or texts are published. The families want the children to learn English, but it isn't taught. Yet there is a desultory support of learning in general—when I was there, some soldiers in an enormous army vehicle would circle the communities, bringing children home from the Tsumkwe school on Friday and picking them up again on Sunday night.

And the men still hunt. One day I was driving a group of people from one community to another when suddenly a poisoned arrow zoomed by my ear, out the car window, and into a kudu which was standing unafraid in the bushes, not realizing that people and cars are related. A man in the backseat had loosed this arrow. The kudu ran, we stopped, the man got out and found his arrow shaft, examined the tracks, and got back in the car. We could go, he said, so we did. The next day he returned to the spot, followed and found the kudu, and with some other men brought home the meat, just like the old days, except the hunter had shot from a closer distance with a greater advantage.

Many white and Bantu farmers, those associated with the government or those who covet the land the Bushmen occupy, repeatedly say the Bushmen are not real farmers and deserve neither land nor help. To some of these farmers, the Bushmen's efforts may never seem "real," since the foundation's experiment has two objectives which run counter to most farming practices of the region. The first is to disturb the ecosystem as little as possible. Due to the amount of ecological disturbance readily tolerated by the whites and Bantus, many white farms are overgrown with thornbush (the result of unnatural fire control) and many Bantu grazing lands are sand (the result of running large herds of cattle and goats on fragile grasslands). I was shocked to see, in a film of western Botswana, that a countryside which thirty years ago looked like Nyae Nyae now has bare sand dunes like a beach. The Bushmen, in contrast, run relatively few cattle while continuing to gather wild foods. Of course, indigenous plants and animals grow better and yield better than exotics and cause no damage. In fact, if allowed to continue, the Bushman farmers will still be farming long after the white and Bantu farms are dust. But to persuade the whites and Bantus of this may be difficult indeed. Environmental eduction has not been part of rural southern Africa's curricula.

- - -

The farming abilities of the various Bushman communities differed with each group. With Toma's son, Tsamko, and other people from the foundation, I visited most communities. One could have served as a model for communities anywhere. The cattle were in top condition and slept at night safe in a high-walled pen. The chickens were glossy. The houses of the people were neat and well built, with roofs thatched heavily against the sun and rain. Beside the houses I saw clean, washed dishes, no trash, and few flies. Within the thornbush fence around the village was a vegetable garden. The people were dressed in clean, mended clothes and the type of clothing matched the gender of the wearer. No little boy wore a dress, and no little girl wore trousers. And no one was very thin, or had flies on his face, or was crying, or had a running nose or crusted eyes or was coughing. Only the dogs seemed ill, starving.

I had come almost straight from Tsumkwe. The cleanliness and apparent prosperity of this village were in such contrast that my eyes must have popped. Noticing my astonishment, a member of the foundation later explained the background of this community. The headman, a Bushman man in his late thirties, had worked on a white person's farm after the government had forced him from his traditional home following the appropriation of southern Nyae Nyae. His hatred of whites was such that he could hardly look at them. He couldn't force his voice to speak Afrikaans or English, although he knew both languages quite well. Luckily for everyone, he had learned of the foundation and had traveled to Tsumkwe to take part in the experiment. He had married a woman whose traditional home was near Gautscha. Seeing him as a prime recipient of cattle because of his farming experience, the foundation had helped him establish the community there. Everyone benefited greatly: the foundation, because he was a successful role model for other people and could show how farming should be done; his group, because he led them to prosperity; and he, because, as he once told my brother with whom in time he formed a friendship, he knew none of the skills needed to live as a hunter-gatherer. It was farmwork or death, he said.

We also visited another community where the cattle had not been let out of their pen for at least thirty-six hours. In midafternoon of the second day they were crying, which was very painful to listen to. When asked why the cattle were still in the pen, the owners explained that lions were around but no one could be bothered to accompany the cattle to protect them while they grazed. The people were too busy producing trade items—souvenir bows and arrows, necklaces, knives in sheaths, and other good-looking things which each month the foundation, taking no commission, sells in a street market in Windhoek, full profit going to the craftsperson. Crafts manufacture is pleasant and popular; people work only when it pleases them, in the shade, talking to others and making good money. This community preferred crafts manufacture to herding.

Shortly before I left, at a meeting of the Farmer's Union (which, by 1987, retained provisional ownership of all cattle given to new farmers until the farmers proved themselves able to give good care), the members—all Bushmen, representing all communities, almost everyone politically savvy—decided to reallocate the craftsmakers' cattle to another village. The next day, Tsamko (chairman of the Farmer's Union) set off to get them. The Farmer's Union felt harshly toward the people of that village and wanted to part them from their cattle because the villagers were endangering the success of the farming experiment merely to indulge their temporary preferences, wasting the very scarce resources of the foundation and risking the already uncertain future of their own people in Bushmanland.

After Namibian independence there will be enormous pressure upon the Bushmen to leave their land. The new constitution proposed by the present interim government of Namibia favors those who want the Bushmen out. It does not recognize or protect any communal land, and will abolish the old tribal homelands with their apartheid connotations. The concept of abolishing the homelands is much favored since it means, in theory, that anyone can live anywhere he or she pleases, which is as it should be. Yet in practice, the living patterns will probably not be fair to all groups, for freehold land, the best and most prosperous land, which includes most farms, but also suburban houselots and town and city properties, has already been described in deeds and will be exempt from land reform. It also seems most unlikely that anyone but the traditional owners will in fact be able to use most of the traditional tribal lands. Perhaps in theory anyone can graze his cattle in, say Hereroland, but I'd like to see just anyone try it. Hereros need the grazing land for their own cattle, and are not a people to be trifled with. I expect they would quickly and easily rid themselves of any interloper. Bushmanland has neither deeds to protect it nor a unified, politically powerful, aggressive, and vocal population in place to defend it.

Last, Bushmanland is politically vulnerable. Today, 70 percent of the people in Namibia live on about 25 percent of the land. These people will certainly press the new government for more land. The new government will also be under pressure to supply land to commercial interests. Any new government faced with such pressure can be expected to expropriate from its weakest subjects. In a visit to Gam, one of the paramount chiefs of the Hereros reiterated a popular Herero maxim: "Wherever a Herero cow sets her foot is Herero land." He added that Bushmen have no property and are like animals. He also said, "No Bushman can own land in Namibia." In anticipation of taking Bushmanland, Herero ranchers are already visiting it, pacing it out, looking it over to see what parts to claim.

In short, there is no room in Bushmanland today for people unwilling to work collectively. Not if they want to survive. Interestingly, the episode of the craftspeople's cattle demonstrates in a manner visible to Western eyes and on a national scale what Bushman culture is all about, why Bushmen seem so concerned with inequality and selfishness. The fact that the craftspeople requested cattle at all suggests that they wanted them merely because other people had them. That they would then waste them was selfish. Here (as is so terribly often the case), the selfishness of the craftspeople—obliviously whittling items to benefit themselves individually, with no thought of the larger group and its struggles for the future—was detrimental to others, to the group in general, so people got angry. Yet no one displayed anger. Instead, a resolution was decided upon by consensus at the meeting of the Farmer's Union after much talk. Very Bushman.

- - -

I found the environment of the Gautscha area considerably changed after thirty years. First, domestic animals had been added, cattle having perhaps the most impact. Early in the morning the cattle were let out to graze where they liked. By 1986, they had substantially reduced the grass around the village and, under the leadership of (I thought) two or three experienced cows, were walking to grass almost a mile away. The leaders then brought them home at night, first to the watering trough by the borehole, where someone would notice them waiting and come to pump water for them, then to the safety of their pen. The grass of the area, which had been supporting this herd for seven very dry years, seemed to be holding its own.

Other domestic animals were chickens and dogs. The chickens ate seeds and minute bits of refuse, and as a result their small bodies were in moderately good condition, thin perhaps but still relatively energetic. Not so the dogs, who were skeletal and weak from starvation. Dogs held a strange position in the Bushman villages: people owned them, named them, and occasionally even spoke of them with pride, but no one fed them. One village was an exception. In this village, the people had cattle but disliked milk, so they gave the milk to their dogs. The dogs of all the other villages scavenged, a practice which people opposed. If people saw a dog taking a bit of refuse from the fireside or licking out a cooking pot, they would stone him or whip him vigorously, sending him away screaming. Consequently, the dogs scavenged secretly. While the people were up and about, the dogs would lie in the shade, keeping their eyes open for possible morsels. When, at about the same time every day, in the hot parts of the afternoon, the people would rest, the dogs would get up and, moving very quietly, very inconspicuously, would explore the village for scraps. If a dog found something like a bone that could not be swallowed at once, he would take it out of the village to eat it in privacy.

I watched the Gautscha dogs for several days and noticed that each dog managed to find approximately the equivalent of a walnut-sized scrap of food each day. I wondered why they didn't hunt, but did not find a good explanation. Perhaps there isn't much to hunt around a Bushman village, though there are some small animals, especially after dark. I saw a hare—I think the same hare—not one hundred meters from the village almost every night. Instead, the dogs ate human excrement, which had a cleansing and beneficial effect on the village. Alas, people whose own nutrition is low probably pass very little nourishment in their excrement.

On a tour of all the villages I counted male dogs and female dogs, reasoning that the physical strains of pregnancy and lactation would be fatal to most females, and, although my sample was perhaps too small, I did find more male dogs. The one female I saw with pups was very young, and her body was nothing but unhealthy skin stretched over bones. The pups she was suckling seemed healthy. With each lesson in abuse at the hands of the Bushman children, the pups cried for her and stumbled after her when she came near. Sucked dry, she avoided them.

At night, the dogs proved invaluable to the village. While I was at Gautscha, almost every night, sometimes two or three times a night, we would hear the village dogs barking, then rushing past our camp in full pursuit of some marauding animal. Several times I was able to identify the marauder: often a hyena, sometimes a jackal, once a leopard!

Since leopards nowadays hunt people (perhaps because their usual prey is becoming scarce), the dogs serve the people better than the people serve them.

One night at Gautscha I was astonished to see a well-fed, long-haired, black-and-white housecat basking contentedly in the warmth of someone's fire. No one fed the cat, I felt sure, but probably it was a mouser and birder, and fed itself.

I found the population of wild animals in the Gautscha area quite different from the population thirty years before. The elands had vanished altogether. No one really knew why. Some blamed the drought. I thought not, since elands and gemsbok are as well suited to a hot, dry climate as any animals in the world. I suspected that the hunters for the biltong companies, whose factories outline the Namibian side of the Kalahari, had killed off the elands.

Gemsbok and giraffes were scarce. The biltong buyers favor gemsbok meat, so the gemsbok may be going the way of the elands. Giraffes have proved susceptible to Bushman hunters on horseback. Since the presence of a horse is soothing to a giraffe, the hunter can ride right beside the giraffe and sever with a knife or a spear the huge blood vessel that lies like a length of garden hose not far below the skin of a giraffe's inner thigh. The giraffe hardly knows what has happened, then faints. A hopeful thought is that Bushmen now realize that hunting giraffe is illegal, and since virtually every hunter has someone, some jealous grudge-bearer, ready to turn him in to the police, most Bushmen don't hunt giraffes. I wish I felt as sure of the biltong companies.

Migrating animals, wildebeest and springbok, are seen no more. Sport hunters are blamed for the disappearance of the springbok, and a great game fence, erected to keep wild animals from carrying diseases to the farms, has kept the wildebeest from their seasonal migration. By the fence lie many dried carcasses of wildebeests and also giraffes, animals who died trying to reach their traditional sources of dry-season water. The only large antelopes still seen relatively frequently are kudus, yet even these are sparse.

The most astonishing change of all is that elephants have appeared in large numbers. Although there is much speculation, no one really knows where they come from or what they are doing in Nyae Nyae. They are possibly refugees from the fighting along the Angola border, where the soldiers are said to use their automatic weapons on every living creature in a belt fifty miles wide. Virtually all the elephants at Nyae Nyae are males. With youngsters in their herds, female elephants probably cannot travel the waterless distance between Angola and Nyae Nyae.

For a number of reasons, the presence of elephants is dismaying. That they have traveled so far to such unsuitable country shows how grim their situation at home must be. And bad as Nyae Nyae may be for elephants, it may soon get much worse. The Department of Nature Conservation intends to include elephants in trophy hunting, in spite of the fact that recent population studies show elephants in a precipitous decline, with their population's collapse so greatly exceeding their ability to reproduce as to make them extinct unless the destruction is stopped immediately.

When I last visited Gautscha about six male elephants lived there, their huge gray shapes an astonishing sight above the low bushes. They ranged in age from mid-teens to late fifties, and they moved about by night, staying quietly and inconspicuously in the deepest bush available by day. They drank from the old Gautscha waterhole, where the water oozed so slowly that to slake their thirst took many hours of the night. They drank a sip at a time.

Sometimes in their thirst the elephants would visit the borehole. Since water had to be pumped by hand from the borehole, something that was done only when the cattle were lined up at the trough, waiting for it, the elephants got only the smell of water there. In the past, in hope of reaching water, they or other elephants had pulled up the pump, then the enormous concrete wellhead, then hundreds of feet of well casing. To stop their destruction, the Bushmen had surrounded the borehole with a densely packed field of large, sharp stones, which elephants can't walk on. Sometimes when the Bushmen were watering their cattle, the elephants could be seen in the distance, looking on.

- - -

One of the first sights I saw in 1986 at Gautscha was Gashe Martin, Toma's son and Tsamko's brother, sitting in the dust, trying with a huge red plumber's wrench to repair a battered ghetto blaster. While he wasn't looking, his son, wearing a frilly blue dress and carrying a cup of water, toddled up to pour the water over the machine. How terribly pitiful, I thought, to see this family struggling with the detritus of the Western world, broken junk for which they have been overcharged and which they don't understand. I turned away.

Not long after, I heard the static of a radio. Improbable as it seems, Gashe had repaired his ghetto blaster. And since the Ju/wasi have always been very sensitive observers, he must also have read my thoughts from my face. Calling me over, he showed me a tape, which he inserted and played. It was a recording he had made of himself playing a guashi and singing a traditional song.

Although much had changed, I thought that the people's underlying ways were unchanged. People still interpreted many things in the old ways. I was particularly moved to learn that the Christian creation myth of Eve giving an apple to Adam in the garden of Eden was seen by some Ju/wa people as Eve teaching Adam how to gather food.

People still arranged their lives in the old ways, too, although this wasn't always obvious. At Gautscha, for instance, people had built permanent dwellings with mud-

and-wattle walls and thatched or tin-plated roofs, some houses patterned on Kavango architecture, some on Herero, and some on Tswana. Yet though the houses were of a new architecture, their placement in relationship to each other seemed traditional, as did the size and relative importance of each house. At the eastern end of the village lived Tsamko with his wife, his brother Gashe and his two wives, these two brothers' married children, and their parents, Tu and Toma. Next to them lived Tu's niece, Nai, with her husband, Gunda, and their married daughter. In the old days, these two groups had also lived side by side, then as Toma's and Gao Feet's families. Beyond them, if not close beside them, lived the widow of Short Kwi, her sister, her sister's husband, and their children, who with their spouses moved back and forth between Gautscha and Tsumkwe.

Not only were the ways people oriented themselves familiar, but the relative stability of the houses they built seemed familiar too. The adult generation seemed to have built the largest, strongest houses. Their married children had built smaller, less substantial houses. And the very old people had, for the most part, built simple little lean-tos, hardly houses at all. This also had been true in the past.

Clothes were made of cloth and the dishes were plastic or enamel, but the speed with which they became junk was like in the old days. In the weeds beyond the village lay a burned-out pot which I believe I could have sand-scrubbed into a useful condition, and I would have, had it been mine and had I been in the financial straits of the person who had thrown it away. Also in the weeds lay a child's wedge-soled violet plastic sandal of a kind I recognized at once—my grandchild in Boulder, Colorado, had one like it. If the sandal had belonged to our family, I would have kept it until the other turned up.

For almost everyone at Nyae Nyae the use of money is relatively new. To our way of thinking, the Bushmen waste it. But, true to their old ways, they have not developed our love for it. To them it is still symbolic, not nearly as important as self-esteem or human relationships, not even as important as the items it buys. One day Nai paid about R 100 for the hind leg of a butchered cow. The cow itself, alive, could have been bought for R 80. When Claire asked Nai why she had overspent so wildly, Nai said she knew how much a cow cost, but she and her family had meat hunger—that was why.

In the same way, people often sell crafts items far too cheaply. It actually cost one woman to make and sell a beaded leather purse, since she let herself be persuaded by the buyer, a tourist, to charge less for the purse than she had paid for the beads sewn on it. Tourists know well how expensive such items are in the curio shops in Windhoek, yet they enjoy beating the Bushmen in trade. The foundation would like to get its hands on these tourists, but they've usually come and gone, their caravans filled with crafts items and their pockets bulging with the money they've as good as stolen from the Bushmen.

For the Bushmen to change their buying and selling practices won't be easy. Money management benefits from math education, and the Bushmen don't yet have much of that. Yet I think the reason Bushmen often undercharge when they sell and overpay when they buy is an old reason: they would rather say yes than no; they would rather be agreeable than confrontational; and in nonviolent social situations they seem to feel less discomfort from defeat than from victory, or, to put it another way, more comfortable bearing grudges than fearing the grudges of others. Possibly for the same cultural reason, nobody from the Nyae Nyae villages steals. In the old days, stealing was unheard of. These days, people know all about stealing but disdain to practice it. Outside of Tsumkwe, the only people who steal, not only by unfair bargaining but by actual pilfering, are the tourists.

I left Gautscha with the feeling that Ju/wa culture has been damaged but lives on, disguised perhaps, but there nevertheless. The people may wear rags, they may be poor, they may—when measuring themselves by a Western yardstick—hold themselves in low esteem. But at least in the villages, the cultural recovery which people have made from the despair of Tsumkwe has been nothing less than amazing. Much of their cultural strength has remained intact. The ability and resilience of Ju/wa Bushmen should never be underestimated.

Even so, in the last thirty years Nyae Nyae and its people have moved from an age-old stability to precarious instability. Hope for the future and even for life itself remains uncertain. With the Farmer's Union and the Ju/wa Development Foundation, the villagers of Nyae Nyae should be able, like other Namibian peoples, to support themselves with a viable mixed economy. They will also be able to raise beef without denuding the pasture, and thus will make an ongoing contribution to their country's food supply. However, they can only serve their country if they can survive—if the present and future governments of Namibia do not adopt a policy of depriving them of their land, the land which has been in their stewardship for a very long time. In fifteen years I'll visit again if I can, and add another chapter.

E.M.T.
June, 1989
Peterborough, New Hampshire

N O T E S

- - - - - - - - -

The information used in this epilogue was gathered from trips I made to Bushmanland in 1986 and 1987. I also used the following sources: a paper by John Marshall and Claire Ritchie, "Where Are the Ju/wasi of Nyae Nyae?" (Center for African Studies, University of Cape Town, 1984); Lorna Marshall's *The !Kung of Nyae Nyae* (Cambridge, Mass.: Harvard University Press, 1976); a report by Marshall and Ritchie, submitted to Secretary F. Stroh, "Husbandry in Eastern Bushmanland"; a review by John Marshall of a report on Bushmen to the South-West Africa Administration by a firm of urban architects; an article by John Marshall, "Plight of the Bushmen," in *Leadership Magazine* (first quarter, 1985, pp. 36–48); and *The Past and Future of Kung Ethnography: Critical Reflections and Symbolic Perspectives Essays in Honour of Lorna Marshall*, edited by Megan Beisele with Robert Gordon and Richard Lee (Hamburg: Helmut Buske Verlag, 1986).

Much additional material was gathered from lengthy personal communications with John Marshall, Tsamko, Nai, Lorna Marshall, Claire Ritchie, John Payne, Ann Edwards, Megan Biesele, and Robert Gordon, to all of whom I am very grateful. I am also very grateful to Gashe Martin, who was most helpful while I was in Namibia, and who died suddenly late in 1987.

E.M.T.

ABOUT THE AUTHOR

Between 1950 and 1956 Elizabeth Marshall Thomas accompanied three expeditions to visit the Bushman hunter-gatherers of South-West Africa (now Namibia) and Bechuanaland (now Botswana). At that time the Bushmen were the last significant population who still lived by hunting and gathering, the economy practiced by all human beings and the ancestors of human beings for millions of years. Few firsthand accounts of hunter-gatherer life were written before this one and because, since its publication, most Bushmen have been evicted from their old homes or forced to change their traditional ways, this book remains one of only a few accounts of the old way of life. In 1986 and 1987, Thomas revisited the people she had known in Namibia and found them much changed.

Thomas, who has spent the last twenty years studying animal behavior, makes her home in New Hampshire. Her other writing includes a nonfiction book about Dodoth pastoralists in northern Uganda, *Warrior Herdsmen*, and a novel about prehistoric hunter-gatherers in the Northern Hemisphere, *Reindeer Moon*.